Cultural & Political Opinions

2016-2019

By

Darnell Clevenger

Chapters

Abortion

It's my body so I should be the one who decides if I have an abortion or not.

How many times have you heard that comment, or something similar, in the good old USA?

Now, I want to make it clear that I'm not against abortion in all ways, shapes, and forms. I'm not against abortion per se. I'm not a dyed in the wool pro-lifer. I agree with the pro-abortionists to some extent. In my mind, there are definitely situations in which a woman becomes pregnant and should have the right to get an abortion if she so chooses. In the case of rape, or what I would call "forced sex," meaning a situation in which a female has been playing around with a guy (dry humping, rubbing and caressing each other's bodies including private parts, clothes in disarray and male hands fondling female body parts with no or minimal evasive tactics on the part of the female) until he is beyond reason and then she suddenly tries to stop the to-that-point mutual wrestling match and he refuses to stop—in the case of rape or forced sex I think the female should have the legal right to get an abortion. I think the same about situations in which it comes to light that the male has some kind of terrible disease that would probably be passed on to any child of his, or even if the female has some destructive disease. I am somewhat undecided about, say, girls as young as twelve or thirteen having consensual sex and getting pregnant and then having an abortion. If the girl's family does not want to raise the child or if there are no adoptive parents who are interested, then maybe an abortion would be the best way. But I think these possibilities should be explored before a girl is allowed to opt for destroying the fetus. I also think these options should be explored in the case of rape or forced sex, especially in the latter case.

But I do not (repeat—do not) believe that any female who becomes pregnant simply because she doesn't for one reason or another use protection or insist that her male lover use such—I do not believe that a child conceived in a mutually agreed upon sexual encounter should be aborted, just because he's unwanted by the mother and/or father.

"But it's my body!" feminists will shout, angrily, scornfully, satirically, whatever. "I have a right to do with my body as I see fit."

"And that, lady," I say, "is where we go our separate ways."

It is not just your body we are talking about. A man impregnated you, so it's his sperm that you are planning on flushing out of your body, sperm that took root and helped your egg create a living being. Maybe he doesn't care, or maybe he wants you to get an abortion, so he won't have to accept the responsibility of his actions and thus dedicate his next "few" years to raising a soft, cuddly little creature who lives and breathes and laughs and cries and gets in trouble and needs tender loving care. Maybe accepting such responsibility would get in the way of his own ambitions and dreams. Maybe he considers himself too young, too innocent, and thus too inexperienced for such extended commitment. Maybe he's too selfish to accept the task of raising a baby to adulthood.

But maybe, just maybe, he would like to raise that child. Maybe his getting you pregnant has caused a parental reaction in him that is warm and dedicated and loving, and he would love to cuddle and raise that creature growing inside you, that creature which is part of him. Maybe his parents would like to help him raise the child. Or his grandparents. Of course the parents or grandparents didn't deposit anything like sperm in your body, so it's not their bodies that are being affected here. But it is their genetic heritage. Is that child an extension of their physical selves psychologically, emotionally? I wonder.

But the father? It's your body, you say. But the creature growing inside you wouldn't be there if not for its father's sperm. A man's sperm. Part of his body. Your egg. His sperm.

But it's your body, you repeat, angrily, disgusted by the thought of a male like me "trying to control your body." Which I'm not doing. I'm simply pointing out that I disagree with you about this "my body" insistence. You might be the oven, but there were two cooks who created the concoction inside you, created it each from his/her own body, not from some recipe put together from outside ingredients.

So, to destroy the fetus is to destroy part of your lover, and the genetic heritage he received from parents and grandparents and….

But that's ridiculous, you say. It's your body. The creature inside you is no more than a concoction made of a female egg and a male sperm. Just part of the waste of evolution. And God knows, that waste is so vast that it is impossible to even imagine its scope, let alone the individual specks that have gone by the wayside untouched and unseen and, yes, unimagined. Any normal male in this modern western world will spit out thousands and thousands of iotas of sperm just like the one you plan on wasting. So I'm not taking anything away from the sperm giver. Maybe, I say. But what is already created is alive in substance as well as in the imagination. What is not is only alive in the imagination, which we all know can never truly merge with reality. Can never be, especially in any human sense.

And I disagree about this "my body" bit: It's not just your body that we are talking about. Ignoring the male sperm, and the feelings of the sperm donor, you still have to consider the fetus. It's a body, I believe. You might insist that it really isn't alive. But I disagree. It is not like a corpse, which has lived its life and is returning to the earth from which it sprang. The fetus is at the other end of the living spectrum, at the beginning, not the end. The odds are that, if allowed to live, it will have years, many years, of enjoying the world around it, of relishing friends and loved ones and new adventures and learning, and crying and laughing at its own foibles and the foibles of others. You would take this away from it. You would take life away from it.

That little fetus you want to eject is a body, which is growing a mind, and a psyche, and is headed toward a whole new world of adventures and experiences that will form it into something like you and me. It is a human being. It just doesn't have all the years of psychological and physical growth that you and I have. But they will come. Unless you destroy his body now. How can a psyche, a whole personality, grow without a body to grow in?

Anti-Trump Resistance

I recently read an article on the internet that, supposedly, came from *The Washington Times*. The title was "Anti-Trump Course at Butler University Offers 'Strategies for Resistance.'" "So," you ask, "what's new?" And you would be correct in so doing. The active anti-Trump crowd seems to be kind of pervasive in the Democratic Party (even among some of our elected officials) and, I would expect, in all left-leaning groups, like, doubtlessly, the Socialist and Communist parties. And they seem to be the present doomsday sayers with respect to our president. And they seem to be pervasive in academia.

A similar attitude about somebody like Bernie Sanders, I suppose, would be pervasive in any far-right groups. I hesitate to say conservative because I think conservatives nowadays are more prone to listen to liberal ideas than liberals are to conservative ideas. I find my conservative friends more willing to discuss their attitudes and beliefs, my liberal friends less willing to discuss and more willing to dictate and reject. This willingness to discuss openly and freely would not, I don't think, pertain to people from the far right any more than it does to people from the left—notice that I did not say "far" left, simply because I think lots of liberals have become very illiberal about social and political differences of opinion.

This attitude seems all too prevalent in and around some of our most elite universities, places which should be the defenders of free speech, not its attackers and delimiters. As bastions of the free and peaceful interchange of ideas, in other words, of learning, are they going to be like the

Alamo to its American defenders or the Bastille to the last monarchs of France, bastions that fell to the invaders? In this case, invaders would mean all those who would destroy, or limit, our right to express ourselves openly and honestly? I truly hope not. I've spent most of my life around institutions of higher education, 35 years of my life teaching and 10 as a student. If I add another 12 years of elementary through high school, well, it would seem that educational institutions are like my second home, places where I feel comfortable.

Or should I say "were" my home rather than "are," and "felt" comfortable rather than "feel" so? The institutions I attended and taught at were not politicized. Not at that time anyhow, not in any limiting or threatening sense. I don't know how they are today, though, since I've been retired for many years, although I can certainly guess given the news about what happens to many conservative speakers. I would hate to think that most of our institutions of higher education are as politicized as many of our elite universities seem to be. Let's see. Ann Coulter was invited to speak at the U. of California, Berkeley, and the speech was later canceled because of the threat of violence from left-wing groups. Hers is not the only proposed speech to be canceled by major universities in recent years.

And just today Education Secretary Betsy DeVos was booed by the students of the all-black university Bethune-Cookman, in Florida, during her speech to the graduating class. Many of the students even turned their backs on the speaker. What bad taste! What insultingly bad taste! Crude, cheap, and tacky! I have to ask myself, are these students learning their crassness and their political attitudes, and their narrow-mindedness, from their professors? Are they learning them at home? Or are they learning them from their parents, friends, teachers, professors, the media, and from our political leaders like Chuck Schumer and Nancy Pelosi? In other words, is this meanness pervasive throughout our American society? Or is it only limited to certain groups? I almost feel like I'm back in the 1960s. Only this time it's not the young and rebellious educated crowd against the establishment, military and political. It's the liberals against the conservatives. It's one large part of the country against the other large part. It is our country divided unto itself. It is a terribly sad and dangerous era in our history and I, personally, worry about the future, for my grandchildren, for my country.

Anyhow, back to where I began this essay: the resistance to President Trump. *The Washington Times* article says that the Butler University course accuses Mr. Trump of "'perpetuating sexism, white supremacy, xenophobia, nationalism, nativism, and imperialism." I think whoever wrote the syllabus must have forgotten several more things to accuse the president of, such as being homophobic and anti-democratic. Maybe, just maybe, that's why they included "xenophobia." But then, maybe I'm being a little narrow-minded here, acting too much like whoever did write the syllabus for the course.

Supposedly, the course is described on the Butler University website as exploring "'why and how'" Trump was elected and how "'Trump's rhetoric is contrary to the foundation of the U. S. democracy.'" So, it won't explore Trump's rhetoric and what it might say about us and what it might mean for our future. It will discuss how such is "contrary" to our whole being and meaning. The use of such a word says it all. The course is like a lot of the "fake" news we read and listen to in the media. It has made up its mind as to the side it is on. It is not an unbiased course trying to shed light on what Trump's rise to power says about our country in the present and, possibly, in the future. It is a biased course, anti-Trumpian, which will study only the negative impact of Trump's election, as interpreted, of course, by the professor.

Anyhow, The Washington Times article further states that the class "echoes the work of a similar 'Resistance School' at Harvard University, the brainchild of distraught professors and graduate students."

Can you imagine that? Resistance schools? That sounds like the French underground against the Nazis during WWII. I find such attitudes both ludicrous and scary. They are ludicrous for several reasons: President Trump is no Hitler or Mussolini, or even a Franco, by any stretch of the imagination. He came to power legally, as a representative of the desires of many of our people; not all of them, of course, but what president has represented all, or even a vast majority, of the people? Moreover, in many ways he's too much of an amateur politician, and even too much of a bumbler at times, to represent a political danger to the country.

Moreover, I believe there is, presently, a greater danger to the country and our political processes than President Trump. One of the major causes of the rise to power of Hitler, Mussolini, and Franco was agitation and, yes, violent confrontation, from the left, from the Communists, Socialists, and world travelers. Trump is an answer from the people to problems presented by the left wing of our political world (by Hillary Clinton, Bernie Sanders, and those who would use street violence to get their way). It is also the people's hopeful answer to an ineffective political system, one which keeps ignoring problems some of which should have been resolved long ago: <u>illegal immigration</u>, our "forever" war in the Mideast, our economy, our disappearing manufacturing base, <u>our debt</u>, our collapsing infrastructure, the apparent lack of morals and ethics in our political class ("Drain the swamp."), racism, and so on not infinitum but definitely for some time.

Doubtlessly the left wing of our political system doesn't see this all the way I do. And I myself am beginning to wonder if Trump is the man for the job, especially with his ego and all the obstructionism thrown in his way by the political establishment and the press. I only hope that he is, or that at the least the right man will step forth in the next presidential election. My feeling is that our future, a peaceful and successful future as one united nation, is at stake.

Basketball Players

Division I College basketball is no longer a competition of student athletes representing the states in which their universities exist, but rather, in the universities at the top of the standings at least, a competition of minor league players hoping to make the majors (the NBA or the professional leagues in Europe, China, etc.). There are exceptions, of course, many exceptions, but most of those seem to be in universities that are not in the top tier of NCAA Division I schools. Those universities at the top seem to have more foreign players and more out-of-state players on their rosters than other colleges and universities, and often more foreign and out-of-state players than in-state players. I personally find this disheartening. In essence, these universities are supporting the NBA and professional basketball in foreign lands by training their new recruits. Moreover I believe that they are doing this on the taxpayer dollar since these out-of-state players and the foreign players have scholarships, probably full scholarships, and since a lot of tax monies go to support these universities in general, not only the faculty and administration and buildings and yearly budget and students, but also the athletic programs. I truly think, also, that universities recruit and support athletics (basketball and football anyhow) at the expense of an academic world where learning in the social and natural sciences, in the arts and humanities, and in business, engineering and other professions should be the number one priority of the institution and should not be continuously undercut by athletics.

I wonder what a Kentucky youth, say, an excellent basketball player and top student, a ballplayer who is top notch, good enough to play in

Division I, a youth who has his sights set on the University of Kentucky or the University of Louisville and has studied and studied to maintain top grades and worked and worked to develop and maintain top notch basketball skills—I wonder what he thinks when he finds that all his work and ability have been superseded by three foreign players and eight out-of-state players at the University of Kentucky and two foreign players and nine out-of-state players at Louisville. Does he think, oh great, I love Indiana or Ohio or California, so I'll apply to them? Or does he give up and apply to a smaller university in Kentucky because he wants to stay close to home and because he loves his state and wants to represent it somehow?

I wonder.

Anyhow, I did a little checking in the 2017-18 rosters of the following universities, and here's what I found, much to my anger since I believe that all athletics and all college athletes should be no more than an extension of the academic program. Athletes should be <u>students</u> who also play sports, not recruited athletes who also have to take academic course work whether they want to or not. They should definitely not be young people who can just barely keep their GPA at a passing level for a year until they can enter a professional draft and so move on. They should not be athletes who plan on leaving the university as soon as possible (after the first year, or the second year) for the professional world of sports. If the professional leagues want a farm club, they should build one and pay for it out of their own pockets; they seem to have millions to spend on their players. And young athletes who want to prepare for the NBA or NFL or MLB should try out for those teams. Those who want an education should make a commitment to the university that accepts them in its ranks of <u>students</u>. And I do not agree that they should be paid athletes. Their scholarships are worth a lot of money and should go, not to athletes or to support a "minor league club" for the major leagues, but rather they should go to <u>students</u> who also want to play some sport for the four years or so that it takes them to complete their degree and to <u>learn</u> at the <u>college</u> level.

But enough of that! Here is what I found about some of the major "athletic" universities men's basketball rosters: This season the U. of Kentucky has two players from Canada, one from Jamaica, and eight others from outside the state. Duke has one player from Croatia, one from Australia, and twelve from outside of North Carolina, none from North Carolina. Villanova's players are all from the USA, but ten are from outside Pennsylvania. The U. of Kansas has three foreign players (two from Africa and one from the Ukraine) and ten not from the state of Kansas. The U. of Michigan has one from Berlin and ten from states other than Michigan. Loyola Chicago has one from Canada, one from Croatia, and seven others from outside Illinois. Indiana U.'s players are all from the USA, but twelve are not from Indiana. Of the UCLA players, one is from Hungary and four not from California. All of UNC's players are US citizens but eleven are not from North Carolina. Syracuse has two foreigners on its roster and ten others not from New York. Michigan State has one foreigner and eight out-of-staters on its roster. The U. of Arizona has three foreigners and twelve out-of-staters on its roster. USC's roster consists of seven players not from California, but no foreigners. The U. of Louisville has two foreigners and nine other players not from Kentucky. Gonzaga's roster includes four foreigners and nine other players not from the state of Washington. And finally, Purdue U. has one foreigner and seven US citizens not from Indiana.

I assume (tongue in cheek) that all these foreigners enrolled in their respective universities and traveled all the way to the USA because of specific majors offered. All of them are probably English majors, right? I assume that all these out-of-staters enrolled in their respective universities for the same reason; of course they couldn't find those majors offered by the universities in their own states. And they couldn't play ball there either, right? All I can say is "Bah, humbug." Given the amount of money in Division I basketball and football, and the amount of money paid to winning coaches, and the amount of money waiting for the top pro-recruits, and even many of those not in the top tier, I guess we can't blame coaches for finding every loophole they can, legal and sometime not so legal, to get the top high school players on their roster. And we can't blame excellent ballplayers for wanting to enter the pros as soon as possible. And to hell with the academic aspect of college. Keep the money rolling from the government and, what the heck, start paying the college ballplayers out of some of that money. Turn them into semi-pros at government expense. After all, lots of government money goes to build professional stadiums and entice teams to certain cities, doesn't it. Hell, the government has deep pockets; ignore our national debt. After all, we all know that athletics are much more important than academics. Don't we? And besides, we taxpayers can afford the expense. Ha! With our national infrastructure going to pot. With our war in the Mideast puttering along like an old Studebaker, soaking up money like a sponge. With the billions we spend on protecting our allies and other nations. With the billions illegal immigrants cost us annually. With the excessive number of public sector workers we have. With our private sector workers making very little compared to what they made in the few decades after WWII, and compared to our public sector workers. And then there's our national debt. But, hell, ignore that. Our government does.

4

Bigotry

Bigotry? Prejudice? Racism? Of course it's out there. Aren't we all attuned to be attracted to and to trust more in what is familiar to us, in what is like us, than we are what is different? Isn't that an integral part of human nature? Isn't that what families and tribes were all about—an innate, comfortable, safe similarity among members? Isn't that what cultures and societies and nations strive to be all about—people of similar genetic and historical backgrounds banding together and forming rules of conduct and beliefs that in turn become religions and laws and social norms. Isn't that what the Melting Pot was all about—differences adapting to the American way, rather than remaining different and forcing America to accept that difference?

And yes, there are always those few who tend to reject the familiar and cater to the less familiar, even the unfamiliar. They are the ones who lead us into the unknown future, the ones who help us advance our knowledge and technology. And, yes, some of them are also the ones who lead us astray, lead us into anger and hatred and wars and persecution.

That can't be helped. After all, we aren't angels, or robots. We are human beings, with all the benefits and faults that the human genome and our environment can give us, and all the differences. And it's pretty obvious that our problems are caused by the differences rather than the similarities. A spiritual mind. A mind that never wanders from the fact-based world around us, maybe can't wander. A rational mind. An emotional mind. A fat person. A skinny person. An in-between person. A realist. An idealist.

A tall person. A short person. A person who makes things. A person who buys and sells the stocks of companies that make things. A person who speaks English. A person who speaks Spanish, or Russian, or French, or Chinese. A black person. A white person. A brown person. A yellow person. No little green men here yet.

However, our similarities are considerably more prevalent than our differences, I suspect, at least among those who have lived here for a generation or two or three, and those similarities are what draw us together and bind us there, not our differences, although differences seem to be becoming not only more acceptable but even desirable—witness the emphasis on "diversity" in college recruitment of students and the anger among certain groups when people speak of social fusion rather than social fission as a model of what America should become.

Yet similarities are what keep us from going to war with each other, or committing ethnic genocide on a grand scale, like in Eastern Europe, or Africa, or the Mid-East. It is our differences, human and social differences, which seem to cause the most havoc on the planet, good and bad. Although those people with different habits or desires or characteristics often lead us into the future, often change us and mold us into something slightly different than what we were, wars too are caused by differences, not by similarities. That's damnably obvious. Just plug the term "ethnic cleansing" into Wikipedia and scan the long, long list of such episodes in Africa, Asia and Eastern Europe. Or consider the causes of wars past, from our revolution and civil war to WWII and beyond, like the civil wars in Korea and Vietnam that we have interfered in, or like the present religious civil war that is going on among Muslims in the Mid-East, again a "civil war" that we are interfering in.

But let's get back to the real point here. Bigotry, prejudice, racism, sexism, homophobia—"differencism" or "differism"? I would again like to make the point that people feel comfortable around what is most familiar, what is most like oneself. That which is "too different" is a threat, not a comfort. Let's take racism, since that along with sexism seems to be the most hated of our isms among our political leaders and other fanatics. Just recently many people are demanding that the governor of Virginia resign because twenty, thirty years or so ago, when he was a young man, a college student, an age when young people pull all kinds of idiotic shenanigans, he dressed up in black face, which of course they see as a terrible insult to black people. Did he also dress up once as Michael Jackson? Or was that someone else? Let's say it was him. I would think any reasonable person would see a great deal of difference in those two episodes. Dressing up as Michael Jackson, if it was not a clown Michael Jackson, should be taken as a compliment to a person who contributed a lot to bringing black culture into main stream America. For a white man to pay homage to Michael is, in my book, a tribute, an accolade, not an insult. I would say somewhat the same for any black face dress-up. It depends on what the dress-up looks like. Is it meant to be derogatory or complimentary or simply a costume and no more. It's like a sports team that goes by the name of Braves. The name, in my book, is a compliment to the Indian male and his fighting ability. It is definitely not an insult, although some Native Americans seem to think it is the latter.

Anyhow, rambling on, I suspect that most black Americans really don't care whether the governor of Virginia dressed up in black face or not when he was little more than a kid, as long as he's not bigoted in the present or future. After all, most young people growing up and becoming adults (those worth their salt anyway) do stupid things, simply because that's what being human is all about—learning and making mistakes and, hopefully, learning from those mistakes—you know, the Christ myth of descending into hell before ascending into Heaven. If we discarded all adults based on the dumb things they did in childhood and youth, we'd discard all except the do-nothings, which (jokingly but seriously also) is close to what we do now if we judge our actions by our leaders in Congress—our do-nothing leaders.

And now to the point, I hope. Take Liam Neeson. He recently confessed that he once wanted to kill a black man, any black man, because a good friend of his was raped by a black man. I personally think that is not such an abnormal reaction. In Neeson's favor, the feeling finally went away as his anger cooled over time. I once, in Mexico City felt a violent hatred for Mexicans when one tried to rape the girl I was with and other Mexicans came to his aid and started a kind of standoff, mostly strutting brawl with my American friends. But my childish reaction also cooled and I have spent quite a bit of time in Mexico since then and have had several Mexican friends. I also felt that way about Germans once, while in the Army in Germany, because of an incident that threatened me personally. But, again, the feeling passed. And then of course there was the hatred instilled in Americans against Germans and Japanese during the WWII by the press and our leaders. That seems to have dissolved over the years. About American fanatics of the left or right? Hmmm, the person who can honestly say that he/she has never had negative feelings about a specific group of people is too good to be true or is too much like a saint for me to understand.

This all leads me to my main reason for writing this essay. I think our leaders are over the top and they are polarizing the nation, using racism and other isms as their ammunition. Neeson is a good case in point, as is the Virginia governor, and as are the following: Gucci pulled a sweater from the market because people complained that the half-balaclava-like top looked like a "blackface." And Adidas included a white sneaker in its Black History Month items for sale. It pulled that white sneaker from the sales items, simply because it was white. Something white pulled because it smacks of racism? Something black pulled because it smacks of racism?

If the complaints about these two items, and about Neeson, and about the governor of Virginia…if the complaints were so suggestive of a terribly deep-rooted anger, even hatred, I would laugh at how ridiculous they seem to me.

All I can say is that bigotry will always exist among human beings, in any society where there is "diversity." All of us have some of it, black, white, brown, yellow, Catholic, Protestant, Jew, Muslim, rich, poor, power-ful, weak. It is more prevalent and stronger in some than in others. The object is to repress it, or to fight it, or to ridicule it, or to ignore it. By con-tinuously making it so important that it destroys people's lives we do no more than continuously drive the wedge deeper and deeper between people of different ethnicities, religions, political leanings, sexuality, whatever. We make our differences a destructive force that brings anger and hatred to the fore, making them the major emotional dynamism between us, rather than acceptance and social comradeship, which any society needs if it is not to dissolve into violence.

Bombs

It's scary. But what could we expect. Ever since President Trump was elected, the fanatic Trump haters have been trying everything to bring him down and occasionally the pro-Trumpians have also staged demonstrations. There were the anti-Trump demonstrations after his election, and at least one pro-Trump demonstration, some on both sides including elements of violence, and, I believe, elements of extremism in the anti-Trump groups as well as in the pro-Trump groups.

In summary, there were the women's march on Washington D. C and some local women's anti-Trump marches. There was the shooting of the Republican Congressman at the softball game. There was, and still is, the continuous negative and inflammatory commentary by most of the media about the president, his events, his comments, and even the people who serve him, seldom any unbiased and reasonable analysis of his accomplishments. Then there was the Kavanaugh situation, a man nominated for the Supreme Court accused with little to no proof of sexual abuse—sexual abuse committed when he was a high school student of seventeen, almost fifty years in the past—a he said/she said situation, and the accusation was made by an anti-Trump and liberal activist.

And then a number of our Democratic Congress members have not only continuously disparaged the president but have also called for their followers to accost his aides and helpers anywhere they can: Get in their face and tell them they're not wanted here! And of course this scary action actually happened a number of times, mainly in restaurants and not only to those who serve the president but also to Republican Congressmen. Then came the bombs mailed to Democrats and liberals, and CNN, who have been highly critical of the president, sometimes in a nasty way. Luckily, meant to be or not, the bombs were all duds. And now…now an anti-Jewish fanatic has attacked a synagogue in Pittsburgh, killing at least eleven worshipers. It is terrible, sad, and frightening. The murderous and uncompromising side of our nature (human nature) is showing its nasty face. We are becoming so polarized that some commentary, no matter how innocent and personal it actually is, can result in professional and personal destruction because we seem to have forgotten that people are innocent until proven guilty, not simply because somebody accuses them. We also seem to have forgotten that we are all human. We all make mistakes. And we all have beliefs that sometimes transgress the values of others and even hurt at times.

I personally don't think somebody should be destroyed simply because he/she believes something that hurts my feelings, and says so; after all, I thought we took great pride in our freedom of speech, not our social engineering skills. Anyhow, witness Megyn Kelly being fired by NBC for no more than saying that she sees nothing wrong with wearing black faces or white faces as part of a Halloween costume. Sure, the comment probably angered many Blacks, but I suspect that most black people are adult enough to have simply passed the remarks off as the type of irritating remark that all of us make at times when we speak without thinking. Yet Kelly was fired. So was the black football player who knelt for the American flag. But some people in the news praise him for his independence. I have yet to hear anyone praise Kelly for her independence of thought and expression, or even come to her defense and say she simply made a mistake and, like the football player, she should not be penalized for her beliefs, no matter who dislikes them. After all, this is the USA and we are supposed to have freedom of thought and expression. Or is it that such went out with all the corporations firing people who express beliefs disliked by the bosses? Or maybe the problem lies with those Democrats and media-lites who hate Trump and insist that his followers be punished for their beliefs. What a terrible place our country has reached when our leaders call for the confrontation of anyone they disagree with, when someone sends bombs to people he disagrees with, or, much worse, when someone commits mass murder against people he disagrees with.

I say, get the press away from its biases and exaggeration and back to ethics and honesty as their basic modus operandi. Yes, we need a free press. But we need an honest one, not one that thrives on exaggeration and bias. I say, get our politicians back to civility and compromise as their basic forms of government, and away from hatred and fanaticism. Move them back toward a democratic form of government, not a tyrannical one. With the continuous escalation of the nasty side of not only the press but also of our leaders, why is it not logical that someone would resort to the use of bombs or guns for political reasons? And now, of course, most of the press is blaming the whole problem on President Trump, ignoring their own role and the role of many of our leaders and others, from comedians and actors to people in public office—organizations and people who ignore their own role in the explosive escalation of anger and violence and invariably blame the other person or the other group. You know, the one I disagree with.

Now they insist that the president must tone down his rhetoric in order to help calm the national anger. I agree to a certain extent. But they say nothing about their own rhetoric and that of our other leaders, especially Democrats, who must do the same and quit calling for violent confrontation of Republicans in public places. I might also add that it is also time for politicians running for office to quit sponsoring negative, nasty ads about their opponents, which politicians from both sides of the aisle do. Those ads appear continuously on television and do little except incite anger and even hatred for either the target or the sponsor. I agree with the call for civility in public life, although I find some of the calls more than a little hypocritical since they come from the mouths of people who must share the blame for the continuous escalation of nastiness and uncompromising attitudes so prevalent in our public life today.

6

Border Wall

We are going to build a wall between us and Mexico, in those places where there is no wall already but where we think one is needed and in those places where we think we need a better wall than the one we presently have—I understand.

Well, I don't think I can make an intelligent comment on this. I simply don't know enough about the methods and places of the movement of illegals and drugs into our country from Mexico. So all I can say to our government is, Go ahead and build the wall if you think its effectiveness will offset the cost of building it. If not, don't build it. (And I'm not only talking here about money, but also about the cost in lives and jobs and health and education, etc. that illegal drugs and immigrants cause throughout our nation.) I too would like to put a finger in the hole in the dike, or put a huge wall in it.

However, I'm not convinced that a wall is the final solution. In fact I believe that it is only a partial solution. As long as drugs are illegal and yet multitudes of our citizens want them, there will be drug smugglers trying to furnish what is wanted—for a good price, of course. As long as foreigners think they can find a much better life in this country than in the country in which they presently live, and as long as our government does nothing about the ones who immigrate here illegally, or is ineffective in doing anything about them, or helps them in one way or another after they get here, they will head this way, illegally if they can't come legally simply because they know that we will do nothing about their <u>illegal</u> entry. And I stress

<u>illegal</u>. For one reason or another many of our governmental leaders (federal and state and local) have decided not to enforce the laws that pertain to our borders.

Why? Misplaced humanism, maybe. Global humanism, maybe. Politics, maybe. Pity, maybe. Racial or family ties, maybe. Workers needed, maybe. I don't know. Maybe they are simply a lot like our Hollywood elites and others of our wealthy people; they spread their charity worldwide, not limiting it to the American poor, or maybe not even considering the American poor because they believe that all peoples of the world should not only have a good life equal to ours but they should have the equality of opportunity, the birthright of equality granted by our Constitution to the actual citizens of our nation, as well as all other rights granted by our Constitution to our citizens. After all, illegals are citizens of the world, as are we who are legal citizens of the USA. Maybe, for the wealthy among us, that makes us all, the whole world, equal under the American Constitution. If so, we anti-illegal-immigrant people have no right to deny anyone access to our country and all its benefits, constitutional and financial. We have no right to pretend that our Constitution only applies to our citizens and the wealth that we earn is ours and should not be spread among the citizens of the entire world.

And here I go again, rambling off target. We were talking about the border wall. I believe that it is but a minor step in the closing off of our borders to illegal drugs and people.

Number one, as long as there are people who hire illegals, either because illegals are cheaper or because not enough American citizens will take these jobs, there will be illegals enticed into the country by the possibility of workers needed. To stop that flow, or to change it into a legal situation, we either need to arrest those who hire illegal immigrants or we need to put into place something like the old Bracero program, giving needed workers legal entry into the country for specific jobs and specific time spans. Of course, I would suggest that we change our welfare program so that any people on welfare who are capable physically and mentally of performing these open jobs have to take them or lose their welfare payments.

We also need to be more proactive in searching out and arresting all illegals who are in our country, those who have overstayed their visa as well as those who have sneaked across our borders. Of course, that will entail a clash between the federal government and those cities, and California, which have declared themselves sanctuaries.

As for the drug problem, I don't think a fence is going to solve that matter although it might slow their movement into our country—and thus raise the cost of drugs and the crimes that go with drug usage. That problem needs to be faced head on by our federal government and our states. The legalization of marijuana is a start, I believe. But we need to go much further. We probably need to legalize some other drugs, especially prescription drugs, and somehow control their usage, as to where and who, on a much stricter basis than we do with alcohol and marijuana. We need to somehow attack opioids and others of the most dangerous drugs, possibly making the punishment for their sale a crime punishable by a prison term equivalent to crimes of violence and even murder. And we need to become much more preemptive in our education of our young about the dangers of drug usage.

I don't think we will ever completely erase the use of drugs from our culture, but if we could cut it in half, or even just control the where and who of usage—that would be a great start.

Capitalism & Socialism

Capitalism and socialism. How many times have you heard that the USA is a capitalist nation, not a socialist one? How many times? In the news media or from a friend or a teacher? Either in a bragging or a derogatory tone?

I'm not sure that I would deny that our economic structure is based in capitalism. Along the same lines, but somewhat in reverse, I definitely would not insist that our government functions as if it were overseeing a nation and economy based completely in capitalism.

Capitalism did once define not only our economic and cultural but also our governmental character, way back before the Great Depression, when there were no labor unions, or social security, or Medicare, or Medicaid, or welfare, or free lunches at school for the poor kids, or government financial support for our schools and universities and students, or government-mandated racial quotas in education and business, or government housing for the poor, or government support for illegal aliens, or a government financed infrastructure, or…. Yes, once we truly were a capitalist nation, a capitalist nation in our very essence. Or, rather, our ancestors were. We? I don't think <u>we</u> can claim that <u>we</u> were once that free of government help and the legal burdens such help so often brings with it, or, admittedly, the benefits it also brings. Our nation was. We were not. None of us…maybe I should say only a very few of the oldest of us were born way back before the Great Depression, when our ancestors were responsible in almost all ways for their own and their family's welfare, and that of their neighbors in times of trouble. When you hear about all the volunteer help in Houston during the destruction caused by Hurricane Harvey, you feel some pride in our people and admit that many of our citizens haven't lost that sense of independence and responsibility that our ancestors had, responsibility not only for themselves and their own families, but also for their neighbors and fellow citizens, and independence from not only government interference in their lives but also from dependence on government help.

But back to capitalism and socialism, we are really a capitalist nation slowly assimilating a great deal of socialism into our national character, and we have been for over a century now, much as Russia and China are communist nations slowly assimilating many characteristics of capitalism into their national character. We are becoming "capi-socialistic" much as they seem to be becoming "soci-capitalistic." I wonder if the democratic structure of our American government will turn out to be the only meaningful difference in the three nations by the end of this century. How ironic that would be after all the petty spitting and spatting between us in the past century, and presently!

Labor unions, representing one small step toward socialism, are one of the most obvious limitations on the free exercise of capitalism, an absolutely necessary limitation many would say, and I would agree. They, more than any other organization, gave rise to the extensive and relatively prosperous middle class which developed in our country after World War II. It's too bad that, in the last half century, they evolved, or, devolved, in the same way as the mom-and-pop businesses, until today most of them "in the United States are aligned with one of two larger umbrella organizations: the AFL-CIO created in 1955, and the Change to Win Federation which split from the AFL-CIO in 2005." And it's also too bad that union membership has dropped from 30% of the work force in 1950 to only 12% in 2000, only 8% of which is in the private sector—according to Wikipedia. Unions themselves, I believe, are partially to blame for that drop in membership. They became larger and larger and more and more powerful as they developed, until, I think, they no longer had the welfare of the individual worker as their driving force, but rather the accumulation of more and more power, like what has happened to our federal government (and state governments?) during the same time span. They drove wages and benefits so high that large corporations took their manufacturing plants abroad, where they could find cheaper labor. The government didn't help any, of course, as they raised corporation and personal taxes ever higher over the years. Nor did the corporations themselves, especially the automobile companies, which found it easier, and maybe more lucrative at the time, to raise prices rather than suffer the losses of prolonged strikes; in other words, they passed the cost of union demands on to the consumer. After all, the middle class could afford to keep up with the rising prices; their wages were rising almost (?) as fast as were the costs of American products, more so at the beginning. So those unions that were a lifesaver for many working families back in the 1930s and well into the 1960s and 1970s slowly became as large and impersonal as international corporations are, as lacking in loyalty as any monolith to the American workers and their needs and way of life, until they ultimately became too ineffective to be a major force for <u>real</u> benefit to the laborer.

Be that as it may, however, labor unionization is a step away from pure capitalism toward socialism, although the forces of larger and larger corporations and tighter and tighter manufacturing job markets in our country seem to be moving us, as a nation, back in the direction of the capitalistic way of life, the "global" capitalistic way of life.

The same is not true of our government, I don't think. Roosevelt's New Deal during the Great Depression started an interventionist approach to government which has expanded in many directions, into many aspects of our society.

Take welfare. According to Wikipedia we seem to provide decently for our needy. "Federal and state welfare programs include cash assistance, healthcare and medical provisions, food assistance, housing subsidies, energy and utilities subsidies, education and childcare assistance, and subsidies and assistance for other basic services." Then there are social security, Medicare, Medicaid, and the State Children's Health Insurance Program, not to mention the more recently approved Obamacare. Social Security, of course, was supposed to be a savings program but has over time included recipients who do not pay into social security. It also pays out retirement monies higher than what was put into the system by many retirees.

Again according to Wikipedia, excluding Social Security and Medicare, "Congress allocated almost $717 billion" for welfare programs in 2010 and the states allocated another $210 billion. By 2013 expenditures for Medicare and Social Security had reached "$1.3 trillion, "37% of federal budget," while "social insurance programs provided to workers by employers" had reached about "$1.6 trillion." As well as being a retirement plan for our workers, Social Security provides help for the old, the unemployed, dependent children, and needy families. In essence, it is no longer just the retirement savings plan it began as, but has become part of our welfare system as well.

So, one of the basic characteristics of Karl Marx' socialist paradise is that each person gives to the common good what he can, what he is capable of giving, and receives from the state according to his needs. We seem to have adopted the latter half of that equation, although some might argue that we aren't yet at one hundred percent of giving according to the needs of our people. Probably not. We tend to see what we perceive as a problem of need and try to solve it, ignoring any potential problems our largesse might cause in the greater society or in other limited groups, or to other people in a specific group. In that sense we are definitely a humane society, or we attempt to be, but not always the most astute one a person could imagine.

But, by ignoring the first half of the Marxian ideal, we are facilitating the erosion of what I have always considered two of our most basic American characteristics, a sense of responsibility for oneself and one's family and a sense of pride that goes hand in hand with a deep-seated work ethic, in other words pride in accomplishment and a job well done. If we are going to continue moving in the direction of Marxian socialism, we need to begin working on the concept that everyone, every citizen, gives to the state according to his ability.

But, you say, there are some people who simply can't give anything. What about the blind and bedridden? I agree, I say. But the idea is to give according to one's ability. If a bedridden person has eyes and functional hands, maybe there are things that he can do, like put things together, or use a computer, or…. If a person is blind, I don't know. I accept that there are people who are simply incapable of performing the easiest of tasks. But I also believe that anyone receiving money from the government should do something for that money if at all possible. He should give whatever he can for two reasons, one because there is a great deal of self-pride in work and giving to the common good, and two because it not only pays back to those who can and do work, but it also keeps that old sense of responsibility for one's self and one's family alive and well.

And so, am I advocating socialism? I don't think "advocating" has a thing to do with what I'm saying here. We as a nation are moving more and more toward being a socialist nation. I can't stop that. But I can suggest that we stop being only a giveaway nation (and probably go broke eventually)…that we stop giving only to our needy and start demanding something from them in return. If we're going to use half of Marx' socialist ideal, we might as well use the other half. I think we would all benefit from such.

Censorship

This rumor was wandering around the YMCA last week and so I looked it up to see just how correct it was. And, except for a little exaggeration about the fights, it was true.

It seems that the Greater Scranton YMCA (PA) banished Fox News, CNN, and MSNBC from the television channels on its aerobic machines because of arguments and near fights. Some other YMCAs, I guess, have done so for some time.

I find that very depressing, but not unexpected. You would think that in a democracy like ours people would want to listen to all kinds of ideas, in order to learn things they might have ignored or not thought about; in order to figure out what all is going on in the minds of their fellow citizens, and thus become more knowledgeable citizens themselves; in order to know more thoroughly what those in the opposite party, or the independents or extremists, are thinking; and, by all means, out of sheer curiosity. After all, we are a free country, right? We are a country which believes in free speech, right? I shudder to think what might have happened to this great nation if our military leaders during World Wars I and II had refused to read anything written by German military leaders simply because they disagreed with their ideas. We might be speaking German. You can't defeat an enemy if you know nothing about the way his mind works. At the least you would find it much more difficult to do so.

So then why all these nasty reactions to what other people have to say? Have we come to the point where the people, or rather certain elements of the people, are going to impose censorship on the rest of us? Are some people saying that if the government won't stop you others from saying things we don't want to hear…if the government won't censor you, we will, with violence if necessary? Are we moving into a cultural atmosphere like that of Russia and China, and, yes, Cuba, during their years of communist dictatorship? I would refer to Germany and Italy under the rise and control of fascism, but our present "censorship" problems seem to come from the left rather than from the right of the political spectrum.

Charlottesville Riots

One of the main political results of the Charlottesville demonstrations? More Trump bashing. Is it purely and simply hatred for President Trump that brings such reactions from the press and our political leaders, and even common people on the street and in bars and other places of business? It does seem like no matter what the president's reaction to anything political, it is either too late, too little, too "incorrect," or flagrantly spiteful, or malicious, or offensive…to someone. The vituperation is something I've never experienced with respect to a president before.

I've lived for 82 years in this great country of ours. I've been voting for 61 of those years, sometimes Democratic, sometimes Republican, but not missing any presidential elections that I can recall. My first vote was cast for Adlai Stevenson in 1956, my latest one for Donald Trump. Between those years I voted for such as John Kennedy, Richard Nixon, Jimmy Carter, Ronald Reagan, Bill Clinton, Al Gore, and George W. Bush. And, I have to admit, I've been happy with my vote in some cases and not so happy in others. But what I am, proudly and, I hope, consistently, is an independent in the political arena.

As for the vituperative reaction to the Charlottesville "riots," ignoring the same relative to the reaction to our president's reaction to those riots, what brings such a reaction on? Is it hatred of anything over to the far right, what some call the alt-right? And if it's hatred for the alt-right, why not for the alt-left? Or maybe the attitude about the alt-left should be one of fear rather than hatred. After all, the destructive tendencies in their marches and demonstrations don't seem to attract much negative reaction, from press or intellectuals or politicians. And that, to me, is kind of scary. It's as if they're saying "Oh, the demonstrators are basically good people. And they have a real beef with the established order because it ignores their calls to help those of our citizens in distress. And they're standing up against the racist right so they couldn't be all bad. Besides they're only destroying property and impeding travel. So cut their anger some slack."

Does that "cutting" then create a domino effect, kind of like Illegal immigration over the decades or a stock market crash, or what might have been part of the elevator mechanism that raised Hitler to power? Or Joseph Stalin? I wonder, and the fear is still sloshing down inside me somewhere. And I ask myself, just what percentage of those people on the alt-left truly are good people who want to help everyone and include everyone in the benefits of our democracy, every race, every class, every age, every religion, and <u>every belief</u>? And what percentage is made up of anarchists, communists, world travelers, and socialists, many of whom would desert any of their fellow demonstrators the moment they found out that those fellows didn't believe 100% as they themselves do, or maybe even 20%?

Of course white supremacists are a nasty bunch. Racial hatred seems to be the only reason for their existence. But are there any differences at all in the alt-right, as there are in the alt-left? I truly think that in the latter case there are not only anarchists, communists, and socialists in the groups that march and sometimes destroy property and cause other disruptions, but there are also intellectuals and students who believe in democracy but have an abiding fear of and hatred for white supremacists. As for the alt-right, there was a black woman on the Tucker Carlson show right after the Charlottesville riots; I'm sorry but I cannot recall her name. She was actually defending President Trump from the accusation that he is the basic cause of the recent rise of the alt-right groups. She had written a book, she said, shortly after the turn of the century. The book presented her belief that many white people, especially males, were beginning to feel disenfranchised, feeling that they had been left by the wayside by a civil rights movement that had gone too far in giving benefits to minority groups, especially Blacks, and thus effectively blocking Whites from those same benefits or equal consideration for them. I don't recall if the woman said that she agreed with this feeling or not, only that she has sensed its existence for a long time and that she believes that the alt-right probably includes many of these people who feel estranged from a government that, in their minds, has deserted them to give preference to others. She called them white nationalists, I believe. They do not necessarily hate Blacks or other minorities. They distrust, are distressed by, and are angry at a government that, in their minds, has deserted them. They demonstrate against that same government as well as against those minorities who are being given special benefits.

Is she right? I don't know since I have not studied the alt-right; nor do I believe that the press or our congressional leaders have, in spite of how quickly they jump on the anti-racist bandwagon, or how loudly they shout in their self-righteous (Do I dare say hypocritical in some cases?)…their self-righteous vituperation against the president.

But let's see! The alt-right appeared, with legal permission, I believe, armed with guns as well as sticks and bottles and other weapons. Guns? Yet no one was shot. The alt-left appeared with sticks and bottles and other weapons, without legal permission. They impeded the movements of the alt-right. Fights broke out. But for some reason the press blamed the alt-right; I was going to say "mostly" but for the life of me I can't recall any positive, even neutral, comments about the alt-right. Is the press saying that the alt-right does not have any right to freedom of speech and needs to be stopped in any way possible? If so, I disagree, no matter how nasty and sickening and hateful that speech is. Or is the press simply saying that they, the media, do not recognize that freedom with respect to the alt-right, only the alt-left and others in between?

Then, tragically, some nutcase drove his car into the melee of counterdemonstrators, killing one woman and wounding other protestors. The press immediately began denouncing the whole bunch of alt-righters for this senseless murder. Now, this is the same press that takes great pains not to blame all Muslims for the terrorism of one, or a few. It is the same press that takes great pains not to jump the gun and claim that a specific act of violence is terrorism until told to do so by government sources. And it is the same press that then takes even greater pains to make sure that only one radical Islamic group is blamed, hopefully the correct one. Not all Islamic terrorists. Gracious sakes, no. Only the correct one! Yet they lay the blame for that one woman being run over, on purpose…they blame the whole group of alt-righters. I find that just as disgusting and dishonest as I find the slogans shouted by the alt-right. If we cannot have an open and honest press, one with integrity, then our democracy is in grave danger, much graver danger than from a small bunch of haters.

What is scary, and disgusting, for me is that so much of the American press has chosen sides and has even become somewhat fanatic about championing its choice, which is the anti-Trump side. It would be easy to point to any number of talking heads or comedians, etc. on television, or to major newspapers, but I am going to point the finger at my favorite magazine. Or should I say once favorite? That is *Time*, the weekly magazine that many of us read faithfully. I have read *Time* since I was 23 years of age and was first introduced to it, not all the time but pretty consistently. And I have had a subscription to the magazine for many years now, and have read it diligently. I have always enjoyed the magazine because it, more than any other popular magazine I have read, has seemed to stand in the middle of the road and present our political reality from that point of view. I could depend, I always thought, on the magazine's editors to present their analyses of the news from that middle ground and to try to present both sides of controversial news stories. However for many years now I have questioned whether the middle ground still pertains to the magazine's stance. With the election of President Trump I have been disappointed by the way the magazine seems to have thrown unbiased opinions to the wayside and has begun to bash the president in any article in which he figures as a main or even minor character. In *Time*'s August 28, 2017 issue, in "Will the Nation Succeed where the President Failed?" after designing that accusatory title and basically blaming the president for "having long petted and pampered the demons of racial politics," and almost for the Charlottesville riots themselves, the author, Nancy Gibbs, says that the nation will "have to look elsewhere for moral guidance…." I don't much appreciate the president of the USA, of my country, being called immoral, especially in a magazine that I have long read because it is, rather, has been, one of the few news sources that presents both sides of problems with honesty and integrity.

In the same issue of *Time*, in "Bigots, Boosted by the Bully Pulpit" (now who does that refer to?) Michael Scherer and Alex Altman vilify President Trump and accuse him of being a major cause in the rise of the alt-right into the limelight once again, stating that he legitimized "a hateful ideology" because he refused to take sides and condemn one group, and one group only, of the face off. They say this even though both sides came prepared for violence. They say this even though no one was shot by all those guns the alt-right had with them. The two authors of the article also accuse President Trump of "demagogic impulses," of using the Oval Office as a "pulpit to tolerate and fan tribal grievances," and of legitimizing "right-wing extremism in the country."

In another article, "What White America Must Do Next," Eddie S. Glaude, Jr. calls the president "mealy-mouthed" because he did not condemn only the alt-right but rather chose to condemn both sides of the Charlottesville confrontation and say that there were probably good people in both groups. And, of course, like the other writers mentioned above, Glaude claims that the White Supremacists and President Trump are on the same side and that Mr. Trump's election has "inflamed and emboldened those who embrace" the ideas espoused by the white nationalist movement.

So, I guess this is not a free country after all, one with freedom of thought and expression, no matter how atrocious that thought and expression is, and that any president not on the side of the alt-left is a step away from being a Nazi himself, if not one already.

Another bothersome thing I find in these articles, and in so much of the press, is that, when they refer to history, they tend to ignore the fact that ultra-nationalists or alt-right activists do not grow from nothing. The alt-right is often as much a reaction to the radicalization of the alt-left as the alt-left is a reaction to the alt-right. And so much of our media tends to ignore the fact that historically both sides have not only been nasty in speech but also in action. Both sides have not only killed millions in war but also during peace time.

I think Ken Shapiro, in an August 15, 2017 article for the *National Review*, best characterizes both extremes of our present American political polarization: "And so here we stand: On the one side, a racist, identity-politics Left dedicated to the proposition that white people are innate beneficiaries of privilege and therefore must be excised from political power; on the other side, a reactionary, racist identity-politics alt-right dedicated to the proposition that white people are innate victims of the social-justice class and therefore must regain political power through race-group solidarity." And he also seems to me to summarize the conflict in Charlottesville in an honest and unbiased way: "There's still no certain knowledge of who began the violence, but before long the sides had broken into the sort of brutal scrum that used to characterize Weimar-era Germany. The two sides then carried the red banner and the swastika." On the one side there was the antifa (Antifaschistische Aktion), a group made up of anarchists, communists, socialists and probably others from the left extremes. On the other side there were the Nazis, white supremacists, white nationalists and probably others from the right extremes. All of these groups are active throughout Europe and the United States.

Me? I fear both groups. The fascists, led by Germany's Nazi Party, took over Spain, Italy, Germany and much of Europe in the 1930s and early 1940s. The Nazis, excluding the number killed in war, supposedly killed over 6 million Jews and 6 million other Europeans, although the numbers could be higher. In their rise to power and during later years, the communists supposedly killed upwards of 73 million of their own citizens in the People's Republic of China (1949-1987) and over 58 million in the USSR (1923-1987), citizens of all categories and classes who supposedly committed "crimes against the Party." (Huffington Post, 1-27-2015) I can only wonder how many innocents the Nazis would have killed if they had managed to win WWII. Frightening! But it's just as frightening to think that the communist element of antifa might take over the USA, or Europe.

I find very discouraging the attitude of our politicians and our media toward the two political poles of our society. That they have chosen to attack the alt-right and accept the alt-left as either our political champions against the alt-right, or as simply something to be tolerated I find scary. I ask myself, are we repeating history, and is this an oblivious repetition or one of conscious repetition? Are we repeating the history of the Weimar Republic? Or is the press blowing this whole thing out of whack, possibly in order to give them a reason to bash President Trump every time some situation requires his reaction.

And if we are repeating history, is it the history of Russia and China rather than Germany? Or will, ultimately, the alt-right prevail in spite of the apparent odds against it? Both political systems have prevailed in different countries.

And, because of the polarization and hate so prevalent around me, I yearn for the days when our country was not polarized, when our people refused to champion radicals of any stripe, but rather truly believed that all of us are "created equal" and that the middle ground, the ground of reason and brotherhood and love of country, must take precedence over fanaticism. I yearn…but then I ask myself, am I actually longing for a time that never truly existed except in my mind?

Civilizations, The Rise & Fall

You know, it seems to me that one of the great ironies of human history, maybe the very greatest irony, is that civilizations are created by the "gimme" type of people, the type of people who take what they want even if they have to fight for it. Ironically those same civilizations are destroyed by "give-away" types. Toughness builds empires, not kindness, as witness our own frontier movement, the Roman Empire, the English empire built with soldiers and strong men of commerce, and the Spanish empire built by soldiers and priests, who were not by any means Christ-like. I might add that business empires are built by the same kind of people as are political empires.

On the other hand, attempts to get along peacefully with everyone and to include everyone among the citizens and beneficiaries of empire destroy those same empires, destroy civilizations that the toughminded have built. The kind people, those people with truly humane depths, humanitarians created by civilized existence, are the people who destroy what created them in the first place. Why? Because we humans, no matter how much we try to live by the creed of freedom of belief and action… we humans, and thus the cultures we exist in, cannot survive profound and widespread disparities in our most basic cultural actions and beliefs. And as we include more and more people in a civilized and unified culture, the linguistic, religious, political, racial differences begin to rip the fabric of unity apart and the spats begin, leading ultimately to disunity and physical conflict.

The United States of America was not created by the kindness and in-clusiveness of good will. The original thirteen colonies were freed from British rule by people who were willing to go to war to establish what they considered their right—the right to govern themselves, the right to do as they pleased rather than as England pleased. The Revolution, as we call it, was led by men willing to kill or be killed in order to have their way. The armies of The Revolution were filled with men of the same stripe. The men and women who peopled our frontier, the men and women who moved out into the wilderness to form homesteads or settlements, were also not of the giving type. By and large, most of them were people who took what they wanted, by the sweat of their labor or the bullets of their guns, even if such meant killing Indians or Spaniards/Mexicans in the process. They were probably normal-acting human beings, not much different from their neighbors who remained in civilized areas, except that they were either more adventurous, or they were more troublesome, or they did not have fertile farm land or a successful business, so they went in search of such, of what has come to be known as the American Dream, meaning success that the unsuccessful or the ambitious or the adventurous or the alienated went into the wilderness in quest of. They didn't adventure into the wilderness for humanitarian reasons. They did it for selfish reasons, to fulfill their own desires or the needs of their families, or to escape some problem they faced in civilized society. The American government helped with soldiers and other means as it saw fit. It too had a dream, Manifest Destiny, although that dream might not have dwelt in all conscious minds.

The point I want to make here, however, is that it is toughness, even ruthlessness, which is the main characteristic that builds our civilizations, not compassion and kindheartedness. Compassion and kindheartedness are noble characteristics, but they do not build civilizations or business empires, or religious empires. Bill Gates did not help build a computer empire by being philanthropic in his business dealings. He was tough and monopolis-tic. His philanthropy came later in life, through the foundation he created to share his wealth with the needy, and it is separate from his business deal-ings. The Catholic Church did not become so powerful that it has its own city in the heart of Rome by being benevolent and humane. The United

States did not become a world power by paying its enemies to be nice and by playing "willing" foster parent to millions of illegal immigrants; that has been a more recent development. First there was the war with England, then the movement westward, killing or forcing onto reservations whatever Indians found in the way of that movement. Then there were the Texan fight for independence from Mexico and our war with that same nation. Then there was the Spanish-American War, through which we took Cuba, Puerto Rico, and the Philippines. Then WWI. Then WWII. And then our military expansion worldwide. And? Are we now trying to destroy our empire, what with all the foreign aid we pass around and the open borders "push" of many of our people and leaders? Benevolence is attractive. It makes one feel good about oneself. People admire philanthropists.

But, when compassion and benevolence become ingrained in government (political, commercial, religious, etc.) it is erosive. Destructive. Simply because, in this world of ours, in order to enlarge their own sphere of influence and control, the strong take advantage of the weak. That is human nature. If it weren't so, we would probably still be living in caves. In other words, Darwin was right, and still is. And the question that keeps eating at my insides is the following: Has the United States reached the point in its history in which its slide into oblivion is underway?

Cloven-Footed

When I was a working man, if you could think of teaching as actually "working," there were these two faculty members who were, as we used to say when we were children, afraid of their shadows. Every time somebody on campus sneezed too often, or too loudly, or off key, or in somebody else's office, or…one or the other of those two guys would appear in my office moaning that the sky was falling. They seemed to see sinister machinations everywhere. That, to me, is one of the most salient characteristics among so many people today, people from all walks of life—races, religions, genders, political creeds, financial levels. Ever since President-elect Trump began, first, his nomination run and, second, his presidential bid, the press, so many Democrats, and, oddly enough, lots of Republicans, have been squealing that he is a racist, a homophobe, a misanthrope, a… that he's anti-Islam, anti-gay, anti-female, almost anti-everything except wealthy and white. Some of it, of course, was simply political diatribe, which is to be expected. But the sad thing is that the rant has continued and even gotten harsher in some ways since the election, even as Trump has tried to soften his diatribe.

Scores of Chicken LIttles have rushed out of the woodwork to screech that Trump is causing the sky to fall and to try to somehow prop the sky up by stopping Trump from assuming office. Me, I'm a little sick of it, to say the least. There have been a lot of people elected to public office in my lifetime that I considered a threat to the wellbeing of the country, to the presidency, to Congress, to state and local government. But have I screamed foul, thrown a public tantrum, or tried in any way possible to keep them out of office? No, I don't consider myself so wise that it is absolutely necessary for the country to do everything my way. But there seem to be a lot of people out there who do.

One of the essences of democracy is that many citizens will be disappointed in specific elected officials, or even dislike or fear them. However, the wheel that keeps the system from toppling and self-destructing is the peaceful and even gracious transfer of power. On the day that many of us start doing whatever necessary, short of violence, to change the results of our elections, that is the day we have taken one step too close to using that very violence we have stopped short of. On that day, if we fail in convincing the country to accept our desires, the only answers are to back off or resort to that violence we have so far rejected. We must accept defeat or take the enemy down by the strength of our arms. It's difficult for many of us, when our emotions have risen to a fever pitch, or when we have publicly committed ourselves to a specific end, to quit, admit defeat, and become reasonable again. The anger, frustration, desire to have our way, dislike, or even hatred, keeps fermenting down deep inside of us, just waiting for another chance to explode, and all the more violently for the waiting. We would be better off tamping it down early on, before it has grown to the level of angry expression in words. For if words fail…?

So many people on the losing side of the election seem to think that Mr. Trump is against everything that isn't white and/or rich. Let me see, if you are black, brown, yellow, white, green, Christian, Muslim, Jewish, Hindu, Protestant, Catholic, big, little, male, female, fat, skinny, ugly... whatever, if you are wealthy you don't really have anything to fear from a Trump presidency, although if you are a rich Democrat you might have a lot to gain if you could somehow stop Trump from taking office. On the other hand, if you are one of those people, except white, and also poor or middle class, you should be quaking in your boots, according to many of Trump's detractors. This, it seem to me, is a Chicken Little view of our country and its political system. After all, we have had 44 presidents over the past two centuries, not all of them worth much. Yet we are still one of the most free and economically sound countries in the world, although we seem to be fast losing the second characteristic. So why should the sky be falling now? And falling just because an unlikeable character has taken over the leadership, unlikeable by some, not all? I didn't much care for Obama, Bush the Younger, or Jimmy Carter. But I didn't shout from the mountain tops that they were bringing the sky down on us. Moreover, I don't really think that a "nice" personality is the be-all and do-all of leadership and accomplishment. In fact it might be a millstone. Competency, I think—competency in the job at hand—is the most necessary ingredient in leadership, competency and the ability to listen to other capable, intelligent, and experienced people before making important decisions.

As for any real threat that Trump's presidency poses to women, blacks, Hispanics, Muslims, and gays, we again have a "sky is falling" hysteria spread among many of our citizens, mainly because of many of Trump's off-the-cuff remarks. He is definitely not very political at times, or politically correct, that is. But then that is part of his attraction, maybe the main part. Many people are fed up to the gills with all the pussyfooting around major problems and differences by our politicians. Blacks, Gays, and Hispanics do have some honest complaints. No rational person would deny that. Women have some too, although not as much as some feminists like to claim. But then, so do white guys. I mean, this is not a perfect world we live in. When government gives one person a benefit under the law, somebody else is probably not going to get that same benefit but will still have to help pay for it. If a university has a certain number of openings in the upcoming freshman class, and 15% of those are reserved for African Americans, well, no White, Hispanic or Asian will be considered for those slots. Why not? Simply because of their race. The rule or this law or whatever you want to call it has nothing to do with ability or financial status, only race. My question is, do you honestly think that Trump will or can do much of anything to change this kind of mindset? I doubt it. He will be more interested in and preoccupied by the major problems that plague the country. Only time and cultural change can eliminate such laws, or practices. The proper question, of course, is, have our cultural attitudes changed enough so that a president can change or eliminate the law? Maybe an even more appropriate question might be, is Trump an elected manifestation of this cultural change I've been talking about? And in that case, will parts of the sky actually fall? Me, I hope so. I'm tired of some of the debris falling from up there in Washington, DC.

12

College Choice

The best national educational system, as I see it? I think there would have to be a lot of changes, especially less freedom for the kids to make their own selections. I think so many of our young base their choice of college on where their parents want them to go, or what college their parents attended, or where a friend is going, or which college has the most prestige among their peers, or where they can have the most fun, or where they can get a scholarship, or where they can play ball or some other kind of sport, or where the cost is the lowest, or….

I doubt very much if the vast majority of kids graduating from high school actually choose a college based on whether it has a specific major that the young person wants to study and whether that major at that specific college (or university) is one of the best in the state, or nation. Many of our high school graduates wind up going to university to study in majors which will have little to do with the jobs they will hold throughout their lives. And many, many of those same youth are pretty much of an academic misfit for university study. In other words they neither have the intellectual capability nor the inclination to profit much from study in the humanities or sciences.

Another problem I have with our higher education system is athletics, not athletics in general but rather the major sports programs like football and basketball, those programs which in many ways serve as filtering and training programs for the next two steps, the minor leagues and the professional leagues. They serve much the same purpose as the minor leagues do for major league baseball, except, in the former case, at the expense of taxpayers and academic standards, not at the expense (and the profit) of owners. At major universities there is a lot of money in football and basketball programs, so much so that the incentive to sign up players who are on their way to the pros is overpowering, impossible to resist for some coaches and universities. So, often, we have programs in which the best players stay on for maybe a year, or two, and then move on to the pros. These players are not recruited as students, or even as student-athletes, but rather as athletes. They might or might not be college material academically.

In smaller colleges, in the recruitment of athletes to play basketball or football, academic ability is also often ignored, for the two reasons that such programs bring considerable prestige to a college and also bring in money from alumni donors, the latter of which is moreover a causal source of considerable money from donors to our major universities.

All of the above leads to a terrible waste of one of our country's major resources, our youth. It is a waste of their time and money. And it is a terrible waste of taxpayer dollars, dollars which could be better spent in supporting students in colleges where they would be a better intellectual and aptitudinal fit, like technical and business colleges and institutions that offer training in the skilled trades or in technological areas like computer science, or in the medical sciences like nursing or medical technology.

Of course, to employ our educational finances and to use the resource of our country's youth more efficiently, we would have to limit the freedom of choice that our young and their parents have to select an institution of higher education. We would have to limit the power of university and college athletic programs to recruit student players based on their sports skills rather than on their academic skills. In essence, we would have to make some profound and drastic changes in the way our colleges and universities recruit students and in the way our young choose the colleges they will attend, some really profound changes. I personally think it's time we did such. We have a major problem with our skyrocketing national debt. Our educational system, especially our higher educational system, is an unnecessarily excessive waste of our money. Our students do not do well academically in comparison to the students of other nations in spite of the fact that we spend more money per student than any other nation. Multitudes of students who shouldn't be, simply because they are not academically capable of doing well in college and are not truly interested in the subject matter colleges have to offer, are moved through our high schools and on into college.

So, what to do? The first thing we need to do is begin testing our young students, at maybe the junior high level, for not only academic ability (intelligence) but also for their major interests related to the work world. Do they test (in the sciences, humanities, arts, language, and mathematics)… do they test in the top percentages of the nation? There should be a general cut-off level below which a student would not be encouraged to continue a college preparatory program, or maybe not even allowed to, but rather encouraged or even required to continue in a program that is oriented toward jobs in technology, the skilled trades, business, nursing, computer science, social work, criminal justice, etc.

Another change that should be made is that of cost. I believe that higher education should be free, like high schools. College and university tuition has simply become too expensive, much too expensive when you think in terms of how much money most college educated students will earn over their work years. College should be free. However, it should also be much more demanding than it is presently, both to get in and to graduate. Much more demanding. And I'm not talking about the GPA or course requirements necessary to go on into law, engineering, medical or graduate school. Those are stiff enough. I'm talking about the general requirements to attain a bachelor's degree: the general degree requirements and the major requirements and, of course, the GPA. Students should not graduate college without the ability to write complicated, lucid and grammatically correct papers of several thousand words. They should not graduate without the capability of solving difficult problems in geometry and algebra. And they should not graduate without a "decent" background in literature, art, history and the sciences, including the social sciences.

As with most people, I suppose, my own personal experiences have been influential in moving me to the above beliefs. As a college professor for many years, I had many students enter my freshman classes who had never read a book, an entire book, in their life. Imagine that! They were high school graduates and entering college freshmen, and they had never read a book in their many years in the educational system. And in the next four years they were supposed to study literature, history, the fine arts, science. Luckily they wouldn't be required to study a foreign language or philosophy. Or, should I say "sadly"?

Another reason I feel that higher education must become more demanding is also from my personal experiences. I wasn't always a teacher. Before my teaching years, I worked in factories, in service stations, and for a construction company outside the USA in the central Pacific, not to mention other part-time jobs. I was also in the Army, in Germany, and I spent time in Mexico City. During those work and travel years I met many people. And there were some college graduates among them. And some of those graduates (I hesitate to say "a lot") had never read a book since they graduated. To learn that, for a reader like I am, was depressing. And it is one of the reasons I think that attending a liberal arts college, a university, should be for those not only with the intellectual ability but also with the inclination, interest, and aptitude. For those who are only interested in getting a "good Job," I suggest colleges that focus on one job-oriented discipline.

13

Conformity

Freedom? Freedom to do what exactly? Or freedom <u>from</u> what? There is no doubt that we are a country with lots of freedoms for the common people compared to countries like Iran or Saudi Arabia, or North Korea, or Russia, or China. And the list could go on and on, but it would most definitely not include European countries such as England and France and Sweden.

Unlike in Muslim countries, our women don't have to cover everything except maybe part of their face. In fact they can wear pretty skimpy clothing if they so wish, although each state has some laws (codes, norms) of decorum (decency), limiting what one can show in public places—laws of decorum that are sometimes more lax than at other times as the cultural cycle revolves, and, of course, are more lax in some states than in others.

Women can drive anywhere they want, alone or with female friends or with male friends, if they have the time and money to do so. They can go to bars, alone or with others. They can go to movies, or plays, or parks, or restaurants any time they want, again if they have the time and money to do so. They can marry the man they want, if he is willing. Or they can remain single. They can work if they so wish and if they can find some place to hire them. Or they can become entrepreneurs. They can go to college, and they can study whatever subject they so wish, if they are intellectually capable of doing so. In fact, they are pretty much free to do whatever they want, within the scope of what is legal, naturally, and within the limits of their abilities and finances, and morals. I guess you might say that they are pretty much equal to men when it comes to legal norms and requirements and limitations.

Men? They too have a great deal of freedom in choosing what they want to do with their life, with their work time as well as with their leisure hours. We don't need to mention that physical and intellectual aptitudes are delimiting factors in all life choices, for all people, as are laws, financial status, and cultural expectations or norms. We also don't need to mention that the decisions of others just might interfere with one's ambitions or other desires, in other words, with one's freedom of choice.

So, our people have considerable freedom to develop their own life-styles, right? Yes, often too much freedom of choice for the very young, many of whom, without close supervision and help from family and teachers, wander into the wrong paths until they, hopefully but not always, find the right one for them. I've often felt that we allow our youth so much freedom of choice that they don't know how to cope with it. They meander through high school without really knowing what they want in the present or future. So they don't take the right courses, the courses that would further their real interests and aptitudes. They wander on to college without any idea of what career they want to prepare for, or they are certain about the career they want and only find out years later that they have little or no lasting interest in, or maybe aptitude for, such a career.

I guess what I'm saying is that there is such a thing as too much free-dom, especially for the young, whose understanding of themselves, of their true interests and abilities, are in the developmental stage just as are their minds and bodies.

But, you know, I think that one of the major forces in human cultures is the force for conformity, maybe because we fear too much freedom, or maybe because we fear differences? That is true of all the countries I've had the good fortune to visit and spend some time in. And it's true here in the USA. Laws not only protect us from those who would take advantage of us illegally, but in many case they are an expression of our culture's moral codes, and its ethical codes as well. Take the simple laws about decency that I mentioned above. We can't go walking about in the nude. Women can't bear their breasts in public whenever they feel like it. A man can't swat somebody else's child just because the child is acting like a brat. A man can't beat his wife just because she disobeys him. All children have a right to an education. One can only shoot another human being in very limited circumstances.

The vast majority of us would agree with both the beliefs and the laws that define the above. But that does not mean that we are free to do whatever we want within the constraints of the law. Being a male, I wouldn't last very long in an office job if I wore jeans and a holey tee shirt. I expect I might last even a shorter time if I decided to wear a dress, maybe a dress that showed most of my chest and my legs up to an inch or two below my rear end. I don't think I would last a very long time in church if I continually interrupted the preacher to tell him how he was misinterpreting the bible, or even to explain to him how he had misused a certain word. In school and college we are expected to show respect for our teachers. And, depending on where the college or university is and the cultural dress norms prevalent in our culture at a specific time, we are expected to dress in a certain way. Men in office jobs, teachers…mostly they dress in suits. In general men don't have hair hanging down to their shoulders. When not on the job, they dress in accordance with the social status they have, or the one they aspire to. Women, I believe, do the same. But only the rebels, or those who are or want to be social leaders, break our fairly lax dress codes.

Rebels? All cultures have those, although our rebels have more legal and social protection than those in many cultures. They have existed throughout my life and in all the countries I've visited. They're the ones who now have lots of tattoos or wear nose or lip rings or dress like Goths or have hair dyed in bright colors. They are also the ones who live at the extreme right or left of our political system, sometimes demonstrating, not always peacefully. Sometimes they become political or cultural or intellectual leaders. Sometimes they add a great deal to human culture, not always good, not always bad, sometimes a mix of both, like Karl Marx or Franz Kafka or our own John Brown.

So we "normal" Americans, those of us who are relatively successful, live and work and get married and have a family and buy a house and save for retirement. We conform to that pattern. I don't see anything wrong with it, since it defines my life. But I recall once when a couple from Mexico City came to visit me and my wife. The couple had two children, in their late twenties, a male and a female. The four of them lived in an apartment with only two bedrooms, a living room, and a small kitchen and bath. We lived in a three-bedroom house with a living room, formal dining room, family room, kitchen, small dining area, and large, usable basement. You know what the woman's first comment on entering our house was? It was something like I don't think I would want to be a slave to such a big house.

That comment has haunted me ever since. I have often asked myself if I have become a slave to conformity and how much it has cost me throughout my life, in time and toil, if I have.

14

Conformity Again

We Americans have always prided ourselves on being a free country, meaning not only do we have the right to vote our beliefs and conscience, and to speak freely, but we have every other right that doesn't infringe upon the rights of our fellow citizens. Or at least that's what we believe, in spite of our legal and legislative systems and their tendency to, over time, place more and more limits on our freedom of expression and action. But then, what bureaucracy doesn't do the same? Isn't that one of the things that eventually bring about rebellion and add to the forces which eventually destroy empires?

However that may be, we seem to forget, or ignore, the irresistible force of conformity that has always been inherent in the American psyche (probably a force embedded in all stable groups of human beings), although I must admit (insist?) that we have had considerable splintering in our culture over the past half century, slowly at first but more swiftly and openly over the past several decades, in dress codes, in body hair, in sexual mores, in racial and religious relationships, and in political beliefs. Why? I suppose one could lay the blame on many people and things, like world-wide communications. But one split, I think, has become dangerous nationally. On one hand, there are the "globalists," who, at the extreme, seem to believe that our Constitution and its benefits should apply to all people the world over. They seem to believe that our peace and freedom and wealth should be shared with all the world's needy. They are the ones who seem to believe that anyone…any foreigner who gets into our country by hook or crook should receive the same benefits as those born here, or as those who have entered our country legally. They seem to believe that those who enter the country illegally should receive the same constitutional and economic and social benefits as anyone. Like all groups, they don't take kindly to disagreement (non-conformity) from anyone, even those within the group.

At the other extreme are those who probably wouldn't let any foreigners into the country, except as visitors maybe, or would be extremely selective as to whom they did let in permanently, selective as to religion, race, sexuality, economic and social ability, etc. They would advocate isolationism nationally and would halt all our foreign aid and our becoming involved in the wars and tribulations of other nations. Like the former group, they don't accept dissent from the party line very well.

That's all to be expected, I think. That's what groups consist of, people (members) who conform to the basic tenets of the group, be the group in question the Catholic Church, the United Church of Christ, the Kiwanis Club, the Elks, the NEA, the AFL-CIO, the Democratic Part, or the Republican Party. If you are a member of a specific group you have to think and act accordingly. Witness the rampant anger at President Trump because he is not acting like previous presidents; in other words, he is not being presidential. There is some leeway for real freedom of thought and personality differences, of course, for occasionally thinking outside the box, but not a hell of a lot, and especially not about anything basic.

If you are a Russian, you think like a Russian. If you are a Chinese, you think like a Chinese. If you are a Christian, you think like a Christian, depending upon your "group's" interpretation of Christianity, of course, not your own individual one. If you are an American? Well, it seems to me that there was a time when we American citizens had certain beliefs in common, like the citizens of most nations, with admittedly the small number of dissenters found in any group. But I am preoccupied here with the basic, normal citizen, or group member, not the fringe elements. We have always had our alt-righters and alt-lefters, just as has any other nation or group or sect or whatever ; we have always had citizens who held extreme views about such things as race and sex and politics and religion, as well as dress and hair codes, and how much lipstick to use on the first date. We, or most of us at least, have always believed that that is their right, the right of the extremists, although our views on just to what extent they can act on those beliefs have changed over the years, drastically in some cases, and not always for the best, I think. But by and large, except for attitudes referring to race and sexual preferences, we are still a free people who have the right to express our inner beliefs without being jailed or otherwise punished by our government for expressing such. That is not to say that members and elements (like businesses, churches, social clubs) of our society do not find ways to punish those who break our cultural norms too badly, as they always have and maybe to a greater extent in the past. It would be naïve to think that they don't. Any society is probably replete with conformist bullies who thrive on attacking those too different and with true-believers who cannot stand others rejecting their (what they see as common and indisputable) beliefs, through speech or action.

I have known many of those types during my years on this earth and in this nation. I have known many people who get extremely indignant, even physically so, at any action or suggestion that they don't consider "normal" or "right" for an American citizen. And I have known a few people who are open to, truly open to, new ideas and ways of doing things. Not many, but a few.

But what I have not experienced before is the polarization of the masses that has slowly taken place in the past few decades in our major political parties, the Democratic and Republican parties. If you are a Democrat, you've got to be a liberal, which no longer means anything from just barely to the left of center to all-out socialism. It means you've got to have a lot of socialism in your thought patterns and feelings. You might not have to believe in all-out socialized medicine, but you do have to believe in free, or at the very least affordable, medical care for the poor and needy, furnished by the working taxpayer. You might not have to believe in the Marxist "to each according to his need, from each according to his ability." Actually, you can ignore the "from" part. And you can ignore some of the "to" part, but not all of it, or even most of it. You have to believe in welfare, welfare not workfare. And, in some ways, you have to believe that minority wants and needs can out-trump those of the majority when it comes to such basics as sexual preferences, religion, politics, race, and taxes.

On the other hand, if you are a Republican, you must ipso facto be a conservative in all matters political and social and religious and sexual, and…. You must believe in capitalism and abhor socialism, ignoring of course that unions and laws that make hospitals treat anyone who shows up with medical problems and lawful restrictions on banks and Wall Street and foodstuffs and laws restricting business practices—all smack of socialistic elements, elements already buried in our laws and culture. So maybe you should actually admit to believing in limited capitalism, just as many liberals actually believe in limited socialism.

But my point is, although I don't think I've made it very well…my point is that our two major political parties are further apart than they have ever been, as are our people. We are no longer a people belonging to political parties both of which are almost intertwined, one just a little to the left of the other, the other just a little to the right of the one, with not a "dime's worth of difference" between them. The Democratic Party has moved much further to the left than it was fifty years ago. The Republican Party has moved further to the right than it was fifty years ago. And those moves, I believe, reflect the political movements of the voters they represent. Maybe that is why there seem to be so many more political independents today than there were a half century ago. But whether or not the last point is true, the majority of our citizens appear to be polarizing in their approach to those social basics that keep any nation cohesive: language, religion, sexuality, and politics. In other words, the basic elements that make up a culture.

Admittedly, the major question is still why. I don't think I've answered that question well, if at all. But I have no doubts that the cause has to do with an inherent American characteristic. We are not deep thinkers like the French or Germans, or even the South Americans. We are a materialistic and practical people. For our population size, we have few really great philosophers or literary personalities, writers who dig deeply into the human psyche and condition, a Faulkner or a Hawthorne or a Twain. Our entertainment genres (movies, television, literature) are slick. They are mechanically excellent, with well-developed plots, enjoyable uni-dimensional characters, lots of mayhem and sex. But they generally lack substance; they lack a depth of penetration into human nature. They are escapist. They are about a quite limited part of our individual lives, a part often only experienced in the news and in the movies or on television: romance and sex, violence and murder, conflict and adventure. They are, by and large, about the extreme aspects of human life, not about what life or people, or our life and our people, are really like.

Our people are conditioned by those same forces. They live in a box created for them by "mass media" school and informational systems, a church, a political party, and a social group or groups. Conditioned well over the years of their growth, the vast majority of them cannot escape that box, not even with their minds. And it is a very shallow box.

So, we are a nation with lots of freedoms. But two black holes are rapidly tearing us apart, the black holes of globalism and nationalism. On the one hand many of us no longer seem to understand, clearly understand, that diversity has its dangers as well as its benefits, that basic differences in language, religion, politics, and sexuality can more easily rip the social fabric apart than sew it together. On the other hand many of us no longer seem to understand that absolute conformity is the very essence of dictatorships, not of democracies. On the one hand many of us seem to have forgotten that our immigrants are supposed to merge with our national essence and help us rise above our limited nationalism and cultural selves, help us become greater than we are. They are supposed to add to our national character, not to diverse or divisive elements within our national boundaries. On the other hand many of us no longer seem to accept that America should be the City on the Hill, the godsend that accepts all comers regardless of those comers' abilities to give of themselves to our nation, or to take from it. In other words, at least politically, we are becoming a nation split down the middle. I can only hope that we are never split asunder in civil war.

Congress

Well, the Republicans passed their tax bill, without any Democratic help. Of course, the latter is not surprising. When Democrat Obama was president, the Republicans dragged their feet every time the Democrats tried to do something. So now it's the Democrats' turn, since Republican Trump is president. For some time now I've described our Congress, to myself and a few others, as a bunch of kids, one side or the other dragging their feet when the other side tries to get them to do something, anything; but I've recently realized that even kids get along considerably better than our supposedly adult members of Congress.

Looking back at my own childhood, long before such as Little League or almost continuous parental supervision had come about, years and years back there in a small Midwestern town, where and when kids could explore the world around them without fear of being harmed in any way and without fear of their parents being jailed and hauled into court for child abandonment because we had been out on our own most of the day…way back in time and place, I recall four possibilities if some of us kids wanted to make a group decision, any decision whether it was easy or contentious: One or more of the big kids, the meanest one or ones, could make us all do what he/they wanted; or we could reach a compromise, usually after a little or a lot of arguing and, maybe, pushing; or we could wind up in a fight to make the decision—winning group rules; or, fourth, we could split up, each group going its own way. Needless to say, we experienced all four possibilities at one time or another. But we did learn one heck of a lot about the need for compromise, without which the future of the day often turned out a lot less fun than otherwise, and sometimes a lot more painful—at least for some.

I don't think any of us want to follow the painful route nationally. We tried that with the Civil War. We lost a lot of young men and crippled many more. A lot of children suffered as they are suffering today in such places as Yemen. Married women were left without a man to help raise their children. The South was left destitute, the North in places not a great deal better off. More: The emotional scars, although softened by the passage of over 150 years, are still with us. Witness our present problem of the Civil War statues. One group wants to take them down. I understand. Some want to keep them up, as a reminder—for good or bad. I understand. I would like to keep them up, as a boost to the historical ego of the South and as a reminder to us all of what we should not repeat—civil war. But, whether they remain or not, the result should come after discussion and compromise, not as the result of angry dictates by one group. Discussion and compromise are democracy in action.

The distressing problem is that we are presently a politically polarized nation. We seem to have lost our way, lost our connection with one of the most necessary and "sacred" characteristics of true democracy: compromise. There are the pro-lifers on the one side and the pro-abortionists on the other. The pro-lifers want no legal abortions at all and do not want any government money paying for them, although I think many pro-lifers would agree to abortions that were necessary in order to save the mother's life or abortions in the case of rape or incest. Many, I hope, would agree to abortions in the case of a fetus that would be born terribly crippled, such as one with no arms or legs developing at all, although I'm not certain about the "many" part given the sometimes fanatic linkage many people today seem to have to their beliefs. Sometimes I think, when talking to friends and acquaintances, and even strangers, that I have been suddenly transported back into the Middle Ages, only with political rather than religious beliefs governing us. I expect to be spirited away by the Inquisition at any moment, even if I suddenly acquiesce to the insistent arguments I am facing. I think I'm facing medieval scholastics discourse rather than one based in reason and understanding, and even good will, no matter how reluctantly given.

Abortion isn't the only thing that separates us. There is immigration. Some on the conservative side of the political spectrum want to halt illegal immigration completely and send <u>all</u> illegals back where they came from, with maybe the dreamers as the only exception—or not. Some on that side only want us to rid ourselves of those illegals who commit or have committed crimes. Many want to change our legal immigration policies, especially changing the laws that allow families to bring in other family members, no matter their level of education or abilities. They want an immigration policy that gives precedence to people with skills we need in the USA. Many conservatives also want Trump's wall to come to fruition. On the liberal side, on the other hand, there is the extreme of the sanctuary city, which has now become the sanctuary state, I understand, with California leading the way as of the first of this year. Many liberals seem to be all for chain migration (families bringing in as many family members as they want, even extended family members) and sanctuary cities (even states) where illegal immigrants, often even those who have committed crimes, are safe from exportation. They don't want a wall. Many, as in California, seem to be happy with open immigration without borders. They insist that we need the manual labor that illegals bring into the country. They ignore or reject the possible problem of illegal workers depressing the wage scale and maybe taking jobs our legal citizens should have, which, we all know in our deepest self, would require deep changes in our welfare programs.

I could go on, easily. We are a country divided on many of the cultural and economic changes that have been developing both recently and over the last half of the past century, and even before that. The political left and right disagree on, and many are polarized by, such as fracking for our great stores of natural gas; our slow but inexorable cultural and legal acceptance of homosexuality and transgenderism; whether global warming, or climate change if you wish, is real and a major threat or not; whether genetic engineering, especially of our food products, is good for us and could help thousands if not millions of people worldwide; whether children are damaged or not when they are raised by single parents, divorced couples, or homo-sexual partners; and even whether free and open sex is good or bad for our young. Now some women are calling for sexual harassment training for males in government and civilian leadership positions. I, personally, laugh at that and wonder if the same thing will happen to sexual harassment that has happened to sexual intercourse among school kids since we instituted sex classes in schools.

Anyhow, to get back to Congress, I wish they would use a little common sense and self-control and get to doing only what, as far as I'm concerned, the legislative branch of our federal government should do—our relationships with other countries, including immigration, bor-der protection, trade and war; interstate commerce, including nation-wide infrastructure of roads, waterways, dams, airways, the electrical grid and pipelines, the internet and, of course, interstate crime; and, fi-nally, tax the people to pay for the government's actions. Congress also needs to listen to the people, all the people, before they make decisions. And they need to quit acting like Big Brother and accept that states have rights—in other words, the people of the individual states have rights. If the people of a specific state (like California) want to legal-ize marijuana and/or other drugs, they have the right to do so, without interference from the federal government. It is not the business of the federal government to tell states what they can or cannot do, unless, of course, what they want to do does great harm to the people of other states and/or segments of people in their own state. By people, I mean legal citizens because I don't believe our constitution or our laws apply to non-citizens unless they are within our borders—<u>legally within our borders</u>. I sometimes think that many of our people and leaders believe that our constitution and laws apply to all people throughout the world, whether those people want them to apply or not. I sometimes think that our leaders want us all to be clones of each other. To misquote George Wallace, they want us to live as if there isn't a dime's worth of differ-ence between any of us. I ask, what happened to our belief in good old American individualism? It is not, and I emphasize <u>not</u>...it is not for the federal government to make laws regulating my drinking habits, my drug habits, my sex preferences or beliefs, my religion and its beliefs, my…. The control of individual actions, it seems to me, should be up to the states and the individual.

Most of all, though, our federal government, especially out Congress, should start acting like a group of people with common sense who live in a democratic nation, not an oligarchic one. They should dig up the remains of compromise and install them in a place of honor in the chamber of the Senate and House, maybe on some kind of altar.

Congress Again

My god! And we pay these clowns, while they do nothing but bicker and spat like a bunch of spoiled brats. Spoiled brats—that is what I think of when I think of US Congress members. Spoiled brats! So many of the Democrats, the more vocal ones anyhow, want everything their way. If they don't get it, they kick and storm around, throwing tantrums. Some of them are becoming really dangerous. The Republicans? Well, I call them the "Do-Nothing Party." It doesn't seem to make any difference who wants to get something accomplished, the Reps simply turn them off and go their own way, either in spite, it often seems, or because whatever it is is not exactly, <u>exactly</u>, what they want. Or, like so many of the Democrats in Congress, they're trying to get re-elected and could care less what is best for the country.

I admit that there are some real statesmen in our Congress. But they are few and far between. And even fewer of them seem to be in positions of power. Maybe they haven't taken enough bribes to acquire and maintain power.

What did Nancy the "Polo si" say? That Trump knows he shouldn't be president. What a childish and idiotic thing to say. And then there's always the question of whether or not she thinks she is a mind reader, something I wouldn't be a bit surprised about. Maybe she has a crystal ball at home and always consults it before she heads to the congressional floor to use her ESP to make one of her "profound" statements about the president. Or maybe she consults Congressman Schiff T. Or one of the other biased (understatement?) members of congress like Disturbed Waters. I don't know, but I sure wish they would start acting like leaders and quit acting like they're just passing through puberty.

Trump knows he shouldn't be president? Wow! How low does one's IQ have to be to make that kind of a statement except satirically. I mean, the man was put in office by our Electoral College, which was designed by our forefathers and entered in the Constitution. Without it, with no more than a popular vote, it wouldn't be long before the cities, with their population, would always dominate the countryside, making their vote (desires and needs) worthless. And, of course, the most populous states like California and New York would soon dominate the smaller states, invalidating their vote, in other words, their wishes. That might just possibly destroy the Republican Party also, making us a one-party nation.

What comes after that? Rule by an elite? I think we have enough of that already. Rule by oligarchy? Rule by a dictator? Civil war? I don't know. Moreover, I don't want to find out either. We have too much corruption in our present leadership, as it is. I can't imagine what it would be like if we wound up with some of the changes the Democrats want.

With all the bickering and nastiness and refusal to compromise (the very heart of democracy), I shudder to think what this country will be like when my little grandchildren reach my age. With all the problems we have (the eroding infrastructure, mass immigration of illegals, apparently unending wars, the flight of basic manufacturing, wages, the seeming politicization of our corporations, the homeless, the healthcare system, and, I think, an ever-more expensive and deteriorating educational system) we need to put our political leaders' noses to the grindstone. Insist that they take these problems one at a time and begin to resolve them. Any member of Congress who doesn't shut up and get busy needs to be recalled and a more democratic and industrious and thoughtful leader installed in his/her place.

Cough Or A Gun

Say you have a cough and stuffed-up sinuses. And your skin feels kind of "sicky-chilly." So you go to a doctor. He prescribes cough medicine and a nose spray and sends you on your way. What would be your reaction? Mine, I have no doubt, would be to find another doctor, one who would treat the cause of my problem as well as the symptoms.

I feel the same way about these mass shootings that have the anti-gun crowd rampaging around the country rather than trying to solve the shooting problem democratically and rationally. Guns are, metaphorically speaking, kind of like the runny nose. When I think of a cold or the flu, I think of sniffing and blowing my nose. When I think of guns, I think of shooting. But, just as it takes some causal factor like the flu or allergies or some other sickness to bring about a runny nose, so it takes some kind of human sickness to bring about a mass shooting. I have to insist that guns don't cause mass shootings just as the runny noses don't cause the flu. Something inside the shooter is the immediate cause of the mayhem just as something inside the sick person is the immediate cause of the runny nose. However, something else, something deeper is the real cause of both, which are no more than symptoms. In the case of the sinus problem, the real cause is probably a virus or bacteria. Any doctor who doesn't treat that real cause when you go to him/her isn't being very intelligent, just as is not any governmental body that doesn't deal with the human factor in mass shootings. Their analysis of the problem is superficial, to say the least.

This does not mean that a doctor should not treat a patient's runny sinuses, should not try to alleviate them as well as the real cause of the sickness. It does not mean that our government should not try to alleviate some of the problems inherent in widespread gun ownership.

I've never owned a gun in my life, so I won't pretend that I know a lot about buying and selling guns, or about the types of guns needed by people for hunting, for sporting events, for personal pleasure, or for protecting oneself and one's family (from an individual shooter out of control or from a government also out of control). I know that I sometimes think I should buy a gun and have it handy, especially after reading about some home invasion or burglary turned violent, or after reading about some good soul being shot and killed by a person he/she was trying to help, or after I myself have been the object of road rage (as I have been three times over the past ten years), which thankfully did not reach the level of physical violence, although once I had to fake acceleration and then quickly cut off the freeway on an off-ramp to avoid an angry driver who was trying to force me off the freeway onto the berm, a driver with a woman and two kids in his car. To this day, I don't know what I did to turn on his rage. But rage it was, all over his face as he shouted unheard words at me and waved his fist.

Anyhow, back to guns. According to *Gun Violence Archive 2018*, there have been 17,123 shooting incidents this year through April 21. Deaths resulted in 4,337 of those shootings, in about 25% of them. What is kind of telling here, what with all the present hype about school shootings, which are generally mass shooting, I believe—what is telling here is that only 66 deaths resulted from mass shootings, although I don't know how *Gun Violence* defines mass shootings. 66 deaths? 66 out of 4,337? That is slightly less than 1.5%. Most of us believe, of course, that even that small percentage is too many. However, several questions do pop into my mind. If there were only 66 deaths caused by mass shootings, how many shootings were there? Four, five, six, ten? Let's say ten. Ten shooting incidents out of the total of 17,123? Ten shooting incidents out of the millions of people who own guns? I personally find it difficult to imagine penalizing millions of people because of a miniscule number of untrustworthy idiots who could care less about the lives of their fellow humans. Such a penalty sounds like what happens in the military. Make the whole company suffer for the problem caused by one. I think that's necessary in the military, where life or death for each member of the company depends on <u>all</u> members. It is also effective because the rest of the company will probably set the culprit on the straight and narrow. But in a democracy like the USA? No way. I don't see how we can trample the rights of so many because of the destructiveness of so few.

To conclude these rambling words about sinuses and shooting, I agree that we should have stricter gun laws, although we know darn well that no matter what laws our Congress makes, they can't take the guns away from the criminal class. Oh, they might make it legally dangerous and difficult enough to take some of their guns away, but not many, I don't think. I also don't think new laws would keep our real rebels, those whose mistrust of government runs very deep, from buying and hiding illicit weapons either. Such laws would more than likely just toss more people into our penal system, some criminals and some just otherwise normal people who mistrust government. So I don't advocate "no gun" laws. However, I do advocate strict registration of automatic and semi-automatic weapons. And I also advocate strict background checks for such weapons.

Then there is that other symptom of the flu, the cough. The cough needs to be treated; otherwise, the sick person will spray other people with his germs. So do those hacking symptoms of mass shootings: criminals and mental cases. They are the ones, along with a terrorist here and there, who seem to do the mass shootings and so need to be dealt with. Otherwise the coughing symptoms might continue getting worse until they spread the flu far and wide. Our national legislature should pass a law defining what types of criminal actions (all felonies or just violent crimes?) and mental problems would make it illegal for someone to purchase or own a firearm of any type. The FBI and state and city police departments should develop lists of people who, under these laws, are not allowed to have a firearm. Those lists should be available to all gun sellers and it should be illegal to sell any kind of firearm to people on those lists.

But to out and out ban all automatic weapons to all citizens in our nation other than military or law enforcement? I don't think so. People should have the right to protect themselves, from the government as well as from other people. But we should treat those symptoms which suggest a deeper problem or sickness. And we should treat them rationally in spite of all the hype that each shooting seems to bring about. However, we also need to <u>try</u> to treat the real cause of these sick shootings (the virus), which is our culture itself, all the way from a corrupt federal legislature which is incapable of getting much of anything meaningful done to a biased mass media which exaggerates almost any news item that comes its way and on down to our individual citizens, many of whom seem to have lost any sense of a moral compass or understanding of what it means to live democratically with other people and the commitment sacrifice and compromise that such mutual existence entails.

Demagogue

Hmmm. President Trump is a demagogue according to a couple of Harvard professors whose book (*How Democracies Die*) I am reading now.

Let me see here. Merriam-Webster's definition of a demagogue is "a leader who makes use of popular <u>prejudices</u> and false claims and promises in order to gain power." That is *Merriam-Webster's* first definition. I myself might add "and hold power." The big question: Is President Trump using the prejudices of the people to just gain and hold power or is he using them to help the country? I think you would have to be in the mind of the president, or be a mind reader, to know what his real motivation is. Besides, I personally think that he is using the hopes and despairs of the people more than he is their prejudices, but then, I admit, I offer about as much proof here for my opinion as the two Harvard professors, in their book, do about their "demagoguery" claim, although I think there's a lot of proof out there for my opinion, if I had the time and desire to track it down and include it in this brief essay.

Now let's go to politician. Also according to *Merriam-Webster*, a politician is "a person engaged in conducting the business of a government," "a person engaged in party politics as a profession," and the disparaging definition: "a person primarily interested in a <u>political</u> office for selfish or other narrow usually short-sighted reasons." One of Wikipedia's definitions of a politician is a person "who seeks political power." It doesn't say why. And then, in *The Free Dictionary* we find that a politician can be someone "who uses public office to advance personal or partisan interests." Hmmm, sounds like any old politician to me.

So, which is President Trump? Many politicians, as far as I am concerned, take advantage of "popular prejudices" to gain office (power) and stay there; that's how they win elections. I believe that Obama rose to power on the need of many Americans to show that at least some of us Americans are not racists. Democratic candidates for office, even the presidency, have called Republicans, including President Trump, all kinds of exaggerated names like homophobe, racist, sexist—it seems to me that these are popular prejudices in both camps, either because the people in that camp do have at least some of these prejudices or have them to some greater or lesser degree or because they believe (fanatically oftentimes) that the people in the other camp have them. One of my personal biases is that there is a degree of prejudice in all of us—every single one.

It seems that almost every time the president or some other Republican comes out against illegal immigration, some Democrat yells racist. On the other hand, the Republicans accuse the Democrats of being prejudiced against our own people, of wanting open borders and thus putting the citizens of other nations before those of our country, before our workers, our poor, and our oppressed.

In their drive for office (power), politicians of both parties sometimes make false claims about the candidates of the other party and, by inference, the other party in general. That is politics. Politics has always been that way, as far as I can recall, although I believe that it has been getting nastier over the past decade or two. And I say that without any "proof" written here in this document and thus leave myself open to the news media spitefully shouting, "He says it without any proof," although of course they won't in this case because they'll never read this and they wouldn't know me from Adam if they did. Moreover, it only seems to be President Trump that so many of them hate fanatically enough to spout something negative almost every time he opens his mouth. That hatred was once called "Trump derangement syndrome," but I really think that a more appropriate term is "fanatic Trump hatred," a hatred so pervasive and deep that even these two Harvard professors, two people whom I for one would expect to be intellectually above such fanaticism…these two Harvard professors put

President Trump in the same political class as Hitler, Mussolini, Pinochet, Hugo Chavez, et al.

They do so at the beginning of their book and at the end. In between they do an excellent job of defining our democracy and analyzing how it has always functioned, how it functions and keeps functioning now. Their major point seems to be that we have maintained our democracy through the centuries by always (almost) having "gatekeepers" embedded in the political process in order to keep the "riffraff" from entering the political process and maybe getting elected. Of course, their basic point is that the "gatekeeper" process broke down and so somehow President Trump, one of the riffraff and a dangerous one, jumped the gate, somewhat like many of those Central Americans in the illegal caravan stalled in Tijuana want to jump our border fence.

Their book would have me worried if I were a Trump hater or if I feared him and what he might do to the country. But I'm not, and I don't. I have seen no evidence, not even one tiny suggestion that he wants to become another Hitler or Franco or Castro or Hugo Chavez. The basic problem that Trump haters have with the president seems to be twofold. One, President Trump is not a progressive liberal. He does not, apparently, believe that every single person in the world has those same God-given rights that our Constitution and its Amendments grant our citizens. And so he does not believe that it is our government's duty to make sure, through diplomacy or force or trade, that all other countries grant their citizens those rights. Two, he wants to put our citizens and thus our country ahead of all other countries. Thus he believes in strict border laws and enforcement. He believes that we should allow into our country only those immigrants (legal) who will benefit our country—immigrants we need in our work force, as engineers, doctors, businessmen, workers, whatever, people we need and thus can use, not people who need or want to use us.

Both of these attitudes of the president are no-nos. He does not believe in a universal welfare system with us on the paying end, and that maddens our many, many do-gooders who would use what wealth we have (or had, sadly) to shower the entire world's poverty-stricken masses with our beneficence. And he does not believe that we should sacrifice ourselves and what hard-earned wealth we have left after decades of spendthrift ways so that the poor from other countries can improve their lot, while our poor and our working men and women sink further and further into poverty.

Me, I applaud President Trump. I have no problem with his tough and sometimes apparently extreme bargaining stances. I am happy that we have a president who believes in putting America first. I have no problem with his twittering and speaking off the cuff; after all, Obama promised to have the most transparent presidency ever, yet he used the back room just like his predecessors and, when he talked in public, often seemed no more than the robotic voice of a teleprompter. I do wish that President Trump would be a little more careful about what he says, both on his twitter account and during his "propaganda" speeches. But then I expect there are a lot of people I know who wish I would think a little more before I speak. I know that I wish that about many people I know.

Demonstrations

Anti-Trump riots in cities across the nation, from Los Angeles, CA and Portland, OR to New York City. In cities, of course, not in the countryside. In cities, where so many of our children are attending universities and where the majority of our population lives. In cities, where the authorities are more willing to put up with violence and threats than the authorities are in the countryside, to put up with anything so as to allow the citizenry to express its childish anger and frustration, a childishness that wants to undo one of our most cherished and necessary freedoms—the freedom to elect whichever presidential candidate receives the most electoral votes in freely held and un-coerced elections, the winner usually being the one who also receives the most popular votes, although not this time by a fairly narrow margin.

God forbid that we stop the demonstrators before they get out of hand! That would be unconstitutional. After all, we do have freedom of speech in the good old USA. It is a constitutional right for our people to express their opinions, without interference from anyone. It is their constitutional right to gather and march…and throw things? And impede traffic? And generally make nuisances of themselves, and endanger the lives of others? Preventive medicine? Yes. Preventive violence? No. We can't have that, not to save your life or mine, or your property or mine, or your or my freedom of access to the streets that the demonstrators have taken over, and to the businesses or homes that line those streets. No, sir!

Personal safety must be sacrificed to the emotional needs of the angry in any specific demonstration area. It must be suspended until the marchers have vented their anger, either through simply marching and shouting, or through adding a little violence and destruction along the way for good measure. Sorry. As I mentioned above, we believe in preventive medicine, but not in preventive violence. We're sorry if you or your child or maybe your neighbor gets hurt or crippled or killed in the march. That's simply an unfortunate accident of freedom of expression.

But I'm running off at the mouth here. Let's get back to the core of the matter. The reason for those fuming marches was the election of Donald Trump as the 45th President of the USA. The demonstrators want him to step down and what? Let Hillary Clinton step up? That's the way I read it, at least in Michael Moore's words. Didn't he visit Trump Towers and leave a note saying something like Trump should be a gentleman and step down, let the person with the most popular votes step up. Gentleman? Is that naïve and presumptuous, and dangerous for our country, or what? It sounds like something one might hear in a banana republic, or in a comic strip, or in a Hollywood movie possibly, a movie directed by Michael Moore by all means—but with a little more threat added for good measure.

All of these people demonstrating were probably perfectly happy in the days leading to November 8. Their candidate was winning, they presumed, as did many of us. But then the upset happened. Trump won the Electoral College vote. He became the President-elect; Hillary didn't. Too bad, but that's the way it happens. You win some. You lose some. I've been an independent voter all my life, voting Democrat sometimes, at other times Republican. I've seen my choice for many offices, not only for the top spot, win and I've seen my choice lose. At times I've not really cared that much. At other times I've really disliked and mistrusted a specific elected person, whether that person became President, Senator, or whatever. But asi es la vida, as they say. You can't win them all, unless of course you live in a dictatorship and you're on the side that wins all the time. That, for me, is the political essence of democracy. You don't win all the time. If you do, ipso facto, you no longer live in a democracy, but rather in a dictatorship.

One of my greatest heroes is George Washington. Many of you would probably say the same thing. After all, he is one of our country's founders, one of the men most responsible for our freedom from England and for our democratic form of government, and for many of our other political characteristics. But what I most admire him for is that he stepped down from the presidency after only two terms in office. I don't recall that happening in any of our neighbors to the south when they won their independence from Spain and Portugal. And I still don't see any of them with governments as democratic as ours, if democratic at all.

It takes a special type of person to do what George Washington did when there was no precedent for such. Now, of course, after more than two hundred years and 44 presidents, a president (or any other elected official at the city, county, state or federal level) automatically steps down after being voted out of office or serving the lawful number of terms in office. It's the way things are done, legally, morally, ethically, politically, in all ways that would avoid any suggestion of a potential attempt at establishing a dictatorship, like a coup d'état. None of us want our country to become a dictatorship, I hope.

Well, what do the demonstrators and their rooting section want? They want Mr. Trump to step down as president-elect, of course. They are within their rights to want him to step aside and let Hillary or anybody else become president. We all have the right to think whatever we want to, and to express those thoughts, with some limitations. The problem is how far freedom of expression goes before it becomes action that interferes with the rights of others.

But that's another matter, something for the courts to decide. Our question is, what would happen to the electoral process if Mr. Trump decided to heed the angry shouts and threats and, yes, violence, and step down, cede the election to Hillary? How would the public react? Well, I suppose there could be anything from acquiescence to blood in the streets. But one thing I have no doubts about. Our peaceful election process, from coast to coast, from the lowest to the highest political position in the land, would be put in harm's way. Maybe it wouldn't be smashed completely, not all at once, but its fabric would have received a snip that could begin to fray, and fray, until it became unrecognizable. Until... until political coups in one form or another became the norm? Until any would-be dictator could send his "brown shirts" out into the streets to demand the resignation of any elected official, and woe be to the official who didn't accede to the demands to step down?

I say to all of you who are upset by the results of the presidential election, those who are demonstrating and those who aren't: If you want to change the presidential voting process, please do so through our constitutionally established political process. And do not attempt to make the change retroactive. Heed the actions and words of President Obama. The election is over. It is now time to try to work together as a nation united. That is what democracy is all about. It is a continual attempt to function as a unit. And "attempt" is the key word here. Nobody…but nobody ever gets everything he wants in a democracy. If he does, there's a problem in Denmark, a deep, deep problem.

Dissing the Flag

Now, let me get this straight. Professional football players are dissing the American flag, and thus America and its people and government, not to mention all our military people, including those who have served in our foreign wars and have come home in caskets or wounded, the latter sometimes to the extent that those wounded soldiers, sailors, marines, and airmen will never be able to function normally again, if they will be able to function at all. Those football players, many of whom are the idols of so many people around the country, think they have the right to disrespect our flag by not standing during the national anthem. So they kneel rather than stand.

They do have that right, of course. We are a country that prides itself on the freedom to speak one's mind, to express one's deepest feelings, as long as that speech or expression does not infringe upon the rights of others. But so do <u>all</u> the alt righters and alt lefters have the same right, including the white supremacists and Nazis and communists and anarchists and anyone and everyone else who is a citizen of our great country. That's what we are, a country whose constitution guarantees freedom of speech. Yet we all know what so often happens when a conservative is scheduled to speak on one of our well-known university campuses, even Berkeley, our supposed bastion of free speech. Out come the demonstrators to keep that speaker from actually speaking on campus. Out come the demonstrators to force the administrators to cancel the speech. And if the speaking appointment actually takes place in spite of the demonstrators, out come not only the demonstrators themselves, again, but also the shouters, to keep the speaker from being heard and the audience from hearing.

These same demonstrators don't take to the streets when left-wingers are scheduled to speak on campus. Nor do they take to the streets when pro football players insult our flag and nation. So it doesn't take a genius to figure that they're left-wingers themselves. They aren't independents or middle-of-the-roaders. They aren't people who believe avidly that all extremists, whether from the right or left, should not be allowed to speak publicly. They are people who would only silence the voices of the right. In that sense, they worry me, just as demonstrators from the right who tried to silence the voices of the left would worry me, and even more so when it is done not through our lawful political system but through violence and intimidation. I have to admit that I would also be worried if people from the middle of our political spectrum began trying to silence all extreme voices, or all voices that do not agree with them. That is the essence of tyranny, to force a unified national voice, one that expresses only those ideas and beliefs that everyone else expresses. That is the essence of *1984* or *Brave New World*. It is also the essence of North Korea and Iran and many other countries on the earth. The ultimate step, of course, would be to force unified thinking as well as speaking, but thankfully such still seems to exist only in the imagination and to be beyond any nation's ability—so far in human history, at least.

But back to the kneeling football players. Here are successful people living the American dream while millions of their fellow citizens suffer from extreme poverty or live paycheck to paycheck: African Americans, European Americans, Hispanic Americans, Asian Americans. On average, according to the *Business Insider* (referencing Forbes) an NFL player makes $1.9 million per year. (NBA players $5.15 million, MLB players $3.2 million, and NHL players $2.4 million.) That's kind of way up there given that the average salary for all Americans is about $41,000 per year and the president of the USA makes only $450,000, including an expense account. Of course he has some other perks like his private jet. But still? Grown men playing kid games earning considerably more than the president of the country? That suggests a mouthful about our country.

Oh well, anyhow, I realize that not all football players make close to two million a year. A few probably receive salaries a heck of a lot higher. Quite a few probably receive salaries considerably lower, but not nearly as low as the average American salary, I don't think.

So what's their beef? That prejudice still exists in America, and raises its ugly head in the form of racism, homophobia, sexism, and a few other isms I can't call to mind off hand? Of course it does! Prejudice lives in all of us no matter what our color, sex, religion, politics, etc. It lives in those football players who insult the rest of us…who insult the country by kneeling when the national anthem is played, just as it exists in every single one of us who blame religion or males or narrowmindedness or inhumaneness for turning people against abortion, just as it exists in all of those people on the political right who blame the news media for creating "fake" news, just as it exists in those people from our middle states who blame the people of the coastal states for our liberal ways (or libertine ways, I might say), just as it exists in those liberals who blame racism or some other ism for why people on the right act as they do, just as it exists in people who believe that all politicians are corrupt and only out to preserve their power and way of life, and just as it exists in all those Whites and Blacks who blame some other group for their own troubles.

In essence, prejudice is our inherent way of shuffling the responsibility for ourselves and our "own group" off on some other group, or of expressing a fear of groups we really don't know very well and don't want to know. It is a rationalization of the worst kind, a negative opinion about someone or some group not based in reason or experience. The hatred that many liberal Blacks and Whites feel about the police and our judicial system is precisely that, prejudice, a feeling not always based in reason or personal experience. And for those of you who would sneer at this comment, I suggest that you read *The War on Cops* by Heather MacDonald. The book is one of the few places where I have been able to find a lot of factual data about crime as it relates to race. I have recommended it to several liberal friends and do you know what the general reaction has been? The author is a conservative, i. e., not worth reading. Now that is real prejudice: a pre-judged reaction to the entirety of something without any experience of it whatsoever. The reaction to that feeling of mine that a person should read the book before judging it has been, well, I've read comments about the book and author. Comments by whom, I might have asked but decided to remain silent and preserve a friendship well worth preserving. But if the comments were about the author's politics rather than about how well written the book is, and how well supported the generalizations, I suspect that they were written by people with a biased, i. e., prejudiced, attitude. And that doesn't mean that I would expect every reader to accept every one of MacDonald's generalizations.

But I'm wandering off target again. My real theme here, at least the one I started out to follow, is that we are, in general, a nation one of whose essential characteristics is freedom of speech. That has been true since our birth, although there have been times when certain segments of the nation have been effectively silenced in one way or another, like in the Revolutionary War, the Civil War, World Wars I and II, and the 1960's anti almost every cultural norm period. And of course the more recent "wars" on free speech on our university campuses and at some political meetings. We are a nation of free speech, but sadly there are many people who believe that free speech does not give anyone the right to say anything that disagrees with what those people believe. I believe that this is a result of the polarization of our political and cultural beliefs. I am uncertain whether this polarization is the result of a trickle-down effect which began in our universities and other educational institutions, and in the highest halls of government (Congress), or if it is the result of a trickle-up effect that began on the streets of our nations, among the poor and disaffected and those who work with them…I am uncertain which, but it is spreading like a plague and is becoming just as deadly.

We need to begin talking. We need to begin listening. We need to find compromises that work. And above all, we need to start using our minds rather than our emotions when it comes to those issues which divide us most. Instead of insulting our flag, and thus our country, we need to rally around it and begin trying to find ways to ease the anger that causes the divide to keep widening.

Maybe even more importantly, all of us need to remember that in a democracy no one group has its way all the time. We have to remember that to allow ideology and/or fanaticism to rule is to begin the move from democracy to tyranny. In a democracy no one has his way all of the time. No one is happy about governmental decisions all of the time because our elected officials rule through pragmatism and compromise and an attempt to do what is best for and wanted by the majority of the people. Or they should rule that way. If they don't, then they are part of a creeping tyranny that could one day smother us until we are but a pale imitation of *1984*.

Diversity

Ethnic differences? Language differences? Religious differences? Racial differences? Difference, that, I have always heard, is one of the most basic characteristics of our very essence as a nation, differences, variety, all that wonderful diversity, all those different cultures and races and religions and languages and world views, all of which become an integral part of the American "melting pot."

Melting pot? Hmmm. Does that mean fusion? Does it mean the merging of all those differences into one united nation, or into one single culture with no real ethnic or racial or religious differences? I think there's a little bit of a dilemma here. On the one hand we talk about diversity as if it is the most positive and greatest thing since the invention of peanut butter, as if diversity somehow makes us a great nation. On the other hand, we seem to expect immigrants to "melt" into our culture so that we can continue to be a unique and unified nation.

I find a deep problem, not to mention contradiction, in these two images. How can we have diversity and a melting pot at the same time?

It we go back to the middle of the 19th century, to the Civil War, there was a basic cultural difference between the North and the South. The former was based in a culture of small farms and factory workers. Oh, yeah, there was the upper class, a class distinguished by wealth more than anything else, and they were the ones that put the blue collar workers to work, so they were responsible for the well-being of a huge section of the working class. It was also through their wealth and work that the small farmers were able to sell what produce they needed to. But the basis of this culture was work to earn a living, work by free men.

On the other hand, in the South there was an aristocracy, one based on plantation ownership and slaves to do the work, not free men working for wages or in order to sell their produce, but slaves.

Two different cultures that clashed in civil war when one decided that the other should free its slaves and the other rejected such an outlandish insistence as interference in their rights as free men to determine their own lifestyle. Oh, of course there were other problems which arose, like states' rights. But the essential division that led inexorably toward war was the slavery issue; in other words it was the basic cultural difference between North and South.

And then there was our Southwest. By the early 19th century Americans were beginning to pour into Texas and other areas already settled and claimed by, first, Spain, and then, for a short period of time, by Mexico. Two cultures clashed, Anglo versus Hispanic—different languages, different religions primarily (Protestant versus Catholic), although both Christian and so not very divided, and different cultural norms, not to mention conflicting governmental loyalties. The differences soon turned to open conflict and finally war. Texas won its independence from Mexico and the USA "protected" the white settlers in the rest of the Southwest by freeing them from "tyranny" in the Mexican-American War and, of course, by annexing the territory they had "settled."

The point I'm trying to make in this wildly simplistic view of the North/South and Mexican/American conflicts is that cultures (or lifestyles, if you will) do not always mesh and live peacefully ever after. I believe that one of the most basic causes of most wars, both within and between nations, is cultural conflict. Our democratic, capitalistic culture has been in a cold war with once-communist Russia for how long? They were our allies during WWII, but not for long afterwards, simply because our cultural norms could not abide each other. And WWII? In essence this war was a war between different political systems (cultures). It pitted the fascism (based on demagogic nationalism and Aryan supremacy) of Germany and Italy against the communism (based in Marxist socialism) of the USSR and the democracy (based in economic and political freedom) of the US. I've ignored Japan and the US allies here.

Again, I accept that the above is a pretty simplistic analysis of the causes of WWII, but I truly believe that differences (cultural, racial, religious, linguistic, political) are the "first cause" of human strife, like God or some other creative principle must be the first cause of any discussion of the existence of this world of ours.

So, in the United States we glory in diversity, in "cultural differences." Yet at the same time we also glory in the melting pot of our cultural differences. Relatively speaking, I think it was probably easy for white Europeans to fuse into one united America, speaking one language, worshipping one God, and, by and large, having one lifestyle. They were all more or less European Caucasian. They worshipped a Christian God, with only minor differences. The cultural differences were minor. The only real problem was the language differences, which in essence was a minor problem when compared to the problem of language differences between English and languages from continents other than Europe.

The immigrants from Europe learned English (not always the first generation) and adapted to American cultural norms, and in the process influenced Americans to adopt some of their cultural norms. It wasn't always easy, witness especially the Irish and Italians.

Then there were the Jews. They had a different religion and a more difficult time merging into the pot.

And then there are the Blacks, the African-Americans. They did adapt to Christianity and in most cases to the American way of doing things, to American culture. But have they ever been completely integrated into the pot? I don't think so. Why? Their skin color, of course. Their integration does seem to be advancing over the past half century, I believe, although many would disagree with me. But it's a long, long way from being complete. And this is a problem that causes a lot of friction, and riots which, ironically, cause the most damage in the black neighborhoods.

And finally there are the Hispanics (excluding the Cubans in the southeastern United States) some of whose ancestors were already settled in the areas of our southwestern states long before the American government incorporated those territories into the USA, and many who have come here illegally, breaking one of our most national protective laws. Have they become integrated into the pot? More so than Blacks, I expect, but less so than other peoples whose ancestors originated in Europe (and, in the Spanish case, mingled with Moors and New World natives over the past centuries). The problem, if such exists, is not religious. Most Hispanics are Catholic. Nor are there any major cultural differences between Hispanic and Anglo culture. One problem could be linguistic, I suppose. But I doubt it. Spanish is closer to English in vocabulary and grammatical formation than German or Polish or Russian. So why have the Hispanics not melted into the pot completely when immigrants from other European nations have? Could it be because of the skin color of many of them, being the offspring of both Native Americans and Spaniards (and Moors)? Or could it be that many of them live so near their heritage, Mexico, that they have much less motivation to adapt?

For the purposes of this essay I have ignored people of Asian heritage.

My point is not that we should stop allowing any peoples from around the world to immigrate to the USA. It is that we should not delude ourselves into blindly thinking that diversity holds no dangers and that it will sooner or later become integrated into the melting pot. It does and it might not. And the greater the differences between the culture of people immigrating to the USA and American culture, I suspect, the greater the odds that these people will not integrate, like many Hispanics, Blacks, and Asians. My final questions then become as follows: Does the diversity that Hispanic, African-American and Asian-American cultures add to our overall American culture outweigh what might have been if they had completely integrated? Does what they add to our overall culture outweigh any threat the differences might hold? What about immigrants from Islamic countries? They are quite different from us linguistically, religiously, and culturally. Will they integrate? Or will they rather add to our diversity? If the latter, will that present any major danger for the future of our country, for our children's children down through the ages?

Doomsday Sayers

Doomsday Sayers? I expect they've been around forever. I mean, there's the coming Apocalypse according to our Judeo-Christian (and Muslim) heritage. At least one of our own Puritan forefathers wasn't immune to the feeling that everything was going to pot: Cotton Mather predicted in 1691 that the world would end in 1697. When that didn't happen, he changed the year, several times in fact. As far back as Rome itself, one of its mythic founders, Romulus, believed that the city would only last 120 years. It was predicted that London would be destroyed by apocalyptic floods in 1524, by an astrologer, I believe.

Well, Rome and London are still with us, both integral parts of western civilization in the present as well as in our history books. There was also the belief based loosely on the Mayan calendar that the world would end in 2012, and the sect of Seekers in the early 1950s who believed that floods would destroy our world in 1954. And so on, ad nauseam.

Right up to the present! Overpopulation, global warming, pollution of our land and waterways—something will get us eventually. Doubtlessly that's a possibility. Nothing lasts forever, does it? Or does it?

The dinosaurs were destroyed. Civilizations rise and fall. Many living species have appeared on the face of the earth, only to disappear. So what's to keep humans from suffering the same fate? Not our peaceful nature, I don't expect, nor our tendency not to trash and waste.

The real doomsday bugbear right now seems to be Climate Change, once called Global Warming, and it's not just a few people, rather many of our "priests" of science and politics and the media, who are predicting an end to at least civilization as we know it, if not the human species itself, because of the greenhouse gases that we humans emit into the atmosphere. There are tons of writings about the damage we do to our world, about global warming/climate change, both pro and con. I have read a lot of them, not by any stretch of the imagination the majority, of course, but I am not enough of a scientist to state that humans are or are not the primary cause of climate change, and I'm not a politician, so I have no popularity to protect and hopefully increase. However, I do know that, unlike what the media says most of the time, there are many scientists who deny that humans are the primary movers of climate change. And I have to ask myself if all of the pro-climate change hoopla is simply one more doomsday prophecy that is, itself, doomed to become precisely that, another unfulfilled doomsday prophecy.

One of the anti-climate change groups is The Friends of Science, "a Canadian non-profit advocacy organization based in Calgary, Alberta." Some say that it is linked to fossil fuel companies. Others deny that fossil fuel companies have any influence on the group, which advocates that the sun "is the main direct and indirect driver of climate change." Not human beings.

Below I have listed some of their denials of global warming, some of their "facts," as opposed to what they call the "myths" that blame humans for climate change. For more information see Friends of Science, *Common Misconceptions about Global Warming:*

1. "The HadCRUT3 surface temperature index…shows warming to 1878, cooling to 1911, warming to 1941, cooling to 1964, warming to 1998 and cooling through 2011."
2. "Significant changes in climate have continually occurred throughout geologic time."
3. "There is no proof that CO_2 is the main driver of global warming.… CO_2 levels move up and down AFTER the temperature has done so, and thus are the RESULT OF, NOT THE CAUSE of, warming."
4. "Greenhouse gases form (only) about 3% of the atmosphere by volume." And they are about 97% water vapour and clouds." So "a

      3% change of water vapour in the atmosphere would have the same effect as a 100% change in CO2."

5. "The sun is a major cause of temperature variation on the earth surface as its received radiation changes all the time. This happens largely in cyclical fashion."

6. In its 1996 report on global warming the UN deleted two statements "from the final draft approved and accepted by a panel of scientists." Those statements admitted that there was no "scientific proof that man-made CO2 causes significant global warming."

7. CO2 is not necessarily a pollutant. "Nitrogen forms 80% of our atmosphere. We could not live in 100% nitrogen." Moreover, "CO2 is essential to life on earth."

8. "There is no scientific or statistical evidence whatsoever that supports" the claim that "global warming will cause more storms and other weather extremes."

9. "Glaciers have been receding and growing cyclically for hundreds of years. Recent glacier melting is a consequence of coming out of the very cool period of the Little Ice Age."

The above article further denies that the "earth's poles are warming and the polar ice caps are breaking up and melting." They state that the "current temperatures are the same as in 1943." And although certain areas of Antarctica are warming, the "main Antarctic continent is actually cooling."

So, what is my reaction to all of this when put together with what I have read from those who blame humanity for climate change? I look around my neighborhood and see all the trash people drop, not only children but adults as well. I think of the pollution of our streams and oceans by runoff from agricultural fertilizers and industry (fracking?). I think of the occasional problems in our drinking water. I think of a recent article about some woman having been infected by a flesh-eating microbe while swimming in, I believe, the ocean. I think of past articles about infections caused by our drinking water. I think of the hundreds, nay, thousands, of square miles of our oceans that are being destroyed by accumulated human waste like plastics. I think of the carbon footprint of the billions of people on this earth, of the waste polluting our lands and seas and air. I think of the continuing increase in our population year after year, and thus of the continuing increase in pollution.

And I think that we really need to do something. But I don't think we need to jump into something like a bunch of frantic children fleeing the ocean because someone yelled shark.

We need to consider the economic, human, and possible resulting cultural, disasters that might be caused by any actions we take. We need to remember that many laws actually do have unintended consequences, <u>so we need to plan carefully as we move our fuel economy from fossil fuels to renewal fuels</u>. And I do believe that we need to move in that direction, not as hastily as some would have us do, but as quickly as we can if we move with consideration for our general economy and the wellbeing of the workers in any specific fuel area, like coal, oil, etc. Take ethanol, for instance. Supposedly its use as a car fuel emits about one half the amount of greenhouse gasses that gasoline does. However, what does it do to the general population and the hungry? Many insist that the use of corn as ethanol greatly increases the price of corn on the food market. Others ask if taking so much corn out of the food market doesn't drastically and negatively affect the hungry of the world.

Those are the types of questions we need to ask ourselves, and to resolve in a democratic way, before we jump totally into something like ethanol use. We have to ask ourselves many questions. We need to have our politicians and scientists and many other thinkers study the potential outcomes of any move we make. What might happen to a large percentage of our population if we suddenly quit using fuels like coal, as opposed to what would happen if we slowly eased away from our consumption of coal at the same time that we slowly replaced it with some renewal form of fuel, like wind or sun power—at the same time training workers in the coal industry to work with wind or sun power?

I, of course, know that we won't do such as this. Our politicians and many of our "greenies" simply do not have that kind of patience. There are much better headlines in jumping into something new with both feet.

Moreover, I think the pollution of our air is but one of three major problems we face: air, water, land. We also need to make as many of our everyday products biodegradable as we can, from grocery sacks and wrappers to clothing and carpets and glass items. We need to make sure that all of our appliances, computers, televisions, lawnmowers, automobiles, etc., when discarded for good, are re-used in one way or another. And most importantly, as far as I am concerned, we need to protect our waterways from all kinds of pollution, from medically discarded materials to discarded personal items to human waste.

I realize that 100% of anything is completely impossible for the human species, but I firmly believe that we need to begin cleaning up our blue planet and keeping it as clean as possible. I don't think that not doing such will destroy the planet, or the human species, but I do think that not doing so might one day not only destroy millions, possibly billions, of people, but also destroy our civilization—to hopefully make way for another one in the future. I cannot accept that we human beings will one day completely destroy ourselves. Is that inability to accept such no more than hope? I hope not.

23

Drugs

Illegal drugs? Marijuana? Heroin? Cocaine? According to Wikipedia, "Over the past few decades drug cartels have become integrated into Mexico's economy. Approximately 500 cities are directly engaged in drug trafficking and nearly 450,000 people are employed by drug cartels.[57] Additionally, the livelihood of 3.2 million people is dependent on the drug cartels.[57] Between local and international sales, such as to Europe and the United States, drug cartels in Mexico see a $25–30bn yearly profit, a great deal of which circulates through international banks such as HSBC.[57] Drug cartels are fundamental in local economics. A percentage of the profits seen from the trade are invested in the local community.[57] Such profits contribute to the education and healthcare of the community.[57] While these cartels bring violence and hazards into communities, they create jobs and provide income for its many members."

So, it sounds like the illegal drug trade is a boon to many of the Mexican people, and, although not mentioned above, to the people of other Latin American countries, like Colombia. What about here in the USA? Historically, except for prescription drugs, which are another but related matter, we don't manufacture illegal drugs. We use them, kind of like we use a lot of things anymore that we don't manufacture; we purchase them from other countries; they make the profits; we don't. I wonder how many millions (billions?) of dollars leave this country every year to feed the drug trade.

However, again according to Wikipedia, "With a large wave of immigrants in the 1960s and onwards, the United States saw an increased heterogeneity in its public.[53] In the 1980s and 90s, drug related homicide was at a record high. This increase in drug violence became increasingly tied to these ethnic minorities. Though the rate of violence varied tremendously among cities in America, it was a common anxiety in communities across urban America. An example of this could be seen in Miami, a city with a host of ethnic enclaves.[53] Between 1985 and 1995, the homicide rate in Miami was one of the highest in the nation—four times the national homicide average. This crime rate was correlated with regions with low employment and was not entirely dependent on ethnicity.[53]"

Moreover, "The baby boomer generation also felt the effects of the drug trade in their increased drug use from the 1960s to 80s.[54] Along with substance abuse, criminal involvement, suicide and murder were also on the rise. Due to the large amount of baby boomers, commercial marijuana use was on the rise. This increased the supply and demand for marijuana during this time period."

The result: "Although narcotics are illegal in the US, they have become integrated into the nation's culture and are seen as a recreational activity by sections of the population.[50] Illicit drugs are considered to be a commodity with strong demand, as they are typically sold at a high value. This high price is caused by a combination of factors that include the potential legal ramifications that exist for suppliers of illicit drugs and their high demand. [51] Despite the constant effort by politicians to win the war on drugs, the US is still the world's largest importer of illegal drugs."

We are the largest importer. Worldwide! So, we pay the people of other countries to poison our people, our children and those people who live next door or maybe just down the street. These people are Americans, American citizens just like you and me. We have laws which force our young people to pay prices for their drugs higher than they would have to if we were the ones who manufactured them, and often forcing them to commit robbery and other crimes in order to pay for the great expense of those drugs. We also make sure that lots and lots of money, our money, goes out of the country to support the citizens (many of them criminals) of other nations rather than into the coffers of our businesses or our government (in taxes).

To me, this smacks of Prohibition on a much grander scale. Prohibition was only a nationwide ban, and on booze rather than drugs. Like our present drug laws, Prohibition was successful in some ways, but terribly unsuccessful in other, more damaging ways. It was a nationwide ban on the recreational use of booze from 1920 to 1933, although there had been regional bans before that.

However, just as with drugs today, the Prohibition laws against the imbibing of alcoholic drinks, according to Wikipedia, "were widely disregarded, and tax revenues were lost. Very well organized criminal gangs took control of the beer and liquor supply for many cities, unleashing a crime wave that shocked the nation. By the late 1920s a new opposition mobilized nationwide. Wets attacked prohibition as causing crime, lowering local revenues, and imposing rural Protestant religious values on urban America.[1] Prohibition ended with the ratification of the Twenty-first Amendment, which repealed the Eighteenth Amendment on December 5, 1933." The nation was split with respect to Prohibition, just as it is today with respect to drug use. My major complaint with both Prohibition and the present drug laws is that both had unintended consequences that led to the rise of powerful and wealthy criminal gangs, as well as to the criminalization and deaths of many innocent people, in the first case, to those who illegally imbibed in spite of the laws, and in the second case, to many who use drugs in spite of the laws.

One of the major criticisms of Prohibition is that it led to "the growth of urban crime organizations and a century of Prohibition-influenced legislation. As an experiment it lost supporters every year, and lost tax revenue that governments needed when the Great Depression began in 1929." My major criticism of our drug laws is almost exactly the same, but on an international rather than national scale. We have created very dangerous drug lords and gangs with vast wealth and power in countries south of our border. And some of those gangs have already invaded our cities. If we keep on as we are, will those gangs in our cities someday have the power they do in countries like Mexico? And will we keep bleeding our needed dollars to other countries, like we have with so much of our manufacturing base?

Our country didn't destroy itself in a drunken binge after the fall of

Prohibition.   Some people did, of course, in uncontrollable alcoholism. They still do. Our country wouldn't destroy itself if we legalized drugs, as some states now are legalizing marijuana. Some of our citizens would, through uncontrollable drug addiction. But I truly believe that the results of legalizing drugs would be a lesser evil than keeping them illegal. There would be more benefits for us and fewer for the drug cartels. And our people would be free to choose to use drugs or not, without so much government interference. And we could use a lot of the tax money we would make to help drug addicts "kick the habit," rather than throwing them in jail as we so often do under our present laws.

24

Education

Education? I would say that education is the essence of any modern technological society, especially a democratic society like ours. Without educated people to fill the working needs of our technology industry, unless we can get enough educated people from somewhere else, from some other society, our technology and the economy it supports cannot sustain itself.

Personally I think we have a crisis on our hands in higher education, one that we need to resolve in order to continue as one of the world's leaders of not only technology, but higher education itself as well. That crisis is one of cost and, to my way of thinking, academic requirements.

According to the National Center for Education Statistics, from the academic year 2005-06 to that of 2015-16 (only ten years), we saw a rise in college/university annual costs (tuition, fees, room, and board) at public institutions of 34%, at private non-profit institutions of 26%, and at private for-profit institutions of 16%. In the latter academic year the annual costs were about $16,757, $43,065, and $23,775 respectively.

Many people I talk to blame the government for cutting back on its spending for education while increasing military spending many fold. But I don't buy that argument. The New York Times has said that spending on education by our federal government is ten times higher today than it was in the 1960s, the years some people think of as the golden years of American education, while military spending today is only one point eight times what it was in that decade. Nor do faculty salaries seem to be the problem. They are barely higher now than in 1970. Moreover, half of college teachers now are part time, while only 18% were part time in 1970. One problem might be the increase in student enrollment since student enrollment is 50% higher now than in 1995 and much higher than in the 1960s. The latter, I believe, is an important problem in both cost and educational quality. I will discuss it later.

But the major cost problem of today's educational system is administration, i. e., administrative salaries and numbers. It is self-evident that an increase of 50% in student enrollment not accompanied by an equal increase in government and/or private support is a major cause of higher educational costs.

But what is not so evident is that administrative growth and rising administrative salaries play a central role in the exorbitant costs of higher education today. Again according to the New York Times, administrative positions in higher education increased by 60% between 1993 and 2009—ten times the increase in faculty positions. Along the same lines, there was a 221% increase in administrative positions in the California State University system between 1975 and 2008, the state leader in the rising costs of higher education administration across the nation. This often hidden but somewhat unfettered rise is reflected in the trend toward seven figure salaries for top administrators.

One might ask how this all comes about. I don't think it's very difficult to understand why the rise in administrative numbers and salaries has occurred. After all, the people with most power in any college/university are the president, his close aides, the deans, and the heads of administrative departments that recruit and control students and collect and account for money from the government and civilian donors. Presidents have the eyes and ears of the trustees. They can usually get approval for whatever they want. And presidents are generally administratively oriented. Even if they came up through the faculty ranks, they moved from department chair to division chair or some dean position or head of some other administrative department. They moved up because they were good at organizing and controlling and finding resources, financial or human or whatever. And they were good at keeping those above them as well as those under their command happy, monetarily and in terms of workload. They gave their people what they wanted, as would any capable politician, which probably often meant adding administrative personnel to ease the load of the people reporting to them.

As for the rising salaries (i. e., cost) of administrators, I would like to simply add a personal experience here, to hopefully show, clearly, why administrative salaries might rise faster and higher than faculty salaries. My first teaching position was in California, at a community college. It was a small college. There were three major administrators: the president, the academic dean, and the finance officer. There were 75 full-time faculty and I don't recall how many secretaries and grounds keepers and other assistants, but quite a few. One year the three administrators received a $1,000 raise each. The faculty and other "workers" listed above received—I can't remember exactly, but I think it was a 3% raise. As a new faculty member just out of college, I was making $6,700 annually. If my memory is correct, and I have no doubts that it is close to the mark, I received a $191 annual raise. Doesn't come very close to a $1,000 annual raise, does it? That was back in the 1960s. Follow my annual raise and the academic dean's annual raise to the present year. Kind of large discrepancy, isn't it?

And do you know one of the arguments given for the large raise to the top administrators as opposed to the rest of us? A cost of $3,000 is a drop in the bucket compared to the thousands it cost to give the faculty and other workers their two to three hundred dollar raise.

I expect that such a comparison might be in the mind of many trustees when they approve raises for faculty, administration, and staff. And, of course, the president and some of his/her top people meet with them a lot and thus have their loyalty, not to mention that many of them are also administrators, of their own businesses or of large corporations. Too bad that boards of trustees aren't composed primarily of faculty members, or ex-faculty members.

And then there is the rise in student numbers: 50% more students presently enrolled in undergraduate, graduate and professional programs than in 1970.

And that is a problem, I think, another problem added to the terrible waste of student time and potential in our present system. We graduate lots of students, especially in the liberal arts, who wind up in jobs that don't really require a college education. We are not a liberal artsy country, with most of our citizens heading out in the evening to a Shakespearean drama or comedy, or going to an art festival or a reading of philosophy. Voters aren't required to have a college education, or even a high school one. Buying a car doesn't require a college degree. Having a family and buying and furnishing a home don't require a college education. From my own experience, lots of my fellow citizens, including many college graduates, don't read books but rather get what information they wish to gather from the television or newspaper or social media, or maybe a magazine now and then. And it doesn't require a college education to understand anything that television offers, or Hollywood.

We are not a philosophical or literary nation. We are a practical people, a people highly interested in technology. And that, I believe, should be our thrust in education. Our present educational system wastes so much student time and potential. Many of our students are not interested, absolutely not interested, in many of their required high school or college courses. We should test our students for interest and aptitude by the time they are in junior high. Those without interest in or aptitude for learning that leads to college, or with interests that lead to work rather than education, should be moved into vocational programs. The same thing is true for those students whose aptitude and interests move them through high school. They should be tested thoroughly before they head for college. And they should be moved in the direction their tests suggest is the proper direction for them— the arts, sciences, humanities, technology, or other vocationally oriented programs like business or education or social work. And the same is true of our college/university students. As they close in on graduation, those who are interested in going on should be tested well (thoroughly) before being allowed to enroll in graduate or professional school.

25

Female Work Clothing

I guess I have a penchant for sticking my foot in my mouth. There's a group I know of that meets one afternoon, late, each week to talk about current events and general social problems. I don't get to the talkfest every week, but I go as often as I can. Well, last week I was there and we were discussing Bill O'Reilly and Fox News. I made the comment that women in working situations often show a little more of their breasts and legs than they should, and that this was especially true on the Fox News channel. One of the women in the group asked me if I thought that women should wear burqas. She seemed a little irritated at my comment (although I know that she is generally a rational, reasonable and intelligent person), so I just said no and let it go at that, mainly because I figured her next question just might be if I thought that females were to blame for sexual harassment in the work place, and that might have led to a heated argument rather than an intelligent and peaceful discussion, because I think that in a way they sometimes just might share a little of the guilt. After all, if a man in the workplace makes a pass at a woman, all she has to do is give a definite no, and I mean definite and insistent, even if she does it in front of witnesses. Then, if the passes continue, or they become more aggressive and physical, she should report them to her boss. If that doesn't work, or if the problem is her boss himself, she should take it all the way to the top, or to a lawyer. If she does nothing, no matter the reason, then, I think, she is partially to blame. I feel the same way about bullies. If a person is too meek or ashamed to bring the bullying to the attention of anyone with the power to stop it, then that person must share part of the blame for the continuation of the bullying. I'm not trying to excuse the bully or the sexual abuser; I'm just saying that we are all to some extent responsible for our own safety and freedom from physical abuse. And I am not saying that there are not occasional circumstances in which the abused has no chance to protect herself/himself. There are, of course. But that does not always excuse the abused from not having taken steps for self-protection.

What I should have said to the woman in our conversation group was no. I should have said that, being a normal male, I enjoy looking at the female body, much like a lot of normal women seem to enjoy showing what they have. I'm no expert on the subject, but this tendency seems to be at its peak during the dating and mate-hunting years and slowly fades during the aging process, depending, I guess, on how well any specific body and mind retain their connection to their youth.

All I can say is great. Keep it up. However…no, I shudder at the very thought of our women wearing burqas or hijabs and those long, shapeless dresses that Muslim women wear. They shout that here is a slave of society, a person whose society has made her ashamed of her body, a second-class citizen at the whim of her husband, her father…all men. And they seem to suggest that the female body needs to be hidden or else it will incite men too shamelessly. They exude the very essence of Sharia law.

They are an extreme, not many steps away from the extreme of not allowing women out in public <u>at all</u>, but rather keeping them in hiding for their entire lives after puberty, keeping them locked up in a room somewhere and not allowing any male but their spouse to visit them, not even their father or siblings. I can't think of anything more horrendous except physical torture.

However, here in the USA women should start a fad that puts them, at work, in suits like men wear—something that essentially hides the sexual parts of the anatomy. Given the natural, physical relationship between male and female of our species, though, I really doubt that such would completely do away with men making passes at women in the work place, or even getting more aggressive, although it might slow the problem down considerably, especially if the change in dress codes slowly brought about a change in our culture's "free" attitude toward sex. I personally have no doubts that men are the aggressors in the game of sex and that women are the deciders (excluding rape or forced sex of course). I also believe that men tend to be much less capable of controlling their sex drive than women. So I don't see a real solution to the problem short of a sea-change in our cultural sexual norms, or physically separating the sexes in the workplace. And I don't see the latter happening short of turning our democracy into a tyranny.

To return, however, to the beginning of this essay, to the real problem I saw in the woman's answer to my comment about women and sexual harassment in the workplace—what she said polarized the problem of work clothing for women. It turned the whole custom of women's clothing into an *Either/Or* situation. And, as we all know, either/or attitudes, stances, etc. lead toward conflict rather than toward honest and peaceful dialogue. It means accept-this-or-else and is indicative of the tyranny of one person, group, nation, etc. over another, or its attempt to tyrannize over another. It should never be an integral part of any democracy. And it sure puts a clamp on free speech and rational conversation.

But it seems to be an attitude becoming more and more prevalent in our post-2000 society. We have become polarized about so much: abortion, health care, illegal immigration, Muslim immigration, elections, our public figures, sex and gender, race, work-fare as opposed to welfare, socialism versus capitalism, environmental problems, global warming. Me, I personally get discouraged by the continuous ideological posturing of our congressional leaders and their seemingly total lack of pragmatism or, all too often, common sense. And I'm talking about the members of both of our major political parties.

We should have honest dialogues, a lot more than we do now, I think. But how does one have an honest, open conversation that leads to any kind of mutual understanding and decision if one or both sides simply sit back and take polarized shots at the other side, if both sides refuse to compromise their ideals? I would say that ideals are nice to worship, to yearn for, but that they can never sink into the abyss of the physical world that we actually inhabit, not without one side or the other tyrannizing over the other. And if that happens, we no longer have a democracy. And we have a heck of a lot of unhappy citizens, even many of those whose side won the battle.

Foreign Workforce

I'm reading an interesting book now: *Strangers in Their Own Land* by Arlie Russell Hochschild. The book is an attempt by the author, a political liberal, female professor from the U. of California, Berkeley, to understand the right side of the political spectrum, the conservative side.

To do so, she travels to the oil/bayou areas of southwestern Louisiana, one of our poorest and most polluted states, where she lives among the people themselves, sharing their lives and trying to figure out what makes them tick politically, why so many have conservative beliefs like small government, free enterprise, and private life without government interference, while at the same time living in a state which needs a great deal of environmental and economic help.

It's a really interesting book, well-written. But what grabs me most, other than the terrible pollution that our supposedly "caring" government has allowed to run rampant for decades in that area of Louisiana, are the author's references to foreign workers in the region. She makes no estimate of the number of them. Her primary interest is in how citizen workers living in that area can still believe in freedom from government interference when their land and bayous are being poisoned by the oil and chemical companies, and when so many of their jobs have been taken from them by foreign workers who are brought in by the multinational corporations simply because they work for lower wages than American workers will.

What she says about this latter problem is kind of startling. I don't think, however, that the foreign-labor problem is limited to Louisiana. According to the PEW Research Center, in 2005 there were an estimated 400,000 to 450,000 illegal immigrants in my adopted state of Arizona, a state with a population of slightly less than 7,000,000. PEW adds that 65% of those were in the work force, which would be over 290,000. According to cnsnews.com, citing figures from the Bureau of Labor Statistics, in September of 2015 there were over 25 million "foreign-born" workers in our national labor force and that number was rising. The news organization further stated that in May of 2015 the unemployment of native-born workers had risen to 5.4% in less than a year while the unemployment of foreign-born workers had declined from 4.9% to 4.7%. (I wonder what percentage of their wages these foreign workers send to their families back in their homelands, a percentage which doesn't do much good for our economy. I also wonder if the annual total of those wages sent out of the US is more or less than the profits multinational corporations in this country return to their homelands annually.)

I also found troubling the following quote from the American Thinker:

As of the fourth quarter of 2011 there were 108,592,000 people living in households in the United States that received benefits from one or more "means-tested" government programs, according to the Census Bureau's estimate. Those 108,592,000 "means-tested" government benefit recipients, according to the bureau, equaled 35.4 percent of 306,804,000 people in the United States at that time.

When recipients of non-means-tested government programs (such as Social Security, Medicare, unemployment, and veterans benefits) were added to those receiving benefits from means-tested programs, the total number receiving benefits in the fourth quarter of 2011 was 151,014,000, according to the Census Bureau. That equaled 49.2 percent of the total population.

Of course a lot of people in the above groups would be children and older people. However a great many would be working people. But almost 50%

of the population receiving some kind of government money free! And the number has probably increased since 2011. I hope not. But given our government's tendency to give things away without expecting anything in return, I consider my hope a little on the forlorn side, kind of like the foolish prayers of a man falling without a parachute from an airplane flying at nine thousand feet.

Now, I don't consider social security or veterans' benefits as government aid or subsidy, at least not for those of us who have worked and paid into the social security system for years, or those who have served faithfully in the military. We social security recipients might be overpaid, and there are a lot of people receiving social security who haven't paid into it, or haven't paid even close to what they are getting out of it. But that's typical of our government: There's a lot of taxpayer money out there so spend it; there're a lot of votes out there so give the people some benefits so they'll vote for us next time around. And not only that, but we might as well continue paying for a quagmire war in the Middle East, and continue doling out foreign aid like we are still living in the fifties, and paying for our troops and military bases in such economically sound countries as Japan, Germany, and South Korea. What the heck! We are one of the wealthiest countries in the world. Or rather "we were." But we've squandered and continue to squander our monetary wealth, albeit possibly not quite as rapidly as we could. And worse, we've put a majority of our workers, our most basic wealth, out of work and on the dole.

But what angers me about this whole situation is that so many available jobs are being taken, not by our native workers, but by workers from other countries, some of whom are here legally, but most of whom are not, some of whom are paying taxes, many of whom are probably not. And, of the jobs our American workers have, I have to ask myself how many are minimum wage jobs, or low paying jobs, or part-time jobs. Do they pay taxes or do they get tax rebates instead? How can our government possibly continue to support all of those people that do get money from it without going further and further into debt, faster and faster? The way we spend money, the way our government does, I wonder how it is that we aren't much, much more in debt than we are.

And then there are the thousands and thousands of well-paying jobs that have been "out-bordered." When, I ask myself, will all of the financial flight stop? Will the present President-elect truly put our country first? Will he truly make bargains that are good for us and not necessarily for our friends and enemies? Will he actually put pragmatism and the interests of our great country rather than ideology at the top of his bargaining goals? I for one hope so. But with all the opposition he will face I have some hefty doubts.

Free Speech

Free speech? The USA is one of the greatest countries the world has ever known for many reasons, from our natural resources and expansion history and education system, to the adventurous and inventive people who have immigrated to our shores, and freedom of speech is right up there at the top of those reasons. Every citizen has the legal right to speak his mind, with a few exceptions like hate speech and inciting to riot of course, or speaking about something a judge has told you not to talk about, or talking to somebody Congress thinks is an enemy of the nation (I always thought that for a country to be our "legal" enemy we had to have declared war on them, but I must be wrong what with all our present frantic anti-Russian fanaticism), or saying the wrong thing at the wrong time in the wrong crowd. I might add that this latter, saying something that is terribly unpopular, is one of those major exceptions to our constitutionally granted freedoms of speech, especially on college campuses like Berkeley and other elite universities, places where free speech means anything that agrees with the campus majority, the liberals, nothing else. But saying unpopular things in public anymore, especially on university campuses, although not illegal, seems to be a great cultural sin. We've got to conform to the popular (liberal?) will. After all, conformity is possibly one of the greatest forces for keeping us safe, by only saying what everyone around us says. As I said, unpopular speech content is not illegal by any means, but it could get you a lot of hate mail and not a little ostracism from those who, on sunny days, for them, are champions of free speech, as long as it agrees with their own beliefs, or is dissimilar only in a few minor and unimportant details. To spout something antagonistic to what is popularly accepted is to court the danger of non-conformity, which in this day and age can get you into a lot of hot water, physically as well as psychologically.

Many of us are adult enough to understand that lots of people the world over, and even in this country, simply don't like to hear ideas or beliefs that deny their own. This, I believe, is especially true of religious, political, or sexual beliefs. Avid Muslims don't like to hear anything negative about Mohammad or the Koran, or Sharia law. Avid Christians don't like to hear anything negative about Christ or the Bible, or our Judeo-Christian heritage. People who believe that sexual deviation is a religious sin and/or a physical aberration don't like to listen to champions of the LGBT community or hear people praise the laws that protect LGBTers and give them equal rights with straight people in such institutions as marriage. Members of the LGBT community don't like to hear that homosexuals should not be allowed to marry like straight people and have all the rights in marriage that the latter have. Liberal Democrats don't like to hear that our borders should be closed and all illegal immigrants, including the dreamers, expelled. They seem to become especially irate when someone, in their presence, praises President Trump or insists that we need to cut back on welfare and make some definite changes to Obamacare. Conservative Republicans, on the other hand, turn away when somebody insists that we need to grant amnesty to the illegal immigrants already living in the USA before we begin to deal with immigration policy or build a wall.

This all bothers me, you know. I believe in a person's right to speak his mind, if he does so rationally rather than hatefully, but even hateful speech should be listened to so that we can better understand those who hate something and why they hate that something. If we never listen to them, how can we possibly decide whether or not, and how, we might improve that something, or maybe help change their attitude toward it? If no non-haters ever enter into a discussion with the haters, about what it is they hate, how will there ever come about any change in the haters' attitudes? I might ask a related question: What if our American military leaders had refused to read anything by their Nazi or Japanese counterparts during WWII, simply because they were the enemy and thus reading anything they wrote would be something like consorting with the enemy? In such a situation, our military leaders might never have learned anything about how their enemies analyzed and planned their military campaigns. They might therefore not have been able to out-maneuver, out-think their enemies. Would they have lost more battles because of a lack of "knowing their enemy"? Would we be speaking German or Japanese now? I find it very difficult to understand why so many people only want to listen to, or read something by, people who agree with their own ideas and beliefs. With such an attitude, how does one expand one's world view? How does one learn? How does one continue to grow intellectually, morally, spiritually, culturally? How can one possibly begin to understand antagonistic viewpoints if he refuses to listen to or read them? And if one does not understand those viewpoints, how can he ever refute them logically?

As far as I am concerned, there is a responsibility that accompanies our constitutionally guaranteed freedom of speech. That is that we are each and every one of us responsible for attempting to understand our fellow citizens, no matter how much their views differ from our own. And they are just as responsible for attempting to find out what our beliefs and attitudes are. Those who refuse to do such are shirking the basic responsibilities of any citizen of our democracy. In a polarized nation like we have become in the past few decades, such irresponsibility endangers us all. It can only lead in one direction, toward further polarization and an ultimate breakdown in communication between our political, religious and sexual extremes—a breakdown in communication, a breakdown in sympathy, a complete breakdown in acceptance and, ultimately, a breakdown in getting along peacefully with each other. And where does that lead us?

Global Warming

Global warming (in one book I read it was called "global weirding") has now become climate change? There seems to be some disagreement about the extent of the human cause of climate change as opposed to the impact of nature's own cyclical patterns. But I don't think anyone would deny that we humans are definitely polluting our planet beyond what is healthy for both us and the planet.

The most important question and a major bone of contention, I think, is how to stop, and maybe even reverse, our negative impact on the earth, not only with respect to climate change, but also with respect to the overall pollution of our lands, our lakes and rivers and oceans, and our air. How do we stop all of this <u>without destroying civilization</u> itself in the process? The easy fix, the one that so many nations appear to advocate, is to switch from fossil fuels to renewable fuels. That seems to be the very essence of the Paris Accords, the worldwide group that President Trump is receiving so much flack for withdrawing us from: President Trump just pulled us out of the Paris Accords. His reasoning: The accords are detrimental to our economy. The aim of the convention is described in Article 2, "enhancing the implementation" of the UNFCCC through:[11]

"(a) Holding the increase in the global average temperature to well below 2 °C above pre-industrial levels and to pursue efforts to limit the temperature increase to 1.5 °C above pre-industrial levels, recognizing that this would significantly reduce the risks and impacts of climate change;

(b) Increasing the ability to adapt to the adverse impacts of climate change and foster climate resilience and low greenhouse gas emissions development, in a manner that does not threaten food production;

(c) Making finance flows consistent with a pathway towards low greenhouse gas emissions and climate-resilient development."

Countries furthermore aim to reach "global peaking of greenhouse gas emissions as soon as possible". The agreement has been described as an incentive for and driver of fossil fuel divestment.[12][13]

The Paris deal is the world's first comprehensive climate agreement.[14] It deals with nationally determined contributions and their limits, I believe.

The contribution that each individual country should make in order to achieve the worldwide goal are determined by all countries individually and called "nationally determined contributions" (NDCs).[15] Article 3 requires them to be "ambitious", "represent a progression over time"… "with the view to achieving the purpose of this Agreement." The contributions should be reported every five years and are to be registered by the UNFCCC Secretariat.[16] Each further ambition should be more ambitious than the previous one, known as the principle of 'progression'.[17] Countries can cooperate and pool their nationally determined contributions. The Intended Nationally Determined Contributions pledged during the 2015 Climate Change Conference serve—unless provided otherwise—as the initial Nationally determined contribution.

The level of NDCs set by each country[18] will set that country's targets. However the 'contributions' themselves are not binding as a matter of international law, as they lack the specificity, normative character, or obligatory language necessary to create binding norms.[19] Furthermore, there will be no mechanism to force[20] a country to set a target in their NDC by a specific date and no enforcement if a set target in an NDC is not met.[18][21] There will be only a "name and shame" system[22] or as János Pásztor, the U.N. assistant secretary-general on climate change, told CBS News (US), a "name and encourage" plan.[23] As the agreement provides no consequences if countries do not meet their commitments, consensus of this kind is fragile. A trickle of nations exiting the agreement may trigger the withdrawal of more governments, bringing about a total collapse of the agreement.[24]

The negotiators of the Agreement however stated that the NDCs and the 2 °C reduction target were insufficient; instead, a 1.5 °C target is required, noting "with concern that the estimated aggregate greenhouse gas emission levels in 2025 and 2030 resulting from the intended nationally determined contributions do not fall within least-cost 2 ℃ scenarios but rather lead to a projected level of 55 gigatonnes in 2030", and recognizing furthermore "that much greater emission reduction efforts will be required in order to hold the increase in the global average temperature to below 2 ℃ by reducing emissions to 40 gigatonnes or to 1.5 ℃".[25]

Although not the sustained temperatures over the long term to which the Agreement addresses, in the first half of 2016 average temperatures were about 1.3 °C (2.3 degrees Fahrenheit) above the average in 1880, when global record-keeping began.[26]

When the agreement achieved enough signatures to cross the threshold on 5 October 2016, US President Barack Obama claimed that "Even if we meet every target, we will only get to part of where we need to go," and that "This agreement will help delay or avoid some of the worst consequences of climate change and will help other nations ratchet down their emissions over time."

Before any of you readers, if there are any, get too upset about the above, I suggest that you read a book entitled *Drawdown* by Paul Hawken. Then get actively involved in some of the efforts around the world that are already taking place, efforts that will not only positively affect our atmosphere and environment but will also help economically, or at least not do us great damage economically.

Guns & School Shootings

It's happened again: a school shooting, this time in a Parkland, Florida high school. Seventeen people were killed, mostly students. The killer was a student who had been expelled.

As is typical, the blame is being placed on lax gun laws; an incompetent mental health system; and a bungling legal system, the FBI and sheriff's office in this case. Police seem to be the 'usual suspects' in mass shootings, when the blame game starts afterwards. The press is already ranting about how inefficient the local law was and the missed clues that should have kept the shooter from ever having purchased a gun. In this case the FBI supposedly dropped the ball when they were notified that the shooter had said on the internet that he would like to become a school shooter. They had the name of the commenter, but they couldn't locate him—or didn't. Of course, they probably have thousands if not tens of thousands of such warnings, so they probably didn't spend too much time and effort on the search. The local sheriff's office is also being blamed for not following up on the calls it received over the years and during the recent weeks about the shooter, up to 45 calls, some reports say.

Then, of course, the anti-gun people are coming out of the woodwork, shouting that we need to ban anything from automatic weapons to any and every kind of gun. (Maybe even cap guns and BB guns, who knows) And marching, of course, marching on Washington DC and the Florida state capitol, shouting and demanding that something be done, now—not very democratic, I say. It sounds a lot like the military, where the mistakes of one or two might get a whole company or more penalized. But the military has to act as a unit if they are going to be successful, so that type of system stands to reason—let the whole unit straighten up the problem soldier. Not so in a democracy where we all, not just an angry few, have a right to be heard and to not be penalized for the crimes of the few.

Many people, on the other hand, put the blame for public shootings on our mental health system. Many of these people seem to think that we let too many of our citizens, and non-citizens, with mental problems go uncared for. I would probably agree with that. But what's the alternative? Put any people we deem dangerous in some kind of asylum? In lockup? Who makes the decision? Or should we just insist that files be made and kept by all law organizations on any person potentially dangerous to society and that extensive background checks be made on any would-be purchaser of any type of a firearm? And that no one who has been deemed dangerous to society be allowed to purchase any kind of firearm?

Maybe we should enforce, really enforce, all the laws we already have on the books before we start enacting new ones. I personally am a little fed up with a bureaucracy that smothers us with laws.

I agree with the more reasonable and rational arguments here, like keeping firearms out of the hands of people potentially dangerous to society. I don't agree with the extremes, like banning all firearms, or even all automatic weapons, or locking up anyone deemed mentally unstable and a potential threat to society.

I also think this is all a lot like treating something like the flu. Say, I go to the doctor complaining of chills, fever, congested sinuses, and a hacking cough. The doctor prescribes cough medicine for the cough and a nasal spray for the sinuses. He also tells me to take cold baths to lower my fever and to cover myself with a sweatshirt or blanket or something when the chills hit. I don't think I would return to that specific doctor again, if I could help it. He treated the symptoms but not the real cause of the flu, not the virus that invaded my body.

I feel that what the fanatics and the angry ask for after a public shooting is similar to what the above fictional doctor did for me. Doubtlessly, doing away with automatic weapons would decrease the potential for shootings in which there are many victims, although people with nefarious aims can often find a way to get the weapons of their choice, whether it be bombs or automatic weapons or a truck. People with dangerous mental problems can always seep through the cracks. And law enforcement can't always catch every potential shooter, not with the officers often being so overworked, not with them receiving so many erroneous warnings from so many people who have an axe to grind with the person they report on, and not with the courts often standing in the way of the officers actually doing anything to put the "blamed" <u>and guilty</u> person in a place where he/she will no longer be a social threat. We live in a democratic society, after all, not in a tyranny where anyone can wind up in prison if anyone on the "right" political side doesn't like him.

So, what do I see as the real cause of mass shootings that keep popping up around our country, although not as often as some would have us believe? What do I think is the real cause, the virus that infects some of our people and turns them into mass killers? Answering "human nature" would of course simply state the obvious and not lead us to anything meaningful. But there is no doubt that we are a murderous species. Our history is crammed with wars and killings of all types, not to mention other forms of cruelty. We are not a species that can live at peace with each other for any long period of time. The irony is, on the other hand, that we tire of war after it has been around for long and sue for, or accept, some kind of peace. Then, the longer that peace lasts the crueler we become with each other until we seem to have no choice but to go to war again.

No, unless we change human nature we will never do away completely with killings, either in war between nations or in war between members of one society. To even suggest that we can stop killing each other is ludicrous. And the more we invent easier ways to kill masses of people the more we will have mass killings. I've been surprised for a long time that we have not yet had, in our country, a mass chemical attack by some lunatic, just as I've been surprised that we have gone decades since the first atomic bombs put a halt to WWII without some nation attacking another with such weapons, or chemical ones. Maybe we are being better protected than some of us think by our law enforcement officers and agents, and our military.

So, what is the real cause of such mass killings as those in the Parkland school or Las Vegas? The first cause, of course, is human nature. However, we can no more change human nature than we can change the first cause of our reality, God. What do we Christians, as well as many people of other religions, blame for the evil in the world? We blame Satan and try in many ways to overcome his evil influence. It's pretty clear that we never quite win that war. And the same can be said of the war on the negative aspects of human nature. Do what we will, the killings go on—and multitudes of people from clergy to teachers and general do-gooders have tried to turn us humans into loving creatures. But the war goes on, just as the war on crime in the streets and in the halls of government goes on, unstoppable.

So, what can we do? Imitate the cops on the streets and the agents in the FBI and other law enforcement agencies: Keep trying. Keep improving our ability to weed the mean from the good. Always staying aware that the war is never ending. But, you might ask, why is it that there was a long period of time, in the 50s and 60s and 70s and….a long period of time when our citizens were relatively peaceful, when our government was involved in "brush-fire" wars around the globe but, except for a brief period in the 60s, and except for our criminal element, our citizens did not commit meaningless killings.

If one ignores the peace/war cycle of human existence, is there something else that turns otherwise non-criminal types into killing machines? Is there an explanation which might lead to the real virus? One of my favorite political novels is Arthur Koestler's *Darkness at Noon*. In the novel, one of the main character's musings is about what he calls "sea change" in human cultural or political settings and the unsettling impact such has on the people suffering such changes. These musings have always remained with me. And, when I think back on my own 80+ years and the changes in the nation and culture which is my native ambient, I cannot help but believe that the USA has seen a sea change of vast proportions from the 1930s and 1940s into this 21st century. A sea change of vast proportions, and that is not necessarily meant as a negative judgment, but rather a simple statement of truth. During those years black people, in my early years considered second-class citizens if citizens at all, have become an integral part of every level and every aspect of our society, from the poorest to the richest, from laborers to bosses and owners, from sports to education and the news media and the entertainment industry. This is true of other minority groups as well. The LGBT community has come out of the closet to gain success in all kinds of places, from business and sports to education and the military. They now have the right to marry. Regional, racial, and class separations by dialect and accent, although not completely gone, especially among first generation immigrants, have been softened if not erased by mass communication forms (like television, the computer, and other technologies) and the ease of long-distance travel, often erasing that sense of belonging one has to his native region. A country, my country, once basically controlled by Mom-and-Pop businesses, is now mostly in the hands of global corporations which have little loyalty to either a specific region or to the USA in general. Our thriving blue-collar class has in many cases become a thing of the past, their jobs having gone to robots or been shipped abroad, or having been taken over by illegal immigrants. Many of our freedoms have been taken away by laws and attitudes which mean well, which are meant to keep us alive, or are meant to help and protect minorities or the country in general, but which make the lives of many of us more difficult and more meaningless: I can no longer pile six to ten children and adults in a car and head off to visit relatives on the other side of the state, unless, of course, I have a car the size of a small bus and enough seatbelts to go around. I can no longer take off across country and let my children play freely in the back seat or in the whole back of a van; I must tie them down with a seat belt. I can no longer send my children off to college certain that they will enter a world where freedom of thought and excellence of reason are not only accepted but are demanded. Colleges and universities no longer choose their student body on academic and extra-curricular abilities only, but rather use diversity "laws" or beliefs as well, sometimes in lieu of. Universities like the U. of California at Berkeley are no longer bastions of free speech and learning, but rather are bastions of "diversity" only in a physical sense. Congress is no longer our primary governmental bastion of democratic compromise and service to "the people," but rather a place where global corporations and large organizations buy votes and where senators and congressmen squabble and spit and spat like a bunch of kids. Uh, make that brats.

And on and on. But enough complaining. We still have a great country. But think how much greater it would be if our senators and congressmen would return to their primary reason for being in Washington DC, to serving "we the people," and to the primary method of law-making in a democracy such as ours, to accepting compromise as a necessity. And just think….but again I'm starting to ramble. The simple fact is that we actually can treat some of the symptoms of mass shootings. We can actually put a lid on some of them, maybe many, by enforcing the gun laws on our books, by maybe making a few more gun laws, by making it illegal to sell any weapon without a background check, by keeping close tabs on people who express tendencies toward violence, and by insisting that law enforcement organizations establish and maintain a lists of those people who have a tendency toward public and meaningless violence. But, unless we give up another one of our basic freedoms (the right to bear arms), or turn back the clock on weaponry, back to the 19th century, say—unless we do that or get involved in another world war, which might take most of the desire for violence out of us, we will not completely do away with mass shootings.

Healthcare

What with Obamacare and the Trump government's attempts to replace it, I've been thinking a lot about healthcare recently. I have to admit, after reading a number of articles about our Constitution, that I was wrong. There is no place in that document that gives the federal government the power to control our health care system, or to make sure that every citizen has access to healthcare.

The above does not, of course, deny the individual states the right to institute some plan of their own, some plan that would make sure that all of its citizens have access to healthcare. It only means that the federal government does not have that right, that power, although that does not mean that the Feds will not preempt that power anyway. They do a lot of that.

The problem with the states instituting and supporting total healthcare access for all its citizens, I think, would be the cost. I doubt that most of our states, maybe all of them, would have sufficient funds to financially support such a plan. I'm not even sure that our federal government has sufficient funds without depending heavily on insurance companies and the strict regulation of healthcare costs, and government debt. Of course, to make such a plan available to all citizens, especially the poorest, the feds would probably have to enact a specific tax for the plan, or find a way to make sure that at least one section of the population paid heavily for it. As far as I am concerned, Obamacare did the latter. Insurance rates first sky-rocketed for those people who for some reason or another could not get on the Obamacare rolls and had to pay for their own insurance, and then later they began skyrocketing for those who were on the rolls. And, from what I have seen of the present Republican bill to replace Obamacare, the elderly will pay through the nose for the plan.

So, should we leave free healthcare for the states to institute or not, as they see fit, or should we find some way that all citizens throughout all the states would receive free healthcare and also help with the costs, something like a general tax, maybe a payroll tax? If it was a payroll tax, all those who don't work, which would include retired people, wouldn't be required to support the plan. If it was a general tax on all income, collected by the IRS at the end of each taxable year, only those who have no income would be exempt from sharing the cost of such a program. If it was a sales tax, those who spend the most would have to pay the most, and all foreigners who visit us and buy things would have to pitch in also.

Me, I think that healthcare should be affordable and available to all citizens, no matter what their financial status. I think it is to the benefit of the nation as a whole to have healthy citizens. Besides, although many people disagree about what the term "welfare" means in our Constitution, when in the Preamble it talks about We the People (meaning the government) promoting "the general Welfare," I have to come down on the side of those who interpret that as referring to the people (promoting their welfare) as well as to the nation as a whole. Why? The nation does not exist apart from the people who compose it. Its welfare is their welfare, and their welfare is its welfare.

Of course I would also change our welfare laws to make sure that any and <u>all American citizens</u> do some kind of work, unless they are <u>absolutely</u> incapable <u>physically or mentally</u> of doing even the most menial of tasks. We have lots of chores, like cleaning up our roadways and city streets to babysitting and house-cleaning for those who do work…chores which could be performed by those people accepting welfare checks from the government.

But back to healthcare, I would accept what is now being called a "single payer" system, what I think we used to call socialized medicine. It is inhumane to exclude some people from access to healthcare simply because they cannot afford it, especially if those "same people" happen to be children, the mentally ill, or people who are chronically sick and suffering.

However, before we begin trying to financially support a "single payer" healthcare system, I think a number of changes should be made to the present system, changes that, hopefully, would make it considerably cheaper. Drugs (prescription medicines)? Why is it that I can drive down to Mexico and buy, across the counter, medicine that here in the USA requires a doctor's prescription? And why is it so much cheaper there unless most of the cost for that same medicine purchased here is paid by our federal government? Is it because medicines are not so widely prescribed in Mexico as they are here in the USA? Is it because the medicines sold in Mexico are manufactured in Mexico (more cheaply) and those sold here are manufactured here? Me, I doubt it. I suspect that the drug corporations (international corporations) price their products according to whatever the market will bear in each country in which they sell their products, and they make up in the USA with high prices (and high profits) for the low prices (and low profits) in other countries.

So, I would control the cost of medicines, and not at cost to the taxpayer (through government subsidies) but rather with laws that control the profits, here in the USA, of multi-national drug companies.

Other changes I would make are in the medical field. Doctors are expensive, and naturally so since they are in short supply and have a lot of college debt to pay off in their first few years, and more, in practice. Given the law of supply and demand, I personally have no doubts that if we had a lot more doctors we would have lower doctor bills when we are sick. So, how do we change that? One way, and I believe it to be the most logical way, would be for our government to ease the educational requirements for general practitioners. We have already begun allowing nurse practitioners to treat patients. Why not go a step further and make it easier for them, and many others, to earn an MD degree as general practitioners. We could still maintain the present standards for specialists in the field of medicine and surgery. I think that the advantage to the people who use our system would outweigh the slight lowering of standards.

Another way to lower doctor bills, of course, would be to make it much more difficult to sue doctors. They should not be sued for just doing their job, even if they do make a mistake. From what I read, the cost of their malpractice insurance is atrocious. Of course they pass that cost on to us, the patients, just as most businesses pass added costs on to their clients.

And finally, I would find ways to rein in the often outlandish costs of hospital care (and medical care in general), and, for many, the cost of medical insurance. Again, malpractice suits might be one of the major reasons hospital costs are so high. Hospitals put patients through many more tests than necessary just because of the possibility of a lawsuit if they don't take every single precaution possible.

31

Hillary

I never had to debate much with myself when it came to choosing between Donald Trump, now President-elect, and Hillary Clinton, now having decided to help contest the election in the states of Wisconsin, Pennsylvania, and Michigan, in spite of her earlier angry reaction to Mr. Trump's refusal to say he would accept the outcome of the election process no matter what.

Hillary had lots of political baggage, negative baggage. There was (and still is) her husband Bill who, if Hillary had become President, would have become "First Gentleman." That would have given him considerable political clout which, personally, I didn't like because he was an erratic president on the international scene and I thought he deserted the blue-collar workers and took the Democratic Party waltzing to Wall Street during his tenure, where it has been ever since, right beside the Republican Party. My fear was that Bill would help keep Hillary in the Wall Street camp no matter what she said. Also, Hillary as President would once again give Bill the White House as his personal hunting ground, for female prey. I wouldn't have minded that a great deal, although there might just have been an iota or two of envy in me somewhere. Women over 18 are adults, after all (most everywhere in the USA, I think), and as such have the right to accept or reject whatever male comes "ahunting." And Bill seems to have a predilection for that female set, women old enough to know better but young enough to say "Yea, man" anyway. That characteristic of Hillary's life, and Bill's, didn't really turn me off that much, not enough to sway my vote, just enough to give me a few sleepless hours wondering why Bill and not me. And enough to be one strike against her.

But what did turn me off was that I envisioned a new investigative committee, headed by another rising Starr, springing up in Congress and spending inordinate amounts of government time and taxpayer money trying to make public every little nuance of Bill's sexual peccadilloes, and those of his partners, and every sticky little detail of what happened in private between two adults. I don't think my anger would have stood quietly by while another Starr tried to penetrate what Bill did, not again. One soiled dress is enough. I can only recall how irritated I was at the Starr Commission poking into Bill's sex life. In spite of my "also" irritation at Bill's lies and half-truths and what I thought of as his job mistakes, in the next presidential election I refused to vote for even one single Republican candidate. Kind of petty of me, right? But I've never claimed to stand above the crowd in character or integrity.

Anyhow, Bill as First Gentleman, although not the major one, was definitely a factor in my rejection of Hillary, a factor that was definitely in my mind before and when I walked into the voting booth. The major factors in my decision not to vote for Hillary, however, were Hillary's character and job record. I didn't see any real accomplishments while she was First Lady, Senator from New York, or Secretary of State. I had no doubts that she would continue President Obama's "ruling" style: avoid Congress in any way possible and rule by decree (directive). I doubted that she would do anything about the economy, illegal immigration, not-very-well-vetted Muslim immigration, Obamacare, the cesspool in Washington, DC, the self-destructive "deals" like NAFTA that we have made with foreign countries, or our continual and kind of ineffective involvement in the wars in the Middle East. And I doubted that she would even attempt to return any of the manufacturing jobs that have fled the USA…return them to our country so that our people and our government (through taxes) can benefit from their successes. After all, she's a Wall Streeter, not a Main Streeter, in spite of all she says, which leads to my belief that she is a terrible hypocrite and will say anything she deems necessary, in any situation, in order to get what she wants—not unlike so many of our politicians, I don't think. Then there was Benghazi: the early-on lie about the cause of the attack on the embassy, and her probable desertion of Ambassador Stevens and the other three Americans who died in the attack. If it was not actual desertion, then it verged on extreme carelessness, and eventually on callousness: "At this point, what difference does it make?"

Carelessness? What about the emails? One has to wonder to what extent her "almost" public sharing of secret material gave our enemies data they could use against us or to what extent it might have caused deaths, or heavy damage, among our secret friends in secret places. And of course there was the Clinton Foundation. While Secretary of State, she might not have given benefits to the Foundation's biggest donors. But then again she might have. The whole situation was quite suggestive. Either way she was extremely careless in her use of the personal server, and afterwards quite duplicitous in her reactions and answers to that use, just as she was extremely careless in whose money was accepted by the Foundation.

And so, my rejection of Hillary had to do with her job performance. At least it did mainly. Bill's sexual peccadilloes didn't interfere with his job performance, I don't think. Hillary's personality quirks did: hypocrisy, carelessness, lack of sympathy for those her decisions destroyed or hurt and a dangerous carelessness not only with the lives of those under her command but with the very essence of what would become her responsibilities as president—the wellbeing of a country and its people.

And then there is our President-elect, Mr. Donald Trump. I admit that I don't know all that much about him and his past. It sounds like he may have raging hormones, like Bill Clinton does. I don't think Bill's affected his job performance as president, and I doubt very much that Trump's will. Besides, Mr. Trump won't be the first president who had a big yen for women. Nor was Bill Clinton! Personally I would find it both odd and disheartening if there weren't a decent number of our past presidents who had a hefty desire for the female of the species.

In any case, Trump's hormones didn't keep him from being a pretty big success in the business world. So why should they keep him from being a success as president? His reactions and outspoken comments on the elective trail sure don't suggest that he's a hypocrite. Far from it! He surely couldn't be as careless and duplicitous as Hillary. Else how could he have earned enough trust from investors and people who wanted to employ his services, and enough loyalty from his employees and associates, to make billions?

And, finally, Mr. Trump is not a professional politician; he's not one of the class of people that I am sick and tired of. I'm tired of promises that are soon forgotten. I'm tired of the bog that our working people have been confined to, sinking deeper and deeper with every president. I'm tired of our say-anything, do-nothing Congress, Democrats and Republicans alike. I want a president who will attempt to re-invigorate our manufacturing base, who will try to fulfill his promises, who will try to balance the budget and decrease the national debt, who will insist on the rule of law and common sense not only on our streets but also in the Capitol and in our immigration system, who….

But enough ranting and preaching. I voted for Mr. Trump for the above reasons and in spite of what often appeared to be a speak-without-thinking character. I sometimes wonder if that was an act, one to link up psychologically with the common man, or if he really does have somewhat of a Jekyll and Hyde character. One thing he has shown about himself, though, is that after the ranting man comes the thinking man, a man who is not an ideologue but rather a pragmatist. Just my kind of man!

History

"Those who don't know history are destined to repeat it."
Edmund Burke (1729-1797)

And there's that political world…that PC world we all have become so familiar with, which refuses to call something what it is. We all are well aware that the vast majority of terrorists today, in the Mideast and the West as well as in other places worldwide, are of the Muslim religion. They might not have been born in Iraq, or Syria, or Saudi Arabia, but they are of the Muslim faith, and they are one way or another linked to Muslim extremism. Yet Muslim extremism seems to be a no-no word for many of our politicians and other leaders, and also for much of the Trumpian enemy of the people, the media.

The same thing can be said about illegal immigrants. In the media and other public places we mostly hear them referred to as undocumented immigrants, or foreign-born workers, or undocumented workers, or some such nonsense. Undocumented immigrants? How silly can you get? They really have broken one of the basic laws of our land, a basic law of the land in all countries, one that keeps a country a country, and not simply a place which other countries can use to get rid of their excess population (you know, like a revolving door), especially their problem people and those who for one reason or another can't make it in their native land, or, truthfully, those who actually are persecuted in their home land. We are not a wilderness, not an unpopulated frontier like our own West once was, not a place for "easterners" (read immigrants from south of our borders) to start anew legally or illegally.

Now I'm not against legal immigration. Moreover I really think that we should increase the number of "legal" immigrants we accept from south of our borders. To a great extent we share a general common historic heritage and religious faith. And I believe that, once we have put our own people back to work, all or the vast majority of those who are capable of working but are collecting some form of government aid, we would probably do well to re-establish what was once referred to as the "bracero" program, or something similar. But there should be limits and rules that we establish, limits determined by the needs of <u>our own</u> country, not the needs a few of our own citizens, and definitely not the needs of other countries or peoples. I don't really believe that we will ever control the illegal immigration problem, not even with a wall, until we go after those of us who hire illegal immigrants, until we quit giving <u>any</u> <u>governmental aid</u> to illegals, until we solve the present problem of all the illegals in our country, until we stop granting citizenship to those who just happen to be born here but of illegal parents, and until we begin (and continue) deporting any and all who cross our borders without appropriate documentation.

I began this essay with a quote about the danger of ignoring history. I would like to continue with my take on historical movements and change. Most of my history classes over the years, from high school to graduate school, presented history from the point of view of the great man (person) and war as the prime movers of change. Great men supposedly have brought about our great changes throughout history. I disagree with that somewhat. My belief is that great men are really manifestations of a zeitgeist, a belief or movement prevalent in a certain time and/or place. The great man who effects historical change is the one who rises to the fore and leads the people in the direction they want to go. He is great in the sense that he can organize and channel the forces already present in the culture. Our founding fathers did not create the basic ideas of democracy as expressed in our *Constitution* or *Declaration of Independence*. Of course they created the specific expressions written in the two documents, and they were the philosophers and doers of the movement for independence. But the general ideas themselves were inherent in the time, among the thinkers and even among the common people, the masses. George Washington and the other Founding Fathers were great men because they stepped up and led the people in the direction the people wanted to go.

I think something similar can be said about war. War is not something that appears out of vacant space in order to change the status quo. It comes about as the result of an unstoppable movement that will brook no opposition and as the result of the attempt by any means by one group or nation to impose its will on another group or nation. It too is a manifestation of a zeitgeist, a general feeling of the people, or some of the people (the most vocal and active?), and their interplay with the thinkers and leaders of the time.

We seem to downplay the real anti-colonial, anti-British atmosphere that led to our Revolutionary War, the latter of which did of course free our country from British rule. We seem to forget the rising antagonism to slavery in the North and the rising anger at northern interference in the South, both of which ultimately gave rise to our only Civil War up to the present time. And most of all, relative to illegal immigration, we seem to forget that it was emigration westward from our eastern states that led to the Texan war of independence from Mexico. We seem to forget that the powers in Mexico City ignored the influx of Anglos into Texas and other western states until it was too late, much like Washington seems to be doing today. And it was that influx which ultimately led the US government to protect the American settlers by going to war and so turning a huge swath of Mexico's northern territories into part of the USA. And, lastly, we often seem ignorant that settlers often led the way into Indian lands and it was the government which followed with its Army to protect the settlers, and to pacify those lands and make them American.

This is the danger I see in an uncontrollable illegal immigration. Uncontrolled immigration into the Mexican territory of Texas in the first half of the 19th century was the primary cause of Texas being an American state today. The same is true of the rest of our Southwest that was once Spanish, then Mexican, and now American. I personally can see the definite possibility of the same thing happening in reverse, in the not-to-distance future. Many people will pooh-pooh this, I have no doubt. Why would people want to become Mexican citizens when they can be Americans, free people living in a wealthy democracy, one of the greatest nations in the world? Well, why did our ancestors want to be free of Great Britain, the greatest empire of the time? Why did Mexico want to be free of Spain? Why did many Mexicans fight beside the Anglos to free Texas from Mexico and later accept Texas's joining the USA?

We are proud of our country. But so are the people of Mexico proud of their country. And so are many Mexican-Americans, and rightfully so. We American citizens are proud of living in a democratic nation, but so are Mexican citizens proud of their democracy. We have a strong economy, but it seems to be declining somewhat, if our trade deficit is any indicator. Mexico, on the other hand, supposedly has the 10th biggest economy in the world, and it seems to be a rising rather than declining economy. We think of our Southwest as an integral part of the USA. Many Mexicans and Mexican-Americans think of it as territory stolen from Mexico. Many Americans would like to see the border become less porous. Many Mexicans and Mexican-Americans would like to see it remain porous, so they and their relatives on both sides of it can connect as families should connect, freely and without outside interference or other obstacles.

So what should be done? I can think of many things, but in the final analysis it is up to our government whether they act or continue to hide their heads in the sand, hoping against hope that the problem will go away if they just ignore it long enough. And that, I think, is something else that helps bring about change in our world, a creeping weakness in government, and in the peoples of a nation, and an eventual reaction of one kind or another to it. The main question here, I think, is whether we will again take charge of our own fate or sit on our hands and let fate take charge of us.

Illegal Immigration

Build more fence between us and Mexico? I guess that wouldn't hurt, at least in places where it's easy to cross into the USA and quickly find civilization to hide in. It would have to be a fence that is difficult for drug dealers and others who would break our laws to clamber over, of course. As for the most difficult terrain along our border, I think a fence might just be a waste of money. It is most effective in cities and other populated areas, I suspect.

But I doubt very much that a fence is the ultimate answer to both the entry of drugs into our country and to our illegal immigration problem. A fence will make it more difficult for drug runners to bring their drugs in. But where there's millions of dollars to be made people will find a way to subvert obstacles, especially a fence along the Mexican border. There is the air, and there is the Pacific Ocean, and there is the Gulf of Mexico. And, of course, as we've seen enough times, men can dig tunnels under fences. Besides there are lots of ways to smuggle drugs through border patrolled gateways—ports of entry.

What so many of us seem to ignore is that the huge financial attraction of our drug market and the even broader attraction of a much, much easier life in the USA than most people can attain in the countries south of our border—those are what bring people north. There is no way we can keep people from risking almost everything (life, prison, rape, enslavement) on the chance of winning whatever it is they dream of: riches from drug running; a life of greater wealth and freedom for themselves and, possibly, their family; escape from continuous poverty and street danger; whatever.

Given the living conditions in Mexico and Central America, there is no way we can stop people from surging north unless we take tough, unremitting action. Such action has been tried before, of course, but it has been isolated and subverted by both our federal government and presently by many of our cities (sanctuary cities). It is also subverted by a dialogue that generally ignores the "illegal" part about Illegal immigration. Many of our politicians, our do-gooders, and those in the media ignore the fact that people who are "illegal immigrants" broke a basic law of our nation by entering our country without appropriate authorization. When nothing is done about it, well, the next wave of illegal entry gets bigger, as does the next, and the….

How far back does illegal immigration stretch into the past? Who was our first president to give amnesty to the illegal immigrants in our country? According to the article "Amnesty for Illegal Aliens" published by *The American Resistance*, for "over 200 years, the United States only granted amnesty in individual cases and had never given amnesty to large numbers of illegal aliens. Then in 1986, Congress passed the immigration Reform and Control Act (IRCA) which gave amnesty to all illegal aliens who had evaded law enforcement for at least four years or who were working illegally in agriculture." Was that, for many, a reward for avoiding being caught while committing a crime?

Anyhow, this resulted in "2.8 million illegal aliens being admitted as legal immigrants to the United States." This amnesty was supposed to be a 'one time only' amnesty. Since then, however, Congress has passed six more amnesties for illegal immigrants.

And how many illegal aliens are presently in the USA? Some people estimate about 11 million, which could, I suppose, be low because others estimate between 12 and 20 million and believe that approximately 85% of the people of Mexican heritage presently living in the USA are here illegally. There are also those who insist that the number is more like 30 million.

So, who has tried to solve the problem? FactCheck says the following: During President Hoover's time in office, "121,000 persons were officially deported or induced to leave." As for President Truman's nearly eight years in office, the same source says that "about 3.4 million were deported or left 'voluntarily' under threat of deportation." Next, President Eisenhower was supposedly responsible for deporting just over 2 million illegals. And now we have somewhere between 11 and 30 million illegal immigrants in our country? And we have a Congress that seems more interested in attacking anybody who tries to deport illegals than in trying to solve the problem. Of course that is a real spark of hope to people wanting to illegally make the USA their home.

So, the more recent attempts of Sheriff Joe Arpaio to round up illegals waiting on street corners for a daily job offer seem like a futile attempt by a lone man in a huge country of over 300 million, with our federal government against him. Our government has made a mountain out of that mole hill. Between the federal government and Arizona voters a stop was finally put to Sheriff Joe's futile attempts to stem the flow of illegals. And now there is President Trump, who is also making an effort to at least deport illegals who have committed crimes <u>after</u> coming "illegally" into our country, although many people are complaining that Trump's rules are rounding up too many 'innocents.' Innocent of what, I wonder. Not of entering our country illegally, definitely not. Who would make such a silly claim? I have to wonder if Congress will grant amnesty to the 11 to 30 million illegals already in the USA.

As for drugs Janet Napolitano, in 2009 when she was Homeland Security Secretary, claimed that the US and Mexico were winning the drug war. Well, I for one can't see any real reduction in the drugs coming across our border or in the drug war in Mexico itself. Witness the opioid epidemic. Witness the number of people killed in the Mexican Drug Wars. And I doubt very much that we will see any substantial decrease in the drugs flowing across our border until we accept that we, not the drug cartels, are the real culprits in our drug epidemic. We are the cause. When a doctor tries to cure an illness (and I mean <u>cure</u>, not simply treat) he doesn't go after the symptoms of the illness, although, I have to admit, that many of the doctors I have had in my life didn't seem to distinguish between pretty obvious symptoms and any type of hidden cause that might exist. What I mean relative to our drug epidemic is that we have to find some way to wean our drug addicts off of drugs and also some way to keep others from becoming addicted, <u>or we have to legalize drugs for recreational purposes—and control that use</u>. At the same time, we need to concentrate our forces against the drugs coming from south of us, as some states have done by legalizing marijuana, so that we have control of the market and can use some of the tax money thus gathered to research ways of curing addicts and keeping others from becoming addicted. And not with laws that make it a crime to take drugs. That hasn't worked worth a damn up to the present, has it? Except to put a lot of our young people in jail. We need to take control of our own destiny, and the destiny of our people, those with drug weaknesses at least, and not leave that destiny to drug lords who could care less about how many people they destroy.

But I'm getting away from the real problem I meant to discuss here—illegal immigration. However I have touched on what I see as the only solution—going after the cause while at the same time treating the symptoms. President Trump is attempting to treat the symptoms and seems to be doing a decent enough job of it: building a "fence" and deporting all illegals who have committed a crime and going after sanctuary cities. Of course, even if he is 100% successful, which I doubt will happen, there will still be a vast number of illegals in the USA. That will be true unless he eventually gets around to dealing with the cause! By cause I mean the jobs people come north to find. That is what most of our illegals immigrate north for. And available jobs, of course, come from people who need workers. If our people are willing to hire illegal immigrants, and our government does nothing to them…do you think they will ever quit hiring them? I don't, not as long as illegals are available and cheaper than "legals," i. e. citizens. And not as long as our 'legal' citizens won't take some of the jobs available!

What I think we need to do is pass a law (laws?) that criminalizes hiring illegal immigrants. Those who knowingly hire illegal immigrants (hiring people who do not have appropriate documentation) should suffer jail time and fines, fines large enough to make hiring illegals more expensive than hiring legals. At the same time we need to re-institute the old bracero program in one form or another, like offer work visas or green cards or something for limited periods of time and for only those jobs which our citizens will not or cannot take. And again, any foreign worker violating those work visas should wind up with criminal charges and deportation.

At the same time, of course, we need to change our welfare system to a "workfare system." All those in the system who can work have to work in whatever jobs are available if they have the physical and mental capacity to do so. Those who cannot work in the jobs available on the open market must needs work for the federal or state governments, in some capacity or another, even if that is babysitting for others who do work, like cleaning up our roadways and city streets.

But most important of all, we need to stem the illegal flow of people and drugs into our country. We need to find a way to cure the causes of these illegal activities before they become more than even our government can handle. Or maybe, just maybe our government can't handle the illegal immigrant and drug inflow now, as weak and apparently uncaring as it is. If that is the case, I tremble for our children and grandchildren and…I have to wonder if we might not be seeing an early 19th century Texas in reverse, a Texas that the government in Mexico City ignored until there were enough "illegal" Anglos in the territory to start a struggle for freedom from Mexican rule.

34

Illegal Immigration 2

Illegal immigration? I agree with President Trump that it has to be stopped somehow, but I don't completely agree with him on how, I don't think. I would probably reinforce the fence we have in places and also reinforce our border patrol. But I would also prosecute those who hire illegals without work papers. Work papers? I would re-institute the old brasero program, carefully gearing it to those jobs which Americans <u>will not or cannot</u> handle, giving limited-time access to non-citizens to do certain jobs, and maybe setting up a pathway to citizenship for those who remained in the program for a certain period of time. However, at the same time I would change our welfare program to one in which all who benefited in any way from government handouts had to do some kind of work to earn what they received.

But let's start with how many illegals there are in the USA. The most common estimates seem to range from ten to twenty million, although we all know how nebulous estimates of that size can be. Presently, a common estimate for the population of our country in 2016 is 324,000,000. Let's say 325 million just to work with easier "round" numbers. If there are ten million illegals in the country, does that mean there are 335 million people in the USA, or are they part of the estimated number? If there are 325 million total, then with 10 million illegals, two in every 65 inhabitants of our country are illegal, one in every 32.5. If the total people is actually 335 million, then two in every 67 are illegal, or one in every 33.5.

If there are twenty million illegals, is that 325 million or 345 million inhabitants we have? If 345, four in every 69 are illegal, or one in every 17.25. If 325, then four in every 65 of us are illegal, or one in every 16.25.

However! However, I've recently read that we might have as many as thirty million illegal immigrants in the country. Thirty million? Wow! That would maybe mean there are as many as 355 million people living in the country, or maybe just 325 still. If 325 million, with thirty million illegals, that means that right at one in every 10.8 people here is an illegal immigrant. If 345 million, then I guess it's one in every 11.5. Whichever way it is, approximately 10% of the people living in this country being illegal is scary as all hell, and even more so since so many people in our federal and state governments are dedicated to making sure that we don't stop the flow from south of our border.

Then there's California, possibly our most crowded state, with an estimated population of 39.6 million inhabitants in 2017 and an estimated illegal population of 2.4 million (low?). Let's round those numbers to 40 million inhabitants and 2.5 million illegals. Again, I'm not sure if the 40 million includes the illegals or not. Let's say it doesn't. So we have two and a half illegals for every 42.5 inhabitants. I'd say that's one illegal in every 21 people. Or if the total population including illegals is 40 million, that's one in every 16 inhabitants. This is all assuming, of course, that the above estimates are correct, or close to correct, which I very much doubt, and that my math is okay. People who don't want to be counted, and people who don't want to count them, can find ways to avoid such. I personally would suspect that the actual number of illegals in California is much higher. In any case, the increase in the illegal immigrant population throughout our country since the turn of the century has been astronomical, and financially and economically devastating, I believe. According to an article in _Newsmax_ by Karen Ridder (9-14-15) the national number of illegals rose by 250% from 1990 to 2007. Has that trend continued to 2018? If so, then I think the number of illegals in the country is a heck of a lot higher than ten million. I have also read more than once that 80% of the illegal immigrants in California live below the poverty line and require assistance from the government. That seems to me to be a logical result of almost 25% (counted total at ten million) of the illegals in the country living in that same state.

What happens if we grant this vast number of people amnesty, or at least grant it to all of those who haven't committed crimes? There can be only one logical answer. Twenty, thirty, forty years from now the number of <u>new</u> illegals (meaning the number of illegals coming into our country after today) will be, to give a round number as estimate (or wild guess?), say thirty million, or forty million, or fifty million, or.... It's only logical that the numbers would increase exponentially. If I began to allow homeless people to camp out in my yard, it wouldn't be long before my yard would be covered side to side, front to back, with people wanting a space of their own. And it probably wouldn't be much longer before some were forcing their way into the house. Moreover, if I also offered free "giveaways" such as food and other "welfare" stuff, I think the fight for a place on my property would escalate dramatically. Would I be forced off my own property?

What bothers me most about illegal immigration, I guess, is that I see a parallel (in reverse) with Texas (Tejas) in the first half of the 19th century. Anglos poured into Texas from the east, much as Mexicans and other Hispanics are pouring into the USA from points south nowadays. The Spanish/Mexican government was erratic in its attempts to stem the flood, sometimes welcoming the illegals with cheap land, sometimes trying to enforce laws to stop the flow; both government and people were divided in their attitude toward and acceptance of the Anglos. That is what the US government and many of our people have been doing for decades with Hispanics, being erratic, inconsistent, and divided in our attitudes, claiming at one point that the Hispanics are needed to take jobs legal citizens won't take, establishing sanctuary cities at other times, trying at another moment to build a wall along our southern border, and occasionally and inconsistently enforcing laws against those who hire illegals.

Well, the Mexican government and the Hispanic citizens of Texas were so inconsistent that eventually the Anglos greatly outnumbered the legal citizens of Texas. We all know what happened, of course. The Anglos had not lost their love of their motherland, the good old USA or they wouldn't have tried to emulate it first and then join it when the emulation became too tough. Me, I think Victor Davis Hanson is correct when he says that, in spite of the fact that many of our illegals from Mexico have fled a harsh, devastating life in their homeland, they have not lost their love for their motherland and its culture, much as many Anglos, who fled failure and a harsh life to migrate to Texas and eventually separate Texas from Mexico, had not lost their love for their motherland, the United States of America. And I suspect that that love of country, probably prevalent among so many Anglos moving westward in the 19th century, is prevalent among many Hispanics moving northward in the 21st century. The real question, I think, is whether or not we will eventually choose to protect our borders and re-establish "law," our law, as the governing force for immigration into these American states, or if we will continue to vacillate until it is too late for us to stop the tide of change turning into a tsunami of separation.

35

Impeachment Anyone

Impeachment. Impeachment. Impeachment. Hmmm. Is the third repetition a charm? A lot of people would really hope so, would really hope that the three-time chant worked like a charm and automatically impeached our president. Of course they ignore the fact that he was voted into office by "We, the people." And they ignore the fact that after months and months of Muellerite investigation, there has been nothing leaked that even approaches an impeachable offense.

The worst part about all this is that many of these people who would impeach the president are our leaders, not only in the national capital but also in many state capitals and city halls. Our leaders. Supposedly intelligent and rational people who believe that one of the most essential characteristics of democracy, other than freedom of speech and all of us supposedly being born equal—one of the most essential and necessary characteristics of democracy is that any person accused of a crime is innocent until proven guilty in a court of law. <u>Any person</u>. <u>Every person</u>. President as well as politician and peon.

And, as I just said, that <u>includes the president of the United States</u>, no matter how much some people might hate him. In this case, no matter how many people have "Trump derangement syndrome," Trump derangement syndrome being a softened and thus more acceptable neologism for fanatic Trump hatred.

Me, I find it kind of scary—<u>it</u> meaning the direction we are headed with this insistence on guilt with no evidence except accusation, which so far has all been politically motivated, as far as I am concerned. And it seems to be a direction our country is heading, a scary direction. First there was the get President Bill Clinton movement, get him for being a man, one, in his case, who couldn't resist sexual relationships with any willing woman, which seems to me to be fairly typical of many normal males, normal sexually, that is. There was no doubt in my mind that the Starr Commission was politically motivated, by our Republican leaders. After all, what does a man's sexuality have to do with his ability to perform as president or senator or laborer? Nada. Moreover, I have always believed that a man's sex life is nobody's business but his own, his wife's, and whatever woman he goes after, or gets. Unless, of course, he actually does come afoul of the law in his escapades—does something illegal.

Then, more recently, there was the #MeToo movement and their insistence that women don't lie about sexual abuse, although any rational person knows that that's a bunch of hooey, as does any reader who is willing to do a little research. Given the right circumstances, many if not most of us will lie—for vengeance, for our good name, for fear, for money, for friendship, for love, for family, for fame, for…. I always thought that a little white lie, if meant to help someone, might just be better than the truth if the truth happens to be hurtful or dangerous. Anyhow, the attack on Justice Kavanaugh is a good case in point relative to the #MeToo movement and the sexual atmosphere it has helped create. Whether Justice Kavanaugh was innocent or guilty, and the evidence thus far suggests to me that he was innocent—whether he was innocent or guilty, his character and good name were terribly besmirched in public, by the media, by many men and women (mainly democrats), and by many of our supposedly rational political leaders. In many ways we seem to have reached the point where Russia was back in the Stalin years, during what I think of as the USSR Show Trials. Only instead of putting our political opponents on trial and then executing them, we destroy them through the media and public opinion. And woe to those, like President Trump, who do not conform to the character and action that is expected of them.

I read now that some state leaders are trying to keep the president off the 2020 presidential ballot by making a state law that anyone who won't make his income tax forms public can't be on their state ballot. My god, what childish nonsense, childish and mean, bullying mean, and terribly dangerous to our democracy. Can you imagine where some of this might be headed? The next thing you know only candidates chosen by the House of Representatives will be allowed on the presidential ballots—and the Senate ballots, and the state governor ballots, and....

I also read that some of our leaders are trying to change our voting laws by getting rid of the Electoral College in favor of only the popular vote, simply because Trump won the Electoral College vote but not the popular vote. Who would that favor? Many say it would make the cities all-powerful and disenfranchise the smaller cities and towns, the countryside, and the Midwest in general. Whatever. It seems to me that both attempts are a step toward rule by oligarchy, and just where would that lead?

I think it's time our Trump-hating leaders stop their childish tantrums and turn to solving some of our national problems—like a skyrocketing national debt, a healthcare system and a higher educational system both financially out of control, a deadly drug problem among our people (one that is creating monstrously wealthy drug lords around the world), a broken immigration system, and a political attitude among our leaders that continuously embroils us in seemingly never-ending wars around the world.

I say let's get back to being a world leader rather than _the_ world's policeman.

36

Imperialism & The USA

It's odd. Or at least it seems so to me. I was talking with a group of people the other day and I mentioned that many intellectuals in other countries consider the USA a nation of economic, political and military imperialism. I immediately got the impression that I had touched on a subject way too far out to be anything but idiotic or anti-American. We did not continue that topic. Nobody said yes, no, or maybe. Actually, only one person commented and she asked me where I got all that kind of stuff. My answer that I read a lot, books as well as magazines, didn't add to the conversation, which simply moved on to another subject.

I find it difficult to believe that people can be so blind, or arrogant, or lacking in historical understanding. It's the same blindness, the same unconscious hypocrisy, that I find relative to our Congressional, and general American, reaction to Russian influence in our last election. It's the same blindness, or arrogance, that has led us to spend, probably, millions of dollars on an investigation that should never have taken place, one that is still ongoing, sadly. We interfere in the elections and internal affairs of other countries all the time, yet we get indignant because the Russians interfered in ours. Where the hell does such hypocrisy come from? Or could it actually be naivete?

Now, I'm not saying that we shouldn't do something about the Russian meddling. I'm not saying that we shouldn't beef up our protection on the internet. I'm not saying that we shouldn't show the Russians what happens to meddlers. What I'm saying is that we should quit blaming our own people. We should quit squabbling among ourselves like a bunch of teenagers. We should go after the real perpetrator. However, I see no reason why we couldn't use the carrot and stick approach. I see no reason why we can't try to get along with Russia, as we do with China and other countries who aren't exactly our friends. We don't take any crap from China, but we try to get along. Why not the same with Russia? The world might just be a little safer if we did.

But back to the topic I began with: Is the USA an imperialistic nation or not? My answer: Of course we are. The USA is a superpower, is it not? What superpower has ever existed throughout history that was not imperialistic? Isn't that one of the basic characteristics of a superpower— a nation that has been able to establish a great deal of control over many other nations of the world; in essence, a nation that has built an empire (territorially, economically, politically, militarily) and has remained the central hub which wields a great deal of control over that empire. Until it was destroyed, of course, as all empires have been

The English established our beachhead in the New World. But we, the American people, or rather our ancestors, after freeing us from the English, followed what was often thought of as our "manifest destiny" and drove ever westward to the Pacific. And they didn't stop there.

First, as they moved westward, our American ancestors took the land from various Indian tribes, who probably took it from other Indians that lived there before them. Isn't that what we humans do? Don't we take land from others of our kind to build empires, tiny or huge, local or worldwide? Don't we destroy empires so we can take land from the inhabitants? Don't we then eventually build new empires? It seems to me that this is one of the most natural and ongoing cycles of human history, empire building and empire destroying.

So, our ancestors are not unique in that sense. They simply began another cycle, one that is not completed yet. Their uniqueness comes, I believe, in what they built out of the destruction: a democracy based in e pluribus unum. And that I am proud of.

But to continue our westward movement: In 1803 the USA purchased the Louisiana Territory from France. In a way that was kind of like buying hot goods. Spain had taken a lot of the area in the southeast from the Indians who once lived there and much later lost it to France. Many tribes still claimed much of the land west of the Mississippi. Spain claimed much of the southern lands west of the Mississippi.

But our nation-building star was on the ascendency. Spain's was on the decline. By mid-19th century we had not only settled much of the northern lands west of the Mississippi, decimating Indian tribes and moving what was left onto reservations, but we had wrested most of our present Southwest from Mexico, which had taken it from Spain when it gained its independence. Also, by the end of the century we had purchased Alaska from the Russians, wrested the Kingdom of Hawaii from the Hawaiians, and, by means of the Spanish-American War, taken control of such as Puerto Rico, Cuba, Guam, and the Philippines. Puerto Rico is still an American territory. Cuba and the Philippines eventually took over their own fate, although we still have a military base in the Philippines, and we still have Guantanamo in Cuba. And, of course, Guam is still an American territory.

With the Spanish-American War, our territorial acquisitions through force ceased, basically. We turned from territorial imperialism to political, economic and military imperialism. In how many countries do we have military bases? I can name a few without doing any research: Japan, South Korea, the Philippines, Germany, Spain, Italy, Guam, Afghanistan, and Iraq. Then there is Guantanamo in Cuba, as I mentioned above. And, according to several lists I just encountered in a few minutes research, we have military bases in sixteen other countries from Singapore to Europe to Turkey and the Mideast. In some of these countries we have quite a few bases, especially in Japan. South Korea, Germany, and Saudi Arabia. Can you imagine the cost of keeping these bases staffed, not only with military personnel but also with staff to support them?

We have these bases, supposedly, as a bulwark against communism and other potential enemies. But I often ask myself why. Germany has one of the best economies in the world. It is a rich nation, definitely on a par with us. So why can't it build an army to protect itself? With the navy and air force we have, we don't really need to have bases in Germany to protect it. If we moved out militarily, and Germany expanded its military to meet its needs, and then they needed help in any given moment against an enemy, we could be there in a jiffy. So why do we continue supporting troops there, supporting their bases, paying them, and letting them spend their wages in a foreign country? Why? I ask myself the same question about other European countries, and Japan. Japan is an economic powerhouse. Why don't they build their own military up to what they think they need? And South Korea? Well, it might be a little iffier, given the character and military development of North Korea.

The real problem is that we have assumed, unilaterally, the position of world policeman, another "duty" of a superpower as we must see it. Something goes wrong according to our understanding of political reality and national relationships and we send in the politicians or troops to "fix it." We have been doing that since the Monroe Doctrine was first formulated. How often have we sent troops into Central or South American countries to rectify what we see as a problem, like in Grenada? I just read a list which included over 50 "invasions" of Central and South American countries and Caribbean islands since 1890. The list also included an extensive number of invasions of Eastern European, Asian, African and Mideastern countries, including the most recent invasions of Iraq, Syria and Afghanistan, of course.

Back in the late 1940s and early 1950s we got involved in the Korean civil war between the north and south. Our involvement left the Korean peninsula divided into two countries, two countries still facing off over a no-man's land, with weapons at the ready. A few years later, 1955 to 1975, we got involved in the Vietnamese civil war. Twenty years! The outcome was probably better for the region. We fled, leaving the South at the mercy of the North. But at least we left a unified Vietnam, rather than one divided between still angry enemies. But now, again, we are involved in a "civil" war in the Mideast, not exactly a war between nations, not exactly a civil war pure and simple, but one that is more like a "religious civil" war. How many years now? When will it end? How will it end? Not with any kind of real victory and unity, I don't expect.

Yet we keep on interfering, on and on. We keep on trying to "fix" the world's imperfections, imperfections that we see, that we create, that we define. We keep trying to superimpose a democratic and capitalistic system around the world, no matter what it costs us in money and people. We avoid trying to do such with the stronger nations, like Russia, China, North Korea, Iran, or with nations under their protection. We are much like Spain in its imperialistic heyday, as it tried to spread the Catholic faith around the globe, or most other empire builders as far as that goes. And like them, we coat our actions with well-intentioned meanings. And like them we are spending ourselves into our grave.

I love my country. I think it is one of the greatest to date. But I think we need to be a little more honest with ourselves and others. And I think we need to back off this self-appointed world policeman bit a little. We need to always consider our own interests before we get involved in any kind of shooting war.

37

Import Deficit

Hey, let's go back to the economy. I read an interesting article on the internet the other day, a 2016 article in *The Balance*. It was entitled "U.S Imports and Exports: Components and Statistics." It claimed that no more than 13% of the goods that we export are consumer goods and that over half of those goods consist of pharmaceuticals, cell phones, and "gem diamonds." The article further said that one-third of all our exports are services, like "travel, passenger services and fares," "royalty and license fees," and "financial services."

Only 13% are consumer goods? And less than half of those would be the basic necessities, say 6%, if nearly that much, which, from the sound of the article, I doubt?

As for imports, the article claimed that "more than 80 percent are goods" like "industrial machines and equipment," foods and beverages, "computers and telecommunications equipment," and "automotive vehicles, parts and engines." All I can say is wow, with a sinking feeling in my stomach. I guess my stomach has a rough time with what my mind already suspected, that most of what we use on a daily basis comes to us from abroad.

Anyway, it startled me even further when I read that the US has an annual trade deficit of about a half billion dollars and that "consumer products and automobiles are the drivers of the trade deficit." How long ago was it that we had one of the, if not _the_, largest automotive industries in the world? My father retired from Chrysler. I have a brother-in-law who retired from Fisher Body. And my wife has a niece whose husband retired from Chrysler. I lived for years in a town that had a huge GM foundry that employed several thousand people. And I've owned foreign cars only twice in my life. Yet I've known for years that my Fords and Chevys were not made but probably only assembled in the US, if even that—that most if not all of the parts were made in some other country.

And it's depressing.

Yet I keep reading that our manufacturing sector is as large as it ever has been, while at the same time our manufacturing jobs have shrunk by a third over the past decade. And the shrinkage is supposedly because of technology, which has made human workers less and less necessary.

I can't dispute the impact of technology. Maybe it has been responsible for our manufacturing jobs decreasing by one third over the past decade. But I have to wonder in exactly which manufacturing industries technology has had such an impact. Would that be in the most, I think, sophisticated industries like airplane and heavy equipment and automotive and computer manufacturing? Or would it be in the manufacturing of everyday things like toys and furniture and food stuffs, and clothing?

And why do we have such a large deficit in the importation and exportation of consumer goods? Why are they being mostly manufactured abroad if it's really technology that is responsible for the loss of manufacturing jobs? Why are the majority of so many things we use the most being manufactured abroad? You know, machines and equipment for what industry we do have, food and beverages, automobiles and automotive parts, and telecommunications equipment.

Well, even if I buy into the idea that our manufacturing output is as much as it ever was, I have to underscore that our limited output, or the decline in sufficient output, of automobiles and consumer products is devastating to our economy. They drive the import/export deficit, as stated above. The money we could be making, or saving, by manufacturing what we need of these, or most of what we need, goes out of the country to support the economies of other countries. It basically causes our deficit of half a trillion dollars a year. No country can sustain such an imbalance forever. For how long can we?

Another problem I have with those who insist that we still have a manufacturing base as big as it ever has been has to do with our population. Back in 1960, say, when we were still world leaders in automotive manufacturing, and when we still created a major percentage of the basic consumer goods we used, our population was about 180 million. By the turn of the century we had a population of approximately 281 million. Over one hundred million increase. In 2016 the estimate was 323 million. That's not quite a hundred percent increase, but maybe it will be in a few more years, and in well less than a century.

So, to brag that our manufacturing base is still as big as it always has been, seems to me to avoid the real problems, that a big percentage of our exports are service oriented and therefore do not create blue collar jobs; that the things we use the most of are mostly manufactured abroad; that we have a big influx of foreign-born workers at the same time that our own people are hurting for decent jobs (or jobs period); that, in order to keep up with the increase in our population, our manufacturing base should have almost doubled since 1960, but at the most it seems to have remained at more or less the same level as it was way back when; that instead of manufacturing our basic necessities we are purchasing them from other countries (with IOUs?).

Individualism

Is there really such a thing as American individualism? Do we really, as a people, have a strong tendency toward independence of thought, opinion, and action, more so than the people of other countries? Is this really one of our essential characteristics? Are we really a nation of individualists? We often claim to be a people who can think, believe, speak, and act as we see fit. We say that we can all be what we wish, within the limitations of our abilities and if we do not encroach upon the rights of others, of course. We don't have to be a carbon copy of our neighbors or of our co-workers or bosses, or politicians. But is that us or a gift from our forefathers and the geographical marvels of our great country?

Like so many of my fellow Americans, I have always believed that we do have a strong tendency toward individualism in thought and action. After all, with such ancestral examples as Henry David Thoreau, Ralph Waldo Emerson, Mark Twain, Ernest Hemingway, William Faulkner, et al, who could doubt the deeply embedded element of independence in our culture? Of course there's always the other example to refer to, the Puritan side of our character, that side of us that has often made us band together to fight against other groups, to group together in wagon trains for the trek westward or in communities on the frontier in order to be safer against Indian attack or other dangers, and to reap certain benefits; there certainly is that side of our nature which motivates us to join in religious groups, political groups, unions, communities, clubs. As with most people the world over, we are pulled in both directions, some of us more strongly in one direction, others more strongly in the other.

Great artists often have a streak of independence in their nature, a streak that alienates them from normal society and sends them off on intellectual or esthetic tangents which others will not, or cannot take. The same, I believe, is true of many great thinkers and people of action, the William Jameses and Abraham Lincolns and John D. Rockefellers and Martin Luther King, Jrs. of the world. So we have a good share of independent thinkers and people of action. But I don't think the character of a culture as a whole can be judged by its great people. Many countries have great people, great thinkers, artists, and people of action.

It is not only true that we Americans have been blessed with great people who showed an inherent independent streak in their character, but also with many common people throughout our history who, although they themselves did not attain the greatness of having their names mentioned in our history books, were an integral part of "independent" groups that did not follow the dictates of convention but rather forged their own paths into the future: explorers, settlers, mountain men, frontiersmen, volunteers in the Spanish Civil War, small businessmen, inventors and artists who never found their way into the history books. That, I believe, is what, along with a wealth of natural resources in minerals, water, and land…that is one of the most essential traits that has made our great country what it is, people who follow their own stars and not the stars dictated by the forces of conformity.

That is not to say that I don't think there is a very strong force toward conformity in our society. We have a lock-step educational system, grades one through twelve and then for many who have the financial and intellectual (or athletic?) ability on to college immediately for four more years; although I must say that the college lock-step has begun to fray somewhat over the past decade or so, I believe such is more a problem of finances than of any kind of independent streak. As for politics, we have only two major parties and seldom has there been any meaningful break in that system. We do have a lot of independent voters, but according to Wikipedia the percentage of <u>true</u> independent voters relative to all voters has not changed since the Eisenhower era, when the percentage stood at 22%. They admit that the number of those who claim to be independent has about doubled. But they go on to say that "…the vast majority of self-defined Independents are not neutral but partisan—a bit bashful about admitting it, but partisan nevertheless."

On the other hand, independence is still alive and kicking in the business world. According to Mike Moffatt in his article "Small Business in the United States" (May 31, 2017), citing the Small Business Administration, "roughly 99 percent of all independent enterprises in the country employ fewer than 500 people…accounting for 52 percent of all workers." This is a little lower than in the 1950s, but only about 5% so.

I could go on like this, I suppose. But when we look at all the technological breakthroughs in medicine, business, education, and our daily lives over the past half century, I don't think there is any doubt that the entrepreneurial spirit, a spirit of independence, is alive and well in the USA.

But I have to ask myself if that individualism, that independence of spirit, is a fading characteristic in sections of our society. I have to ask myself if the movement away from small private enterprise to large national corporations and, ultimately, to monstrous international corporations hasn't taken away a large part of our individualism. It is much, much easier, financially and socially, to work for Safeway or Google or Walmart than to try to compete with them in some kind of a start-up. It is much easier for a man to wear a suit in situations where suits are expected than to forebear such. It is much easier to follow our educational lock-step than to find slower, meandering, less acceptable paths out into the work world.

But, you say, what's new? The social and personal tug-of-war between conformity and independence has always been with us. We've had huge companies ever since the formation of such as Standard Oil, Ford Motor Company, and Sears and Roebuck. And there always seems to be an unoccupied niche for another entrepreneur to fill (like Mark Zuckerberg did with Facebook) or a way to include previously separate groupings into one corporation, much as Walmart is a grocery store and department store and nursery all in one huge store and much as Amazon is becoming a Walmart enclosed in a mail order house (like Sears and Roebuck once was, but with "mail orders" becoming "computer orders").

Yet I find the forces for conformity stronger than I once did, although I sometimes suspect that the finding might be within me, a result of aging, rather than out there in the actual world. Of course, the attraction to conform, to not rock the boat, has always been strong. In my childhood and youth there were always social groups to belong to and social forces such as peer pressure to incline a person to join one group or another. There was the church. Most people I knew belonged to one church or another. There were the social clubs. There were the unions for the working class. Even at school there were the ins and the outs, and even in the out group there were certain conventions relative to dress codes, attitudes and beliefs, just as with the in groups. I don't see that this has changed. Witness the American gothic movement among our youth, how they all conformed to black in their dress codes. And witness the more recent Tattoo Culture. So many of us seem to want to be a part of something, even if that something is supposed to represent an independence of spirit, a social rebelliousness. Dress fads are simply a manifestation of that need to belong. Women who look terrible in short dresses still wear them because not to do so sets them apart from their group. Men who would rather have an easy life living in a small apartment rather than a house with a lawn and flowers and shrubbery to keep up, still buy the house for their family simply because that's where families of a certain class live.

So, the forces driving us toward conformity are always with us. But what would we do without them? I don't think I would care to live in a world of total anarchy. On the other hand, I wouldn't want to live in a world of total conformity either.

The real problem is just how far along the road to conformity do we want society to move. Do we want a culture in which everyone has to dress the same, eat the same foods, get up at the same time and go to bed at the same exact hour and minute, have the same type of car and the same size home? Do we want to force everyone to belong to the same church and thus conform to the same dogma? Do we want everyone to belong to the same political party? I don't think so.

But let's get back to my original point. There's little doubt that we still have a great deal of individualism in our country. The real question is whether that individualism, that independence of thought and action is slowly giving way to the strong forces of conformity. I can't answer that question in the amount of space I have here. It would take a tome or two, I believe. And then any conclusion would probably be little more than a personal opinion.

Yet I do bemoan the sometimes outlandish, even petty, forces toward conformity in the present political world, especially relative to President Trump and his family. The president has been chastised over and over for not being presidential. Being presidential seems to mean being like most past presidents, which in turn seems to mean only doing in public what your minders tell you to do and only saying what the teleprompter tells you to say. Of course, what your minders tell you to do must be what other presidents have done, how they have acted in public. Any tantrums or personal quirks or discussions of important things and personal beliefs and feelings must only appear behind closed doors. Otherwise you're not being presidential. If you tweet, and your tweets show your true personality, you are not being presidential. If you tweet, and your tweets show that your hide is a little thin and your reactions too quick and off the cuff, and not well thought out as if they had been written over a week or two, well, you aren't being presidential. If you go visit an area or state suffering from a nasty hurricane or earthquake or some other catastrophe, and you don't visit with the families of those killed in the catastrophe, well, you aren't being presidential (in this case you have no feelings for those suffering). Never mind that, if you do go into the danger area, while first responders and volunteers are still trying to find and rescue people still in danger, many of those first responders and volunteers will have to put their rescue work on hold in order to protect you for however long you remain there. Never mind that some of the victims waiting to be rescued might die because a potential savior had to suspend his rescue efforts to protect you. You just aren't being presidential.

And your wife? She has to dress like presidents' wives always have, in the high style of the style dictated for women of stature. She can't wear a cap and slacks, no matter how comfortable and appropriate they are. She's not being first lady-ish, I guess.

My question from this attitude in the press and elsewhere is whether or not it is representative of the American people as a whole. If it is, then I bemoan the loss of a spirit of independence in our political life. If it is not, then I lament, deeply lament, the loss of that spirit of independence of thought and attitude in the majority of our media; and I fear for a future in which our news media is more lock-step in thought and expression than the first twelve years of our educational system is in subject matter and student advancement.

Islamic Terrorism

Well, there was another terrorist attack in London Saturday night, with seven killed and 48 injured. Since 2005 there have been 65 innocent people killed in terrorist attacks, with hundreds wounded. And London is but one city where Islamic terrorists have attacked innocent people. The attacks are worldwide, from Europe to Asia, from Russia to the United States, from India to the Philippines.

And what was British Prime Minister Theresa May's reaction to the attacks? She said, "Enough is enough!" She said the government and the people needed to be more vigilant and set up more obstacles to stop the terrorists. And what did President Trump say? He blamed political correctness.

And those seem to be the typical responses to terrorism, mostly Islamic terrorism in this century, and previously.

My problem with all of this is that it's all about defense, nothing about offense. Terrorism is most definitely not a game, but it is definitely a form of war, and war has certain characteristics in common with games like basketball and football. One is that it too consists of both offense and defense. Can you imagine one of those games in which one of the two teams involved only played defense? What do you think would happen? There is no way, absolutely no way, that a team that only plays defense can win a game. Now I'm not saying that a team (or an army, or a nation) should ignore defense. No. Defense is crucial. No team, no army, no people can win a game, or a war, without a good defense; defense is crucial to protecting the basket, the end zone, the nation and its army from major intrusion. So I actually agree to some extent with PM May. We do need to become more aware of potential threats around us, hopefully without sacrificing our freedoms of movement and gathering in crowds. We maybe need more obstacles and police presence at large gatherings, for safety reasons.

But we can't go on forever waging a defensive war against Islamic terrorism. We can't afford the cost, in money and lives and social stability. A few people killed every year can mount up to a lot of deaths, and a lot of financial expenditure, and a lot of emotional harm to the people as a whole, both in those countries not at war but nevertheless targeted by Islamic terrorists and in those countries in the Mideast like Afghanistan where the war against terrorism goes on and on and on and kills thousands every year, slowly destroying the will of the nation and the will of the poor people who are, for all practical purposes, on the front line.

We have to do something. We have to expand our offense enough to win the war, to destroy the will of the terrorists to continue their fight. We have to play an offensive as well as defensive game, and that offense has to be one built to win, not just to keep the enemy from holding on to territory they have won by means of their offense.

Which leads to another question: If hundreds and even thousands of people are killed in the Mideast annually, not only those on the front lines of battle but also those murdered in terrorist attacks, and if thousands of others are wounded and maimed for life in this on-going war, and thousands and thousands of others displaced into foreign countries for life—if all of this is true, then wouldn't it be humane (more humane than the way we are presently waging the war) to destroy the terrorists (Al Qaeda, the Taliban, etc.) no matter where they are and no matter what the cost in lives of innocent civilians among whom the terrorists are hiding? The cost in civilian lives would probably be much less than it has been and will be if we continue with the defensive war we have been involved in for years—our longest war ever.

Learning To Think

You would think that institutions of higher education would be havens for the study and discussion of ideas and beliefs of all kinds and stripes, not only inside the classroom but also in campus life in general. That, I believe, would include all political ideas and organizations; all cultural, spiritual, and economic ideas and realities; all attitudes and systems of thought from the political far right to the political far left; beliefs from atheism to theism; anything and everything that helps the mind grow and learn to weed the chaff from the wheat. You can only learn to reason through the new and the complex in its relationships to the familiar, not through the familiar in isolation.

The ideal university would be one in which students ultimately come to a personal world view that is precisely that, a personal world view, not one that comes unchanged from a specific group of professors or students and has been superimposed in some way upon the campus in general. The ideal university should be one in which students continue functioning on their own after they graduate, as thoughtful and curious creatures, when confronted with the unknown or the generally rejected, making their own conclusions irrespective of the pressures from other minds. And above all, it should motivate students to become ever curious, to become inquisitive humans hunting for *new truths*.

But, of course, the ideal thinking human would be like Spock of Star Wars. He would be a rational creature, without emotions to interfere with reason. I've never met such a person and I doubt that I ever will.

Anyhow, institutions of higher learning should be places where students learn to think, to analyze, and to come to their own conclusions, not only in alien situations but in their own personal and public world, the world in which we all function daily and must either blindly follow others or make our own decisions as to which fork of the road we will take in any given confrontation of beliefs or possible actions, any time we must make a personal decision or simply follow our leaders. After all, how can our young truly learn to think both inside and outside the box if so many of the ideas they come into contact with are little more than variations of the same system of beliefs or attitudes? How can our educated citizens and leaders of tomorrow lead a nation of such cultural and spiritual variety as ours if they have only, in their education, been confronted with the limited world views of a certain group of people, their professors and the fellow students who are little more than echoes of those professors?

But they are, you say; they definitely are: Students in higher education are subjected to a variety of world views. There are foreign language programs, where students can immerse themselves in languages and cultures other than their own, cultures in which the citizens don't always approach problems the same way we do in the USA, where they don't always have the same attitudes toward politics, history, even reality, as we do, where even the problems we see around us are completely foreign to them. There are courses in philosophy, literature, art, the sciences, and history itself. In many of these courses the student is subjected to a variety of thoughts and attitudes, and feelings.

Most professors assign texts to supplement their class lectures and, in some cases, discussions. In a few cases they invite guest lecturers into their classes. Too often, though, the guests and the texts simply expand on the ideas the professors themselves develop in class. They don't set forth opposing ideas, opposing theories or hypotheses, or contradictions, for consideration and discussion. So, education can limit thought, especially if most professors consider themselves the ultimate authority on the material under consideration in class and, on their tests, base their grading system on how much of that material the students have assimilated and/or how well the student can develop a rational analysis of the class material, all based in the professors' own view of the subject matter. This does not always allow for much latitude in student thought and often leads to the regurgitation by students of the professors' own analyses. Why? Well, I believe that it is very difficult for any of us (including our professors of course) to read an analysis of a subject with which we are familiar, very familiar, and to which we have a very profound personal attachment and strong beliefs about the conclusions that can be drawn about it… it is very difficult to read such (as a student might express on an exam) and accept as logical those arguments and conclusions which vary widely from our own, or disagree with our own. As supposedly rational creatures, but ones with a great deal of emotional attachment to the familiar, we tend to find rational that which agrees with our thoughts and feelings and irrational, or of weaker reason, that which does not. In other words, the familiar seems rational. The unfamiliar does not, or seems less so. That, I believe, is true of the highly educated as well as of the uneducated. It is true of students as well as of their professors. Since their early childhood, education has given our students the same pattern, an all-too-human one: What I believe is rational. What those who disagree with me believe is not necessarily so.

So why is it that so many speakers from the right side of the political spectrum, and not from the left, are turned away from speaking engagements on college campuses, or boycotted, or harassed? There are probably a number of reasons, but of the three which I find most influential on student minds and, therefore, choices one I have discussed above—that students aren't really taught to think outside the box. They have not really learned to mingle literary and historical and psychological and scientific and…they have not really learned to apply analytical methods and knowledge used in one subject to problems in other subjects. *Madame Bovary* is a novel. It is analyzed as a novel and as literature. I don't think I've ever heard of it being used in a psychology class, or in a history class., or in any class other than a literature class. And in literature classes it is taught as literature, although in some classes it might be placed in its historical context. In my own years as a student I don't recall ever having a class that studied the relationship of two or more disciplines until during my graduate years at the university.

Two other characteristics of our educational system which tend to limit the development of students minds in a horizontal but not necessarily in a vertical way are the professors and students themselves. Three political systems vied for power in the world during the twentieth century. They were fascism, communism and democracy. The first found its ultimate expression in the Nazi parties of Germany and Italy. Especially through Germany the rise of fascism led to the extermination of multitudes of Jews and other dissenters throughout Europe before and during World War II. What widespread political influence fascism had, destroyed itself through the above and through the vast amount of death and destruction during the war, especially in Europe and the USA.

Communism lost much of its international appeal through the dictatorial and murderous rule of Stalin in Russia, and his successors, and through the brutal rise and rule of communism in China. That left democracy which, it seemed at the time, might turn out to be the ultimate human governing form.

But, in the example par excellence of democracy, the USA, many found a deep national problem, inequality. From that problem rose the Civil Rights movement and the struggle for women's rights to equality with men. An added problem was that the USA was not only democratic but also capitalistic. Of course, during the first half of the twentieth century we had moved further to the left politically, by establishing unions and helping them become more and more powerful. The struggle for racial and feminine equality moved us further in that direction, further toward socialism, since such a political system offered the ideal possibility for true equality, equality of races, of the sexes, of social classes, and of finances. Add in the sixties protests against the Vietnam War and other social injustices, and I think you have the mix that prepared today's professors at most of our major university and college campuses, not to mention many teachers in our schools.

The height of the Civil Rights Movement was 1955 through the 1960s. Many of our professors and teachers who grew up during that period, or who entered college then, would have begun teaching by the 1970s. Their ideas would have had great impact on their students, many of whom would have become educators themselves, thus adding to the domino effect of liberalism in our educational institutions. Add to that that the country itself was becoming more and more infused with socialistic ideas and programs during the last half of the twentieth century, and you have what might be called creeping socialism, or maybe even rushing socialism: not only civil and feminine rights and unions, but social security, welfare, graduated income tax, Medicare and Medicaid, educational quotas for specific types of students, food stamps, belief in the need to redistribute the wealth, etc.

I personally would find it odd if most of the professors and administrators of our major universities weren't far to the left politically, and those in most of our other institutions of higher learning. Add to that that the majority of the students in those institutions aren't there to learn. They are there to get decent jobs after they graduate. They aren't interested in becoming intellectuals. They aren't interested in becoming members of the intelligentsia of the country. They aren't really interested except tangentially in politics. They are in essence the silent masses, the silent majority, of our educational system. They aren't the ones who boycott and harass conservative speakers. It is the vocal minority of professors and students who do that, just as it is the vocal minority who do all the shouting and foot stomping on the real political scene.

And why don't the vocal students of conservative beliefs speak out? Why? For the same reason that the political right has been comparatively silent outside the voting precinct for over a half century, until the Tea Party movement changed the atmosphere a little. Conservatives too believe in some of the things that the left believes in. They disagree with others. But they don't like to speak out against people who, rather than reason with them, call them names and try to shame them—boycott and harass them.

I don't know if Donald Trump's election will in any way change the political atmosphere on our university campuses. He is most definitely a role model for speaking his mind, and his emotions. I hope so.

41

Media Schizophrenia

Here we go again, or is it simply a <u>continuous continuation</u> of a <u>continuing</u> "Fanatic Trump Hatred," what has often been called "Trump Derangement Syndrome." Whatever one wants to call it, it truly seems to be a fanaticism born of hatred. And, sadly, it defines our news media and its polarization as well as our political leaders—I came very close to saying schizophrenia rather than polarization. But I didn't, although I should have. After all, as Wikipedia says, schizophrenia "is a mental disorder" and that, I believe, is precisely what our news media has.

And maybe that is the real problem, although our news media should be well past its young adulthood, when schizophrenia seems to show its ugly head so often. But, then, maybe not. Maybe the nineteenth century defined our news media's infancy, while the twentieth century became the time of its childhood and teen years. And now, in the twenty-first, we are experiencing the movement into adulthood of all those people we used to call the "press corps," while at the same time we listened to what we considered their honest analyses of our nation's problems—used to. Of course all those supposed reporters exaggerated. Of course they sometimes took sides in political squabbles. Of course they gave us their opinions about world and national problems.

But I don't recall a lot of continuous, angry and spiteful bias against one specific public figure. Against totalitarianism? Yeah. Against Fascism or Communism? Yeah. Against some dictator in some country, like Hitler or Stalin? Yeah. Occasionally against an American politician? Yeah, but not hatefully or spitefully almost every time those reporters opened their mouth. And <u>occasionally</u> is the key word here. I don't ever recall continuous and nasty attacks on any of our presidents except Richard Nixon, and the press has to take some of the blame for destroying his mental balance. But I don't ever recall the news media continuously and spitefully denouncing whatever any specific politician said or did, and not denouncing it in a subtle or <u>humanely decent</u> way. Or even in a rational way a lot of the time.

Anyhow, according to Wikipedia, the symptoms of schizophrenia typically "begin in young adulthood." I smile, somewhat sadly, definitely sarcastically, when I ask myself if that is our news media. I wonder if most reporters and "talking heads" (Is there really a difference that I can't see?) would insist on having my words "fact checked" and, if they did, could I possibly convince them that this is really an opinion, not a fact. Why do I ask such a stupid question? Because I sometimes find myself in doubt as to whether many in the press corps/news media know the difference when it comes to President Trump. Why? Fanatic hatred? I think so, but please don't fact check me on it. Let me jabber in peace.

Two other characteristics of schizophrenia listed by Wikipedia are "abnormal behavior" and "a decreased ability to understand reality." Is not a continuous and unrelenting attack on a president of the United States, a man in an elective office…are not the unrelenting attacks on the president abnormal behavior by a group of people who are supposed to report the news to the people, breaking it down and analyzing it in a rational and unbiased way, and then letting the public make up its own mind about the reasonableness of the actions or comments being reported? Is not the continuous and opinionated use of exaggerating nouns, verbs, adjectives and adverbs when discussing the president, his comments, and his actions, and the continuous jumping to conclusions about the "Russian Affair" every time Mueller blows his nose—is not all of this abnormal behavior for a group of people who claim an unbiased approach to what is happening in our world? And isn't the inability (apparent or real?) to understand some of the reality behind what is happening, or to ignore it…doesn't this suggest a possible decrease in our news media's grasp of the reality of our world.

Another characteristic of schizophrenia, which Wikipedia mentions and which makes me grin when I think of it relative to the news media, is anxiety. And wow! Does the news media ever have anxiety attacks every time the president twitters an off-the-cuff comment, or every time one of the White House staff quits, or every time somebody like Comey or Pelosi calls the president names? It's like some person who hates his neighbor with an unrelenting passion, so much so that he/she screeches to his dog, "Get him, Fido," every time that poor neighbor so much as sneezes or says "Hi." And when the other neighbor asks, Why?" he/she shakes his/her fist and screams, "Didn't you see him try to kill my dog?" Or, "Are you stupid or do you just not care if he ruins the neighborhood? Nobody trusts us anymore because of him. The world hates us and he's to blame. He's a maniac. He's not human. He doesn't care about anybody but himself and the dumb working people. He won't let anybody move into the neighborhood unless they get permission first? He…he's deplorable and so is anyone who listens to him." And so it goes. And we poor "deplorables" put up with it. Why? Because we believe in freedom of thought and speech. That, to us, is the very essence of democracy.

And so, an important extension of that argument, or maybe the very essence of it, goes that no democracy can exist for long without a free press, no matter how imperfect it is. "Even if it is motivated by the frenzy of a fanatic hatred so deep and unrelenting that it warps almost every reaction?" I ask. That question, of course, usually sets off a tirade of anger directed at me and the president.

My usual next comment generally brings out even more anger, if it is possible to elicit more anger than that directed at President Trump by the "hate fanatics." That comment is that I really don't believe that a free press is a basic necessity of democracy. In fact, it just might be a danger to freedom of thought, expression, and action.

I believe in a <u>free</u> and <u>honest</u> press. A press that is free but dishonest is dangerous, very dangerous. It passes itself off as the arbiter of public opinion, yet its opinions are often not only exaggerated (got to sell papers or news programs by beating the other guy to the punch and then sounding as if what you have to say is the most important news to come down the pike—right on the cutting edge of great change or destruction), but also deeply biased.

Exaggeration is the essence of a dishonest press: thirty million people in the path of the storm; Trump bashes Theresa May (Actually he expressed his opinion, but, hell, those words don't sell papers or news programs or express the fanatic hatred for the president felt by many); the boy in Washington with his school mates smiling at a Native American playing a song and the press whaling on the boy for "smirking" and "threatening" the Native American, an exaggeration and lie that at least some of the news media later retracted and apologized for; and then the Russia probe—every time Mueller the "Buller" makes another arrest for "lying" or some such "dastardly crime" the news media begins slobbering all over itself and praying, in print or on television, for the president's impeachment, and all that after how much time and money wasted on the investigation? An aside: Much of this reminds me of the communist show trials under Joseph Stalin.

There's no doubt that the country is polarized—the people, the news media, Congress. And there's no doubt in my mind that the press should be an arbiter of the free discussion of our problems, not the leader of one side or the other in the fray, not the element that brings about more and more polarization. But it's not. Instead of leading us in free discussion of our problems, it takes sides and becomes the very essence of the problem. We can't _honestly_ talk about race in public; otherwise, the news media will shout racist. We can't _honestly_ and _openly_ talk about the sexual problems we have as a modern society in which women are trying to establish an equality of freedom with men; if we do the press will shout sexist, unless we happen to be on their side. President Trump can't _honestly_ discuss illegal immigration with Congress and possible ways to solve the problem; if he does, or our political leaders do, if they are not on the right side of the aisle, the news media will accuse them of racism and inhumanity and anything else they can come up with.

So, I say no to a free press. And I say no to a dishonest or biased press. I say yes to a free and honest press, one that tries to present both sides of all important problems. A dishonest press is a danger to free speech, to the very basis of democracy. An honest press is a boon, an absolute necessity. And I sure as ever shake in my boots every time the news media's schizophrenia shows its ugly symptoms, which is often anymore.

42

My Country

My country! My country! Where did you go, my country? Were you taken away by the fanatic "anti-Trumpers" or is it that you are still here and have been all the time, only in hiding, embarrassed by our childish politicians and tantrum-prone citizens? Is it that you, the real US of A, is not what I thought it was but rather what I thought it was only existed in my imagination? Were you but a fiction of a dream world I created to insulate myself from the real you?

I never thought that you were perfect, not even in my wildest dreams. But I did believe that you were one of the best. You represented a model of democracy, a country where freedom of expression and thought are a reality, not a camouflage for corruption and hatred and disrespect and, yes, tyranny. You represented a country where a person could disagree with his government representatives or his neighbor without fear of retribution, without fear that the secret police might show up one night to whisk him into oblivion or that his neighbor might set his house on fire, in anger. You were a country where a man or woman, <u>a citizen</u>, could disagree with the neighbor, on matters political or religious or sexual, without fear that that neighbor would turn away forever or seek retribution.

Or at least that's what I thought you represented. Until Donald Trump became president. Oh, I'm not naïve enough to think that there haven't been personal or public vendettas brought about by political or sexual or religious differences, by disagreements about such. We had our civil war. We have had our problems with racial differences, and sexual and religious differences. We still do. I remember the first Catholic family, which I know of, that moved into my hometown. I remember that there was a black man who lived east of town, on a small farm. I also remember that he was never in town after dark. And I recall the attitude of many neighbors about homosexuality, not a positive attitude by any means. People didn't come out of the closet in those days, not out into the public eye.

Then there was the Civil Rights Movement, which many black people don't think has gone far enough, even to this day, and which many white people think has gone too far. There are the petty wars we have gotten into since WWII: Korea, Vietnam, and now our seemingly endless fighting in the Mideast. Lots of disagreement there. I for one think we should have avoided all of them. But I'm not sure what decision I would have made if I were leading the country and thus had a lot more info than I do as a simple citizen.

And, speaking of freedom of thought and expression, why is it that it's mostly (with a very few exceptions) Democrats who are out there in the streets trying to bully our political leaders (and, yes, our people) into championing illegal immigration? Why? Why is it that they ignore our own poor and downtrodden in order to champion the poor from south of our borders, down Mexico and Guatemala and Honduras way? We do have children in places like Louisiana and our big cities that are as impoverished as the poor in other countries. At least that's what I read. Yet I hear almost nothing about our poor and downtrodden from our political "street people." I hear lots of ranting about our supposed unjust and harmful immigration policies and practices, nothing about helping poor American citizens. Why, I wonder. Is it because the immigration situation is the latest democratic fad, kind of like miniskirts were at one time?

Or is it something more profoundly ingrained in the very essence of democratic government? I firmly believe that government in the USA is pendular in nature. We move to the left until enough people become fed up with what our leaders in Washington D. C. are doing. Then we swing back to the right. The election of President Trump represented a definite swing back to the right. Was it the final motions of the swing, or was it more toward the beginning? I guess the midterm elections this year will let us know.

But what really bothers me about this what-I-think-of-as-natural political swing in our democratic lifespan…what bothers me is that a big segment of our liberal citizens are not accepting the pendular motion peacefully, as citizens of a democratic nation should, even when they disagree with where that motion is headed. They should be intelligent enough to know that the pendulum will stop and begin its return swing, if only they will wait patiently and continue advocating for their beliefs peacefully. But they are now taking to the streets much like the Communist International did in the 1920s and 30s, when they too advocated the destruction of state barriers (borders)—in other words, the "abolition of the state." They, our citizens out there on the streets ranting about unfair and unjust immigration laws and practices—they must know that what they are really advocating with their insistence on open borders is the complete "abolition" of the USA as a nation.

Or are they so naïve that they think we can serve as a safety valve for Mexico and Central America and many other parts of the world indefinitely…without becoming more like Honduras, or Guatemala, or Mexico, or…than like what we have been up to the present. If they think so, they need to read about our own frontier. Our frontier served as a safety valve for our country as the latter grew into what it is today. Not bad, huh? Not bad for the USA. But what about for the wilderness land itself? What about for all the Indian tribes that lived out there in the wilderness? Was our growth good for them? And what about Spain and France relative to our Southeast? And what about Great Britain and Canada relative to our North and Northwest? And what about Mexico relative to Texas and the rest of our Southwest? And what about the native Hawaiian islanders?

Are we, as a safety valve for the countries south of our borders and many other countries in the world…are we to suffer the same fate as did the Native American tribes beyond our frontier? Are we to suffer…? Or are we going to pick and choose who joins our nation as an immigrant, only allowing in an amount we think sufficient and those who will add something of value to our "melting pot"…only letting them become our fellow citizens? In other words, are we going to close our border to illegal immigrants and keep them open for legal immigrants? Or are we going to open them to a rising flood of illegal immigrants that might someday drown us?

North Korea

For some time now I have thought that the Mideast was our greatest threat from abroad. I figured that we might get embroiled in a shooting war with the Russians over Syria and its ruler, Bashar al-Assad. Or Iran might decide to go ahead with its program to develop nuclear weapons and, once that was accomplished, attack Israel. Or all the fighting against ISIS might cause greater friction between the Kurds and Turkey, fighting might develop, and we might become involved somehow in the fighting. Of course any of this could still happen. A miscalculation might put us in a shooting war with Russia. Turkey could go after the Kurds and we might feel obligated to defend them. And Iran could decide to go ahead with its original plans to develop weapons of mass destruction and so ignore any sanctions that we put on them, kind of like North Korea has been doing.

No doubt any of the above could happen. And if not, the war we are presently involved in against ISIS could take a turn for the worse. After all, the war began against Saddam Hussein, continued against the Taliban and other terrorist groups, and segued into the present conflict against ISIS. It wouldn't surprise me at all if, as the fight against ISIS winds down, another rebel group decided to take us on.

But North Korea now—it has become the major bogey man in my closet of potential flashpoints. The essential problem is, I believe, that North Korea will use, and has used, any method necessary to develop nuclear weapons. In that sense it hasn't changed its character much since the Korean War or, maybe for that matter, since the end of WWII, when

Korea was divided between the USA and Russia, much as was Germany. The peace talks during the Korean War ran from October 25, 1951 to July 27, 1953 (almost two years), while the fighting was still going on, and only stopped when Russia and China turned to their own interior problems and lost interest in the talks. Nothing was finalized by the talks. There is still an armed demilitarized zone between the two Koreas. They still express wishes for re-unification, but nothing along those lines has ever been done. And both countries are still armed to the teeth, South Korea by the United States more than by its own hand.

I don't think North Korea has changed its character since the Korean War. It is still ruled by Kim II Sung's family. It is an absolute dictatorship. And the successive rulers almost seem to be clones of Kim II Sung himself.

As I see it, those successive rulers have probably been developing nuclear weapons for decades, even while they signed non-nuclear weapons pacts with the IAEA and major countries like China, Japan, Russia, and the United States. We have held non-nuclear proliferation talks with North Korea and the above nations off and on since 1985. North Korea has signed a number of pledges to not develop nuclear weapons and then later reneged on those pledges. We have unilaterally withdrawn all tactical nuclear weapons from the Korean peninsula, under President George Bush, in 1991. In that same year the president of South Korea signed a pledge not to use nuclear weapons and not to build uranium processing or reprocessing facilities in his country. Yet by 1994 North Korea had developed an atomic weapon or two. And now we know that it has developed a hydrogen bomb, not to mention intercontinental ballistic missiles. All of this development has had to occur over several decades and during the same time that North Korea was talking and signing non-nuclear weapons pledges. (See the Arms Control Association's "Chronology of U.S.-North Korean Nuclear and Missile Diplomacy" for a much more extensive outline of the above.)

So why in the world would so many people think we need to set up talks with North Korea in order to talk it into halting its nuclear and missile programs? I think that's wishful thinking, and very naïve wishful thinking at that. The Sung dynasty has one overriding desire, and that is to join the world's nuclear weapons clique, which, in turn, will give them a path to re-uniting the Korean peninsula under their own terms, not those of South Korea, or the United States, or China or Russia. It will make Kim Jong-un as powerful as his image of himself. It will give him a chance to blackmail us and the world, something he seems very good at.

So no, I don't think talks between us and North Korea would be worth the time involved. As we talked they would simply go ahead with their development of ever more powerful nuclear weapons and missiles. We have two possibilities: Let them continue developing their weapons or stop that development with war. Which would be the best route?

Obamacare

Obamacare, or the Affordable Care Act, was doubtlessly well-intended. Among other things, it was meant to cover the medical costs of those American citizens who could not afford to purchase health insurance on the open market without considerable government help in supplementing the costs of that insurance, and it was meant to give coverage to some sections of our society who could not get insurance because of certain pre-existing health conditions.

The problem is that the Affordable Care Act has had some costly un-intended consequences. In one instance, at least, it is costly for a certain segment of the population. I cannot claim a lot of research data to back up such a claim, only anecdotal evidence from friends and acquaintances, and from occasional comments in e-mails or internet articles and in the media, and of course from my own personal experience.

In 2004 our oldest grandson, 18 years of age, had to move in with me and my wife. He had major problems of asthma and allergies and a few years later began to have gran mal seizures. At first, the policy cost us $94. By 2006 the monthly premiums had only risen to $116, by 2009 to $150, and by 2011 to $202. Not too bad, we thought nervously. We still didn't consider that amount atrocious, not with the seizures and all, but it was over a one hundred percent increase in seven years, way above the inflationary rate. Then October of 2013 hit and Obamacare kicked in. The premiums for our grandson's policy jumped to $254 that month. And now, slightly over three years later, they stand at $435.

When the premiums jumped so much in 2013 I began to consider Obamacare. I remembered that our premiums had jumped quite a bit in 2011, the year after the Act became law, and quite a bit after Obama became president, in the two years leading up to the enactment of Obamacare. Then when Obamacare became actuality our premiums began to shoot up like jets off an aircraft carrier catapult. Since 2004, when we first purchased the policy, our premiums have risen almost 250%, the vast majority of that from 2009 onward. How much of that do I blame on the insurance company and how much on Obamacare? (I now hear that premiums under Obamacare are going to rise quite a bit starting next year. Will that mean another great increase in the premiums for non-Obamacare policies?)

Whatever! Our grandson is now 31. We have had the policy on him since he was 18. My questions at this point follow: Are exorbitant increases in insurance premiums the norm for young people say 18 to 40 or 50, people who have to purchase their own insurance policies because their employers won't, or can't, people who are now, under Obamacare, required to have insurance? Have their insurance policies risen exponentially like our grandson's? And are those raises mainly because the insurance companies are raising their rates to recoup costs for all the pre-existing and other "problem" conditions they are now required to cover? In essence, is it that the insurance companies are recouping their excessive costs under the Act by exorbitantly raising the rates for the policy holders not covered under the Act? I can definitely understand why so many private companies are presently, whenever possible, avoiding purchasing policies for their employees, although I find it difficult to sympathize with them?

So far we have two possible culprits: Obamacare and the insurance companies. Those members of Congress who voted for the Act (with or without reading it) didn't take into consideration that insurance companies are private companies and so could be expected to find any way to recoup whatever losses they accrued, losses like having to write policies for expensive consumers such as all of those with pre-existing conditions—recoup their losses by passing them on to the consumer. After all, as I said, like all private companies, insurance companies are profit based, so why wouldn't they make as much profit as they can?

So, as I see it, there are two culprits to the rising costs of insurance. And what about a third one, medical care (like hospitals, doctors, health organizations, etc.)? While bemoaning the rising costs of our insurance premiums, I hadn't thought much about the cost of my own and my wife's medical bills. Our policy is Medicare based (HMO) and so I don't receive bills much. Like right now, I have been sent to physical therapy by my doctor, because of a pulled, possibly torn, rotator cuff. I go twice a week. I made a negligible co-payment on my first visit but have paid nothing since (after three weeks). And I don't receive any bills at all. So I haven't the slightest idea how much this costs my insurance company, which is in essence the federal government, and thus the taxpayer. It could be pretty exorbitant.

What I do know is that a little over a month ago our middle grandson was in a car accident and was taken to the hospital even though there was nothing wrong with him. He spent fourteen hours there. I think he was probably tested for everything under the sun, and under the moon also. After looking at the bill, I have to ask myself, a little sarcastically, if he was tested for HIV and Zika as well as the flu. His bill was slightly over $47,000.00. Yes, that's forty-seven thousand. For fourteen hours. And there was nothing really wrong with him! My eye teeth are lying somewhere on the floor near where I first read the bill.

And so there are three culprits to the skyrocketing costs of health care: Obamacare, insurance companies, and hospitals. I expect there is a fourth, or maybe it can be included as part of the hospital-cost problem—doctors.

Expert and expedient health care for those in need is, of course, one of the main ingredients of a strong, happy and healthy society. I believe avidly in that sentence of our Declaration of Independence that refers to the same: All people "are endowed by their Creator with certain unalienable Rights, that among these are Life, Liberty and the pursuit of Happiness." It would be difficult, I think, to pursue happiness if you were terribly sick and/or hurt but with no appropriate help available, never, none. Moreover, if we are endowed with life by our Creator, is it not incumbent upon our government to help us maintain that life as best we can, to help protect and keep it as healthy and vital as possible?

I think so. "Help" is of course the key word here. The government is there to aid us, not to take over all responsibility for our welfare. It provides a legal system and an army. We do our part by obeying the laws of the land; at least most of us do. We also do our part by paying taxes to cover the costs of our legal system. What do we do relative to national support for health care? And our roads, and…, but that's another topic. I think government does a decent job protecting us—decent most of the time. But I think it does a lousy job helping keep us healthy and fit. People go bankrupt because of catastrophic health problems which lead to catastrophic expenses. Health insurance is so excessively high that many small companies cannot afford it for their employees, and large companies reject it, so their employees go without…before Obamacare, and maybe even now in spite of the fines. Hospital costs are…$47,000 for fourteen hours? And there's nothing wrong with the patient? We have an Affordable Care Act that penalizes the young and healthy, yet at the same time our elderly are often covered from stem to stern? What we need in our health care system is a little common sense and equality. Equality—you know, that stuff that is supposed to exist in every nook and cranny of our great nation, that stuff that's supposed to be the adhesive that holds us together.

What I say to the government is, do something to control medical costs and insurance premiums, so that employers can once again maintain health and accident insurance on their employees. Find a way to take care of those people with permanent or terminal illnesses that lead to catastrophic expenses. And please, read the Affordable Care Act and then make lots of common-sense changes. That's what we need in our government right now, and especially in our healthcare system—common sense and lots of good old American pragmatism.

45

PE In Education

In my book, our American educational system no longer serves the best interests of either its students or the country which supports it. That is true both academically and extra-curricularly. Let me qualify this last sentence a bit. What our schools attempt, I believe, they in general do well. It's what they no longer do and what they ignore that are the problems. In this essay I'm going to ignore the academic world of our educational system and talk about one specific extra-curricular problem, physical education (PE, for short). Not band, or choir, or theater—all of which seem to do well in our school system as it is presently constituted.

I keep reading about the obesity problem in our country and I ask myself why we have such a problem and how we can reduce if not solve it. The cause seems, to me, to be pretty clear. There are all the mechanical and technological devices which keep people sitting in one place for long periods of time, thus making them more susceptible to weight problems. (I'm not going to mention the ease for most people of getting food too high in caloric content, or of buying all these devices. Nor am I going to discuss our hunger problem and the types of food the government furnishes the hungry. Nor am I going to lay blame where a lot of it should fall—the wealth that has made so many of our lives too easy and toil free.) There is the automobile, which has made it easier to get from one place to another without expending much energy; driving beats walking or riding horseback or biking or taking a bus or train, after walking to the station. The auto changed life for the multitudes in our country. More and more it has replaced shank's mare, until today I see people getting in their car to drive a block or two to the grocery store, or to visit a neighbor or relative, or to take a child to school, or…and not just some people, I expect, but most people who own a car or truck and have the money or mechanical knowledge to keep it running, which seems to be the vast majority of people in our country.

Just drive around your neighborhood some Saturday morning and count the number of cars parked around each house. Not many will only have one car. Or stand on a street corner and count the number of cars that actually have more than one person in them. You know, passengers.

Those who don't have cars have to take a bus or some other form of public transportation, of course, which does cost a little more energy than walking outside or into the garage and getting in the family car, or one of the family cars.

Television is maybe the first entertainment device that has kept more and more people sitting in place for longer and longer periods of time. As we all know, there were movies before tv became very popular. But movies were not a daily (or nightly) attraction, simply because movies weren't available in most of our villages and small towns (or living rooms), so small-town people had to drive or take a train to a large nearby town to see a movie, or wait until Saturday night when one showing of a movie was available on the street downtown or in the high school gym or maybe in some business building reserved for the event. In most towns, I think, it was a small minority of the people who traipsed on a weekly basis to a nearby city to see a movie, or attended the local showing of one. Many of the rest showed up at the local gym or diamond to watch a ball game, another pastime that keeps people sitting in place for a couple of hours or more. As for city people, I expect that they were a lot like small-town people. Most only attended movies on weekends, if at all. But not so television, and most houses and apartments have at least one television.

And then there came the computer and the cell phone and all the variations on them and all the apps and games that have become a national addiction.

Oh, I still see people out walking or biking, kids too, but not very damn many of them, and I don't see bunches of kids playing ball of some kind in the parks and school ball diamonds, or gyms. And I still see people who look like they are in good shape physically, but definitely not as many as in the past, I don't think. So many of them, kids and adults, except for the athletes, look like they might only do three or four things: eat, sleep, and watch tv or play games on their computer or one of its variants.

And so just what can we do about the obesity that besets the country? We surely can't pass laws that our citizens have to exercise daily for an hour or two. That would be a little difficult to enforce and would probably increase the prison population exponentially. We can't close down all the bars and movie houses and take away all the cars and television sets and computers and…. Nor, I doubt, can we really enforce laws that regulate what and how much people eat and drink, in spite of the few mayors who seem to think we can. After all, we are not Syria or ISIS. So what can we do?

Me, I think the answer is pretty clear. Exercise, like so many leisure-time activities, can become a habit; and many of our habits are formed in our early years and, with a little help, can carry on into our adult years.

There was a time when there was such a thing as required PE in our school system, in many high schools and colleges. There were recesses in elementary school, during which the children were required to get outside and play—move around, get the old body maybe even sweating a little. PE was also required in many colleges and universities, usually for a couple of years only. And I don't really think there was much of a commitment in high school or college to making sure that every single student did some kind of physical exercise at least three times a week, for at least an hour or so each of those days.

And the schools got bigger and bigger, as did the universities and colleges. And somewhere along the way PE disappeared from the curricula. The only students who continued getting sufficient exercise were those students in intercollegiate athletics, and those who were wealthy and good enough to play on intramural or club teams. So here you have these schools with only the top athletes getting any consistent weekly exercise (not to mention that they are the only ones using the expensive gyms), and that sometimes for only the limited duration of a seasonal sport, like wrestling or football or volleyball or baseball or track or soccer or tennis (or golf?).

As much money as we put into our schools and colleges, as much time as the students spend in those institutions, I think the faculty and staff owe us and our children. They should help their students develop physically just as they help them develop academically. Recesses and noontime breaks already exist in most elementary schools, I believe. But maybe they should be a little more structured so that <u>all students</u> not only get outside for a certain amount of time but also do something physical, even if it's just moving around continuously, for the time they are out there. By the time students are in junior or high school, there should be organized activities to help the kids develop their physical stamina and agility, even if those activities consist only of walking for an hour three times a week, anything to lower obesity and help the kids feel better about themselves and their bodies. Sweating some of their excess energy out of their bodies might just help them concentrate better in their classes too, all the way from the first grade through the university or college. And, if done several times a week, it might just improve the nation's obesity rating. I would exempt the intercollegiate athletes, of course—for example, those who play a varsity sport or compete in swimming or track, or march in the band. But I would exempt them only during the season in which they were actually training and competing, unless they trained year around. I would also make exceptions for those who competed in intra-mural or club sports, or those who could prove that they exercise sufficiently on their own.

And what would the students be expected to do during their exercise period of a minimum of three hours per week? Anything from walking or swimming or running to playing pickup ball. And under the supervision of a teacher. The <u>participatory</u> supervision of a teacher. That just might help the obesity problem among our nation's teachers as well as among their students.

46

Perks

Is it just the good old boy/girl system? Or is it something even more nefarious, like a complete lack of moral integrity? Or is it a combination of both? Like the good old boy/girl system has become saturated with amorality. Or, even more frightening, has our whole culture lost any sense of how to follow the path of righteousness?

Me, I don't claim to be the most moral or ethical person in the world, neither now nor when I was young man, neither relative to my sexual relationships with women nor relative to my work ethic. Like many males, and females, I suspect, I've had my moments of weakness. I've pushed harder than I should have in trying to get some young woman into the bedroom, or just to get some kind of sexual release, and pleasure, of course, from her. I've misread a woman's negative reactions for positive ones. I've made passes, overly aggressive ones, where they weren't wanted or shouldn't have been made. What normal male with normal hormones hasn't? What normal male with normal hormones hasn't pushed too aggressively at times and hasn't misread, or ignored, a woman's reactions to his insistence.

As for my work ethic, I have to admit that there have been plenty of times when I goofed off more than I should have, or called in sick when I really just had a hangover, or lied to my boss about a certain file that I was supposed to have completed, or screwed the pooch on some job I had been assigned and then found some way to hide the screw-up from my boss.

At times I wound up being penalized for my incompetence or chicanery. But I don't recall ever being rewarded for my screw-ups or for not accepting my responsibilities and following through with them. But then, I was never at the top of the work ladder, where rewards often seem to come no matter how incompetent a person is, no matter how much a person avoids the duties and responsibilities that go with the job.

How often do we read that some CEO or even a slightly lower echelon person has screwed up, lost his/her job, and yet has received a huge severance pay?

47

Polarization

Polarization? Violence? Liberals refusing to read something, or even accept it as something having any intellectual and unbiased potential, simply because it is written by a conservative. Conservatives doing the same in reverse. Our Democratic Congressmen immediately trying to find anything and everything wrong with a proposal that comes from our President or the Republicans in Congress, much as the Republicans did with the previous president and while the Democrats had a congressional majority. Many Republicans doing the same thing because they don't expect the President to toe the conservative line, or the Tea Party line, or the Libertarian line, or whatever line they have drawn in the sand around them.

I am so tired of ideologues, so tired of our government leaders who seem completely unwilling to bend a fraction of an inch to consider the ideas of their opponents long enough to make an intelligent counter proposal so that the haggling can begin. I'm so tired of the minority party in Congress dragging its feet like a kid being dragged off to the woodshed. We live in a democracy. Or at least we used to. Or so I have always thought. But what the heck? Maybe I've been wrong. Maybe I'm wrong about the political actuality of my country. I always thought I lived in a democracy. I always thought unbending ideology was a characteristic of dictatorships, while pragmatism and compromise were characteristics of democracy. Do I actually live in a squabbling oligarchy?

I do think I live in a country that defines itself as a democracy, but one that has become ideologically polarized, just like so many of the people themselves seem to be. One of my problems, I have to admit, is that I don't know whether the people became polarized first and that began to reflect itself in Congress, or if Congress became polarized and the people have slowly, unconsciously begun to reflect that polarization in their own voting and other habits. I don't suppose, of course, that it makes a great deal of difference. What makes a difference is whether or not we will be able to overcome our polarization in the near future and again begin governing our country in the democratic fashion—with compromise and pragmatism, rather than with continuous, unbending insistence on our own principles no matter what. If we cannot do that, if we cannot make that change, then I weep for the future of the democracy in which I have always thought I lived.

Look at all the problems facing us. There is Obamacare. The ACA has some quite good points, such as not allowing insurance companies to reject potential clients simply because they have some pre-existing health problem and, on the other hand, helping poor people afford insurance by paying for some of their policy costs. On the other hand, it has some very negative effects on the cost of insurance, especially for those who have to purchase their own policy because they are not old enough for Medicare but have too much money to qualify for Obamacare. For many of these people premium costs have gone through the roof, often in such as copay prices as well as in premiums. For that reason it is only logical that part of Congress' approach to improving Obamacare would be to control premium costs as well as hospital costs, much as it does for Medicare. So, my solution would be for Congress, all of Congress (Republicans and Democrats alike), to start going through Obamacare step by step, trying to improve or fix what needs fixing, rather than trying to throw out the whole thing and start over. But will that happen with our present Swamp Figures? I doubt it.

And Obamacare is not the only thing that needs a careful overhaul. For most of my life I did my own tax returns annually. Years ago, when I first began filing with the IRS, the form took me maybe a half hour or so, at the most. But the years passed and by the time I was middle aged I was sometimes spending as many as two days getting the <u>forms</u> ready to mail. Of course, my returns were a little more complicated by then. I had more assets. I had a family, a wife and children. My wife also worked. My costs were more complex. Innocently, I figured this would change and again become simpler as the children left home and my wife and I moved into old age, with little variation in our annual income. But that did not seem to be the case. The laws kept changing, becoming more complex. I eventually began having a professional do the work.

That cost me, of course. It was a little added tax, not to the government but to someone who might as well have been working for the government. The complexity of the tax laws definitely supported his job, keeping it from disappearing.

I could go on rambling like this. We have so many problems that our Congress should be helping us with, not only in passing and changing laws but in giving us guidance by their personal actions if not their professional ones. There is the terrible and, as far as I am concerned, unwarranted distrust of the police and our judicial system, which seems to me to be often increased by the statements and actions of our leaders. There is the problem of our open borders and the effect on jobs, the economy, and public morale. There is the continual <u>hypocritical</u> preoccupation with such as the Russian interference in our last presidential election, and the amount of time and money our federal government is spending on their investigations of such. To me, it smacks of the childish, hypocritical investigation of Bill Clinton by the Starr Commission.

It smacks of vengeance. Each political party often acts like a pack of bullies jumping on and trying to destroy anyone in the opposite party who might have made a few personal mistakes. But most fearful of all, it smacks of unrelenting demagoguery mixed with unbending ideology.

Police Shoot Unarmed People

The news media goes bananas any more when an unarmed black man is shot by the police. So does the black community. And, of course, both groups blame the police and call for "justice," meaning revenge against the police officers involved. Few in the news media mention the lack of common sense, and the extreme danger, in a black man, or any man, or woman, jumping over fences at night in a dark neighborhood and then hurrying up to police officers with something in their hands—and that in an era in which the news often has an article about an ambush and murder of policer officers. Few in the news media mention the lack of common sense in a person who darts up to a police car in a dark alley, with something in her hand, up to a car containing two officers who have been called to the neighborhood because of a reported possible rape and who are, doubtlessly, on edge because of all the unprovoked shootings of police officers over the past several years. How do those officers know that they haven't been lured into an ambush? It's easy for all the second guessers to say that they should just have rolled down their window and said, "May we help you, Ma'am?" But it was a dark alley, so they probably didn't have the slightest inkling that it was a woman who had suddenly appeared at their window and that what she had in her hand was not a gun. They were called there because of a reported <u>violent</u> situation. They weren't on television where an officer always sees the bad guy first, or soon enough to be the hero. And where a tv officer and a bad guy

"

are faced off with pistols pointed at each other and where instead of pulling the trigger immediately, as all common sense in reality says he should, the officer stands there, pistol pointed at the pistol pointing at him and screams for the bad guy to drop his weapon and get on the ground. Any intelligent person watching that program knows damn well how silly and childish it is. All that bad guy has to do is crook his finger and the officer is dead. But on television, of course, he doesn't pull the trigger. He either obeys or the officer pulls the trigger first. Great drama! Too bad life isn't like that, with superhuman officers unafraid of being killed in scary situations and bad guys afraid of or simply unwilling to pull the trigger first. With an open face-off before the killing. With the dead person a proven bad guy. With no greys, or all-too-human errors, in between black and white. Too bad so much of our news media slavers at the possibility of excoriating the police in any situation in which they kill in any way other than clear-cut, slick-fiction self-defense.

The reality is that police officers are human and they are being killed for little or no reason, and so they have an all-too-human "right" to be on edge in any situation that suggests danger—dark areas at night, sudden movements of suspects, people appearing out of nowhere, especially if they have something in their hand and are pointing it in the direction of the officer(s). According to Wikipedia 69 police officers were killed in the line of duty in 2011, and that does not include dying in automobile accidents while on duty, or dying of heart attacks, etc., stats that would double or more the number of police officers who died on duty that year. The 69 above were shot. In 2012 49 were shot and killed; in 2013 27 were; in 2014 51 were; in 2015 42 were; in 2016 64 were; and in 2018, as of 3-29-2018, 20 were, with only one-fourth of the year over, which suggests that this could be a dangerous year for police officers, with maybe 80 killed by the end of the year if the surge continues.

The first question related to the killings of cops that comes to my mind is who the perpetrators are. *Newsweek* (I no longer recall the date) pointed to a study of 74 police officers shot and killed in 2013 and 2014, a study by a Prof. Michael Stone of Columbia College of Physicians and Surgeons. Stone says that the killers were all males. One-half were involved in crimes before they killed a police officer. One-half simply killed a cop because of hatred or mental illness. "In 2013, 46 percent of the cop killers were white, 37 percent were black and 18 percent were Hispanic." In his article "New Study: Who Kills Cops?" (April 18, 2015, in *The Truth about Guns*), Robert Farrago also cites Dr. Stone. Stone supposedly studied 66 cases of officers deliberately killed. According to him, 75% of the killers were 18 to 37 years of age. Also, although "comprising less than 13% of the population, blacks constituted 37% of cop killers in 2013 and 26% in 2014." That is almost three times their population percentage in 2013 and two times in 2014. It seems only logical to conclude that blacks are much more likely to kill cops than other races are. So, if I were a police officer, black or white, I think I would be more afraid of blacks than of other races.

According to "Narrative Collapse" (March 16, 2017), 62 cops were shot and killed in 2016. The known suspects were 28 blacks, 27 whites, 5 Latinos, and one Alaskan native. Also in that year four corrections officers were killed (two white females, one white male, and one black male). The latter were all killed by black males. Again, with blacks making up only 13% of the population, the conclusion of this article is that "Blacks are underrepresented among crime suspects killed by police, but greatly over-represented among people who shot and killed police."

And then, in "Police Officer Deaths on Duty Have Jumped Nearly 20 Percent in 2017," (July 5, 2017, *Fox News*) Lauren Goldstein states that Randy Sutton (national spokesman for Blue Lives Matter) said that "last year approximately 50,000 law enforcement officers were assaulted, that ran the gamut from pushing them to shooting them and causing disabling injuries," or death. I ask, is it any wonder that police sometimes shoot unarmed people who point things at them, who suddenly move toward them with something in their hand, who refuse to obey commands, who become aggressive at close quarters. After all, a police officer not only has the duty to protect the public and to enforce the law, but he also has a duty to himself, his family, his friends and relatives, and his fellow officers to protect himself and his partners. And, most importantly, he/she is human like the rest of us. Those who complain about the police shooting civilians, even unarmed civilians, should ask themselves what they might have done in a similar situation—and they should answer themselves honestly, and keep television and movie fiction and personal bias out of their answer.

49

Police Violence

You know, I'm getting awfully tired of the blame game. Every time I turn around, it seems, I'm running into an article where one group blames another for problems that have become so deeply embedded in our daily lives that it will take a lot of "togetherness" to solve them, if we even can solve them without a civil war. Yet no one looks for solutions except in changing the other groups' way of doing things, rather than trying to figure out how the "blame thrower" can change itself to meet the other group half way. I get awfully tired of this mantra that "me and mine" are perfect and you and yours are defective and need to become more like us, or we will have to destroy you.

A recent article in the New York Times ("How Phoenix Explains a Rise in Police Violence: It's the Civilians' Fault" by Richard A. Oppel), of course, points to the problem, but still stays on the anti-police side of it. According to him, the police say that the community, or that part of it which is the problem, is too aggressive, yet the anti-police activists say that it is the police themselves who are too aggressive in their reactions to civilian aggression.

I personally think that there is some truth in blaming both sides. But I think that the root cause lies in our culture, i. e., in the community, in the totality of the community not in any one specific group or any part of it. And this blame game raises its ugly head all the way to the top of our political heap. I mean, what happened when President Trump was elected? Left wing nutcases, Antifa leading the way, began demonstrating, the demonstrators often showing their anger and indignation through violence, by obstructing traffic, breaking windows, burning and looting businesses, and attacking the police.

Then there was the left-winger who shot up a Congressional ball game and put a Republican congressman in the hospital. And let's not forget those Democratic "congresspeople" (like Maxine Waters) who raised the violence ante by telling her followers to get in the face of all Trump's workers and followers, when they were in public places, and tell them that they weren't wanted in those places. Can you imagine how some liberal fanatics might have taken those words? Not as a peace offering—that's for certain. We saw some of the reaction on television, when Republicans and their families were accosted in restaurants and bullied and cursed into leaving. Those verbal and threatening attacks must have been emotionally devastating for any children caught in the vituperation.

The Battle of Hate of course escalated with the attack on the Jewish synagogue by a right-wing nut, the ultimate in sad commentary on American politics at the present time. And it continues with the seemingly never-ending Mueller investigation, a liberal persecution of the president of the United States at excessive and meaningless costs (I've heard both 25 and 30 million)—excessive and meaningless costs for the American taxpayer, an investigation that is supposed to be about collusion of the Trump campaign of 2016 with Russian interference in American politics but has become nothing but a continuous search for anything Mueller and his people can find (or create?) that will hurt and even destroy anybody associated with President Trump and ultimately destroy the president himself, and I expect their hope is to destroy all the Trump family as well. The Battle of Hate continues with the fanaticism of anti-Trump hatred embedded in the Democratic Party, manifested in their continuous threats to impeach the president as soon as the new House is seated after the first of the 2019. It is, sadly, fanaticism at its worst and most devastating, something that is supposed to be foreign to our political system, but which has become more and more prevalent over the past decade or two. The progression scares me, as does the continuous calls from the besieged Republicans for an investigation of the Clintons and their foundation—Bill and Hillary, sexual abuse and pay for play games.

But what scares me just as much, maybe even more, is the amount of dishonesty and politicization that has been uncovered and "suggested to be prevalent" in the many branches of our government, from the Congress itself to the FBI and elsewhere.

And worse. Worse! The fanaticism, the hatred, the often seeming politicization of even our morals and ethics is like a disease spreading throughout our culture. And the blame game is there too. Take illegal immigration. The Democrats want us to take care of all comers—by "us" meaning of course the taxpayers, the workers. Anyone who doesn't agree with them is immoral, inhumane, racist, or worse. The conservatives, or at least many of them, want to take care of our own before we take care of the others and would rather take care of the others from afar—send them foreign aid or send the soldiers to straighten their government leaders up. Whatever. To the Democrats the conservatives are immoral and inhumane to try to stop illegal immigration. To the conservatives the Democrats are immoral and inhumane because they would rather help foreigners than their own poor citizens and because they could care less about our own working people, who have to foot the bill for foreign aid and government aid and…. But wait now! The conservatives haven't tried to cut back on foreign aid or on the aid given to illegal immigrants, at least not that I know of. And, until President Trump came along, neither Democrats nor Republicans did much of anything to cut back on foreign aid or taxes. And they still haven't cut back on foreign aid, I don't think.

But let's get back to where I started, or at least to where I thought I was heading. There are a lot of reported police shootings any more. I don't think any rational person can deny that, although I don't think it's completely clear that there are more per capita per annum than <u>ever</u> before. However, there are one heck of a lot of crime-related, gang-related, hate-related, anger-related, sex-related senseless killings in our society, especially in cities like Chicago. The major question, however, is the one of the chicken or the egg. Did the police develop itchy fingers first, or did the itchy fingers arise in our society before it did among our police officers? Not being an expert on the subject, I can't say for certain. But I <u>believe</u> that the escalation of police shootings is a parallel reaction to the escalating violence as a whole and, especially, to that part of it which threatens our police officers as they go about their daily task of trying to keep the peace in a society becoming more and more prone to hatred and violence, senseless violence. A hatred fed by some of our political leaders.

I ask you. If you were a police officer, would you be kind of afraid now? You read, almost daily it sometimes seems, about some police officer or officers being shot while trying to serve a warrant or stopping a speeder or just sitting in their car checking the flow of traffic. Senseless shootings and general killings don't just happen to civilians. They happen to police officers also. While the police are simply doing their job. Completely unprepared for an attack, with their weapons holstered and their minds on their task. It also happens occasionally to others, like to a woman jogging on an isolated trail or to people enjoying a night of dancing and laughing, such as in the bar in Paradise, CA or in Las Vegas. Most people, I expect, simply forget the potential danger, because they don't belong to a specific group that has been the continuous target of senseless killings. But we Americans are the target of Islamic terrorists, you say. I say, just so, but there are millions of Americans to diffuse the threat and there are a lot of people out there (cops, FBI, etc.) to protect us. But police officers? They are on their own. They are their own protection. And the killer can come from anywhere. He can be anyone with a gun or other dangerous weapon. It is not any external threat, but an internal one, internal to our society. And the police officers, like anyone attacked, have only a split second to react— to die or live. And they are human like the rest of us, and so are nervous, even afraid, especially in situations in which they run into someone who, they think, has a deadly weapon and is trying to use it. And then, in their memory, exist all those other officers who were not prepared, not ready to react, and so lost their lives. And…well, they react in a split second. They shoot or they don't. They live or they die. Be honest. What would you do? Ask the danger, politely or authoritatively, to put his gun down?

I wonder how I would react. I don't know. But I have deep sympathy for the officers put in such a situation and then judged by those who have never been there and cannot imagine the blind reaction and possible following anguish, no matter whether the shooting was good or bad. I cannot imagine and thus do not blindly shout: Guilty!

50

Politics versus Religion

I can't believe this. Religious and political beliefs are now being equated? That's what I read anyhow, that if the Supreme Court says that a man can refuse to bake a wedding cake for a gay couple, because gay marriage is against his religious beliefs and thus abetting such would be a sin, then a restaurant owner can refuse to serve a person whose political beliefs she disagrees with because it would be what? A sin against her political party? Or against her personal political beliefs? Or just something that she doesn't like? And, by gar, if she doesn't like it then it needs to be done away with, before someone gets his feelings hurt.

Crap! I am shocked. Literally shocked. I'm an independent, so I don't owe my allegiance to either American political party. Now, let's see. Does that make me an atheist? Or maybe just a political atheist. Or, eureka, maybe I'm a political agnostic. Does that mean that a believer in the Democratic Party can refuse me service? Oh, yes, maybe if the owner of some restaurant thinks that I'm a political agnostic he/she can shuffle me over into a corner, away from his normal customers so that anything I say won't be heard and thus corrupt some "innocent" soul, or so that my very presence won't upset anybody, especially the owner or one of his/her waiters (servers). Or maybe this latter comment of mine, not knowing if I should say waiters or servers, is what is so dangerous and upsetting about me. I'm not up to date on the latest neologisms and so I could easily insult someone, in public no less, by calling him by an old fashioned word, one that has been changed over time to another word that, since it has no historical connotation relative to its referential meaning, is less socially hurtful or some such idiotic thing.

But back to the real topic here: verbal, even physical, aggression by the Left (Socialists? Communists? World travelers? Democrats?) against conservatives, especially against those who support President Trump. I think that it is terribly dangerous. One day the Left will hurt someone, a politician, a Trump employee, an innocent, maybe the child or spouse of a conservative. Or maybe the Right will strike back at the Left by accosting liberals in public places and physically abusing them or driving them out. Maybe there will be a clash in the streets of one of our cities and several people among the guilty parties will be hurt, maybe killed. Will that stop the mean nonsense or will that cause it to escalate? I don't know. I hope all this nasty confrontation stops soon. I hope this all is just another bump in our road to national adulthood. But I worry. Our politicians like Pelosi and the Waters character act like two agitators on the sidelines of a Little League baseball game, two agitators trying to motivate their team to kick the you-know-what out of the other team, legally or illegally. Just do it! They're not really human, you know. And besides, we're in the right and they're in the wrong. That's the truth. I say so.

51

Press Unethical

My subscription to *Time Magazine* finally elapsed a week or so ago. I think I've been reading *Time* since my mid-twenties. Say, close to 60 years. Oh, I don't suppose that I've read the weekly magazine consistently cover to cover over all those years, definitely not during the many years I was in undergraduate (a late bloomer, I was) and graduate school. Maybe not thoroughly during the years my children were little, when my weekends and evenings were filled with family doings. And I don't recall when it was that I first subscribed to the magazine, rather than read it in the local library or at a friend's or in a doctor's or dentist's office. But I still remember when I was first introduced to the weekly, and it was back in the late 1950s, out on Eniwetok Atoll, by a roommate who had graduated from Berkeley with a major in English. He believed in thoughtful and rational discussion of whatever. He believed that reason was the essence of true human discourse, not argumentation, not insistence on one's righteousness, not the refusal to listen to others and to weigh their opinions rationally before making up one's own mind, or before spouting off. And above all, I don't recall him having ever included a person's personality while weighing that same person's opinions.

Time, for me, for years, was a magazine I could depend on to wander the middle ground in the political world and to show both sides of a political argument as it developed its own opinions. It was not a magazine for fanatics, either of the right or of the left. It was not a magazine for the thoughtless or for those whose minds were already made up. I liked it. Reading the magazine provided a time of reason, or mental security, in my world, one often filled with indifference to or intolerance of opposing views.

Then President Trump was elected to office. When I look back, I wonder if maybe the magazine had become less and less tolerant over the past decade or two and I simply had not noticed it. I wonder, but I don't know for certain and I don't have the time or inclination to research past copies. All I know is that once Trump became President Trump, *Time* became one of the fanatic anti-Trumpers. Any article about him included negative and derogatory adverbs and adjectives, even nouns and verbs, about something he had done or said.

So I dropped my subscription. I don't like personal attacks on the president of the United States, or on any public figure as far as that goes. I didn't like it against President Obama, or the Presidents Bush, or President Clinton, or…. I never went so far as to call anyone who spouted off about President Obama a racist. That's even nastier than the attacks on President Trump. And nasty and/or other personal attacks I simply do not like. We are supposed to be a country in which freedom of thought and speech are protected. And that I believe in: reasonable and rational discourse; not fanatic dislike or personal attacks. Disagree all you want with a person's opinions, but leave his character out of it. Unless you are perfect. Then you may throw the first stone. Because when you start throwing stones, so might another person, and another, and another, and…. Before long the war is on, and it is no longer a war of words, but rather of stones and worse.

What bothers me most about this war of words that seems to be escalating, is that it is led by the press, as well as by our public figures. The press is supposed to be our beacon of reason in this dusky world we live in. Yet anything that President Trump or one of his family or adherents does is denigrated, no matter what. President Trump began spatting with Kim Jong Un of North Korea. The two leaders threatened each other. The press began writing that President Trump was putting us in danger of a nuclear war. They said that he was acting like a school kid out of control. It wasn't Kim Jong Un doing that or unable to control himself, even though he was testing nuclear bombs and rockets and sending the latter over Japan and threatening Guam and us. Then the president scheduled a meeting with the North Korean dictator. The press immediately began writing, almost ranting at times, that the president was not prepared for such a meeting. Of course the meeting came off quite well. But the president had the gall to say that we were now free of nuclear threat (unspoken: because he thought he and Kim Jong Un had reached a good personal rapport). He did not say that there had been any written agreement, or any overall agreement on nuclear disarmament at all. But anyway: verbal explosion! Many in the press began to scream about how the president had given away the ship, especially after he cancelled our joint military war games in South Korea, something the press had earlier said was a threat to North Korea, and something the president had probably decided to offer as a sop to North Korea.

The real fanaticism, though, is that the press' anti-Trump hatred affects his family also: Ivanka; her husband; Trump, Jr.; Melania. When the first lady kept out of the public eye after her operation, many in the press were beside themselves with frustration, even anger that she would have the nerve to hide from them and not bare her operational scar. And then she traveled down to our border with Mexico to see what was really taking place with the children of illegal immigrants. Even worse, she wore a jacket with a sentence on the back meant for the press: "I don't really care" or some such wording. Of course the press decided to interpret that as her comment about the immigrant children. That was to be expected, no doubt about that. Nothing our president or his family does is ever interpreted in any way but the worst possible way by our press corps, except Fox stations.

And even more discouraging, anyone associated with President Trump, or anyone who defends him, is fair game for the press vultures: Take Sarah Sanders. She was asked to leave a restaurant in, I think, Virginia. Imagine yourself such a fanatic hater that you evict someone from your restaurant or other business because you don't like the politicians they work for. Imagine a country where such hatred expands until it infects both sides of the political spectrum. At what point does it explode into violence? That is where our press is leading us, I fear.

However, back to the point. The press, as well as our politicians, did not defend Sarah Sanders' rights. They have not defended the personal smear that went with such an eviction, or the nobility of Sarah Sanders herself when she left without making a fuss or threatening a lawsuit against the owner of that restaurant, which I think many people would have done and followed through with. No, Sarah left and only later defended her position on what the press is now whining was a government instrument. Thus she, not the restaurant owner, is guilty of an ethical violation. What trivia! What petty, petty trivia!

I've reached the point where I find our press not only unethical and fanatic in its anti-Trump hatred, but spiteful as well as petty. And they even had the nerve to print something by Walter Shaub, "federal ethics chief under Barack Obama and now a fierce critic of the administration." Can a "fierce critic of the administration" treat a member of that administration with integrity? It sure doesn't sound like it here. And it is even more telling that the press would use such a biased person to try to prove a point. But then what can one expect from a biased press like we have here in the good old USA?

52

Real Value of Sports

Of what real value to education, and to the nation as a whole, are sports, either organized competition between institutions or within the student body of any single institution, in other words, intramural sports? So many educational institutions have expensive gymnasiums and football fields and, to a much cheaper extent of course, fields designed for baseball and track. Public and private educational institutions from high schools through community colleges to graduate universities spend millions of dollars on sports structures, not to mention on coaches, team uniforms, transportation, scholarships etc., also not to mention the considerably less expensive gyms at elementary and middle schools. No doubt the schools (and thus the communities) do receive some of that expenditure back in the form of the cost of tickets to games and events, and in donations from specific alumni or parents, and in some cases in having a large venue in which to hold various meetings. I truly wonder, though, if any of these structures actually pay for their construction and upkeep, or if they are rather something people are willing to pay for because of communal pride, like the professional stadiums cities are willing to help pay for with tax breaks and other incentives, even though the profits for the owners of those teams and the salaries for the players and coaches and other staff are astronomical compared to those of most of the taxpayers, the people who really foot the bill.

Except for a few at the top of the NCAA conferences and tourneys, I doubt if any educational institutions actually make a profit on their gyms and other sports structures. Rather I expect that those structures are quite costly, to the taxpayer as well as to donors at the public institutions, to donors at the private institutions. But is there any real benefit that makes worthwhile the cost of these athletic structures at our educational institutions? Even more important, how many of our students actually get to use these structures except as a place to go, sit and watch others perform?

I don't doubt at all that athletics do help our young people learn to function better in the world as it is, rather than as we wish it were. Some of the benefits that I see are the maintenance of the body in good physical shape, the development of good exercise habits that just might carry over into later life, the development of sportsmanship, of a competitive spirit, of learning to work with others, of learning to apply yourself to attaining a distant goal, of developing self-discipline, of understanding that loss and victory are both part of the human experience and, most important of all maybe, of learning to accept your own strengths and weaknesses and to capitalize on the former. But the question is, what percentage of students actually get to participate in athletics, and thus benefit from the structures? I would judge that it is a small percent of the student body at any given institution, and really small by the time students enter college.

According to an article by *Bridging the Gap*, in September 2012, about sports participation in secondary schools, 40% of high school students and 23% of middle school students "attend schools that report zero participation in intramural sports." I might add that, as far as I know, not many schools any more require PE of their students.

The article further states that the "percentage of students participating in interscholastic sports during the school year is relatively consistent across the 8th, 10th and 12th grades at 31 percent, 30 percent and 30 percent, respectively. For intramural sports, 22 percent of students in 8th grade participate. Rates of participation among students in 10th and 12th grades are almost half of that." Does that number become half again, or less, for college students?

As for student participation in intercollegiate athletics, according to NCES about 5% of college students will participate, although in some of the more elite colleges a high percentage of the students will play some kind of intramural sports. I think that is probably a small percentage of the total numbers of students who attend college across our nation.

I guess my problem is that I think we as a nation spend a tremendous amount of money on athletic structures that, in the final analysis, turn most of our young people into spectators rather than participants. And if the number of professional teams in the country and the number of games one can find on television during any given week, not to mention the salaries of professional athletes, are any indication, the habit of sitting and watching athletic events is definitely one habit that most of our high school and college graduates continue throughout their lives.

So I guess I'm between the proverbial devil and deep blue sea here. I too like to watch athletic competitions. But I pretty well limit my time watching them to college basketball, and only two college teams consistently, along with the NCAA tourney at the end of the season. I have other things I prefer to do, like read, write, exercise daily, and spend time with my wife and family, and with friends. And I enjoy cooking.

One of the things that bothers me most about the money we spend on athletic structures in our educational system is personal, I have to admit. It has to do with the vast number of our students who, I feel, are forgotten, except as spectators to fill the gyms and football fields. I taught at the college level for 35 years. Year after year I watched these seventeen and eighteen-year-olds come in as freshmen. Many, you could tell, had long since given up doing anything much physical. Many others came in with the physiques of athletes. But they were no longer athletes. They didn't have what it takes to compete at the college level. Some of those would continue doing enough in the physical line to stay in relatively good shape. Most, however? Within a year they no longer looked like ballplayers or runners or swimmers. They had become chubby, fat, even obese. What a waste, I have always thought. With the amount of money we spend on athletics in our educational system, we should be serving all of our students. From grade one through the last day of college, we should be helping them develop good exercise habits. Bring back PE, everywhere, I say, even if it's just having students walk for a half hour, or hour, several days a week. And put much more emphasis on intramurals. The extra cost in time and money would be well worth it.

53

Respect

My country has changed during my lifetime. I mean really changed. Much of that change has been for the better I believe. Sports have come a long way since Jackie Robinson first broke the color barrier in baseball, sports all the way from Little League to the Olympics and professional baseball, or football, or basketball. You can add music, education, public safety, the military, business, and politics to that. In all walks of life, including housing, the races are more integrated than ever before, for better or worse. One of the greatest examples, of course, is our first black president, Barrack Obama, who has less than three more weeks to serve in his second term. I was not an Obama fan, and I don't care for some of the changes that he seems to consider his legacy. But one change of note, one that I have never heard anyone refer to, is how his tour in the White House has affected television, and thus the very essence of our cultural norms and life. Today, there are many, many more all-black and biracial ads and programs on tv than ever before, and I'm sure I see many more interracial couples out in public than I did eight years ago. There are no doubts in my mind that this is the result of having a black man and woman in the White House for eight years.

But not all changes over the past seventy years have been for the better. In fact, I shudder at some because they weaken the very fabric of our peaceful society. Two such are courtesy and respect—respect for the law and for those who enforce it, respect for our fellow citizens and for their right to go about their daily lives without violent and threatening disruption, and, of course, respect for our government and for those who govern, no matter what we think of them personally. And with that respect, of course, should go the courtesy neighbors and citizens owe each other, not to mention courtesy for the offices of our elected officials, like the presidency, which entails in my estimation a show of respect for the people who fill those offices.

I read a short news item the other day about a guy who was driving in the snow and came across a car in the ditch. Like a decent citizen and fellow human being, he decided to stop and help. But then he saw a bumper sticker on the car in the ditch. It read "Trump." There was a lone woman in the car. So what did our potential good neighbor do? He pulled out and continued on his way. He wasn't going to help a Trump supporter.

Can you imagine such a reaction? I can't. I have always thought that democracy entailed not only freedom of speech and action, as long as the latter did not infringe upon the rights of others, but that it also gave us the right to our personal beliefs. Oh, I can imagine someone, at the moment of recognition, spontaneously reacting in such a way. I can imagine an anti-Trump person being irritated by a Trump sticker on a license plate, just as I can imagine an anti-Obama person having a similar reaction to an Obama sticker. I can understand that, especially if the viewer is an avid Hillary advocate and passionate anti-Trump supporter, or vice versa. I can even understand a momentary desire to drive away and let the poor woman fend for herself. I can understand that. After all, we are all human beings and thus have our angers and frustrations and cowardly moments as well as our more positive reactions. But what I cannot understand is the cold action that follows, the actual physical desertion of that person, that woman, in need. I don't think I would care to live around such people, or have them in my family—or in positions of leadership in my country, although I realize that such a wish is quite a little on the naïve side, to say the least.

Anyhow, this example is not the only one to happen since Trump's election. I read that a member of the Mormon Tabernacle Choir resigned rather than sing at President-elect Trump's inauguration. And our news media keeps trumpeting about all of our professional entertainers who have refused to perform at the inauguration and the clothes designers who will not design inauguration dresses for the First Lady-elect and her family.

Luckily we have some real Americans in our country (a lot of them probably), people who realize that they can't always get their way, simply because we do live in a democracy and in such a political system compromise is the key to continued peaceful co-existence, as are occasional emotionally devastating losses and failures. We do have real citizens and many institutions that truly believe in democracy and act accordingly, in spite of the problems that might be involved. One of those institutions is Talladega College of Alabama, a private, all black, liberal arts college. The Talladega College band will be performing at the presidential inaugural. The members of the band and its leaders and the college's leaders are to be commended. To me, they are what America and its democracy is all about, as are the members of the Mormon Tabernacle Choir who will be performing in President=elect Trump's inaugural. Not those who have refused, of course.

I find those who stand forth and accept the election results, in spite of not liking them—I find them admirable. I find those who reject it in their many petty ways—I find them pitiful, and dangerous. All of this pettiness is beyond me, although not unexpected. We had a big share of it in relation to presidents Obama and Bush the younger, and to earlier presidents. But I really think it has gotten worse and worse over the past few decades. And the recent intensity and nastiness of it worries me. It worries me because it is terribly disrespectful and divisive. Our country is becoming divided not because of a specific president, either Obama or Trump, or others before them. It is becoming divided because more and more people refuse to compromise. So many people, even our rulers, seem to be ideologues any more, rather than pragmatists. And ideologues do not compromise unless forced to. That is why we are divided. We are divided by more and more of our people. We are creating a divide that no president can heal, in spite of the promises to bring us together. It is We the People who are to blame for our ills, for our divided country. And only we can close the divide, with more courtesy and respect for those who disagree with us.

I truly believe that the increasing lack of respect and courtesy for the president-elect and his office is but an example of the lack of respect and courtesy that is spreading throughout the USA, a worrisome lack of respect for out electoral system and for the president-elect that has sparked riots from "sea to shining sea," a lack of respect which, if not somehow overcome, can only lead toward more and more dissension and violence.

54

Road Rage

Road Rage? Well, there is plenty of other angry violence in the world today and, of course, in our own America, violence from the carefully plotted attacks of Islamic extremists to the Billy the Kid types who carry hidden pistols and pull them out firing away when they think someone has "dissed" them. So I guess road rage is but one more manifestation of an anger embedded in all of us and finding violent expression in so many trivial ways in our modern world of "the forgotten man," a world in an upheaval of traditional values and in a depression of decent jobs which, if we had them, would give us back a self-esteem lost by so many workers over the past few decades.

Anyhow I don't find it difficult to understand why people get upset at other drivers. I myself get upset at other drivers often enough. Our roads and streets seem to be clogged by drivers who are in such a hurry that they ignore lines or stop lights or the right of way of other drivers, or pedestrians.

On a personal note, I was sitting at a stoplight the other day, on my bike, on the sidewalk; I have an old sprocket bike and so I ride on the sidewalks since there is very little pedestrian traffic in the area where I live and I don't pedal very fast anyway. But anyhow, I was sitting there at a busy intersection waiting for the light to change so I could continue on my way home. It finally did. The light turned green in the direction I was headed and the walk icon came on. I was heading east. I was on the left (north) side of the street along which I was biking so car traffic was coming from my left into the intersection. I started to push off, to pedal on across the street, but noticed movement from my left, so I hesitated, my front tire right at the curb. It's a good thing I did, lucky for me anyway. A pickup truck, moving maybe twenty to thirty miles an hour, roared past me and turned right, without stopping or even slowing. If I had pushed off into the street I would have been hit. I caught just a glimpse of the driver, a female. She had a red light but didn't even slow down. And I don't think she saw me sitting there with my front wheel on the curb, a few inches out into the street, maybe a foot from the right side of her car as it sped around the corner. And she was not texting or talking on a phone, just driving with her eyes staring left to make sure no car was close enough to endanger her. I cursed to myself and pedaled on my way. I don't think I would have chased her down if I had been in a car. I'm not that type, generally. But I do have a temper, like so many of my fellow human beings. So I cursed and pedaled angrily on my way.

I've also been the object of road rage a couple of times in the past two years. Once I was exiting a local freeway, planning on turning right onto the surface street I was approaching. There was also a one-way surface street paralleling the freeway. The freeway exit was two-lane, but those two lanes opened into four lanes as they merged with the parallel surface street. The cars exiting the freeway had the right-of-way. The parallel surface street had a yield sign as it merged with the freeway exit. The freeway exit came out onto the second lane from the left. In order to turn right, I had to cross the two lanes onto which the surface street exited.

So, with my turn signal on and my eyes darting from in front of me to the rear-view mirror, in which I could see the traffic coming from the surface street and back over my shoulder to make completely sure that the way was clear, I cut across the two lanes to the right-turn lane and stopped at the red light. (There was a no right turn on red sign.)

But lo and behold, suddenly this motorcycle whipped around and stopped right in front of me, blocking my path. The driver jumped off and stormed my way. I realized immediately that I must have cut him off. I had not seen him. And I had the right of way. He stomped up to my window, shouting. I shrugged and said "I didn't see you and I had the right of way."

He stood there shouting for several minutes, then turned and stormed back to his bike and raced off, taking out the rest of his anger on his bike, I guess. The knot in my stomach began to ease. I realized that I hadn't understood a word he had said, not because he didn't speak English, but because his anger garbled his words and my fear must have stopped up my eardrums, or my mind.

My other experience with road rage came once when I was returning from Tucson to Tempe on the I10. I was driving along minding my business, probably doing between 65 and 70, which is my normal highway speed any more. There I was, just driving along in the right lane of two lanes along that stretch of the I10, when suddenly this car (a sedan, not new) darted past me swung wildly into my lane, effectively cutting me off and making me slam on the brakes to keep from tailgating him. Then it swung out into the left lane and slowed until it was moving alongside me. The driver was shouting something (all I could see was his mouth moving; I couldn't hear anything) and waving his fist.

There was a man, the driver, and a woman in the front seat, maybe in their thirties or so. There were two children in the back seat. They were maybe in their pre-teens. The woman was staring straight ahead. The two children were staring at me. I slowed down. The other driver braked to remain by my side. I sped up. The other driver goosed it and slammed into my lane and slowed down again. I whipped into the left lane but he sped up and cut me off, slowing down again. We did this dance for a few miles and then I saw that we were approaching an exit. I kept the other car beside me, on my left, until I was almost past the exit opening and then swung into it.

What happened to the other car? I haven't the foggiest. I parked on the berm of the exit for about five minutes and then re-entered the freeway and continued on my way. I was happy not to run across the other car again.

Like most of you, I've also read about the road-rage killings, stupid violence over a silly mistake, or carelessness, or maybe too much aggressiveness.

I'm presently reading a book entitled *The Age of Anger: a History of the Present* by Pankaj Mishra. Mishra points out that the world today is pervaded by anger, an anger that stems from reaction to the failed liberal promise of freedom, equality, and well-being and an anger like that which led to the rise of Nazism and Fascism and Communism and to both world wars in the past century, and to the cold war between the West and Russia.

The book is fascinating and extremely insightful. The anger Pankaj discusses is the cause, as he sees it and to which I agree, of so much violence in our present world, from the negative reaction to President Trump's decision to reach a friendly relationship with Putin's Russia, to the demonstrations against Trump's presidency, to the lone-wolf, senseless killings in Europe and the United States, and to the wars in the Middle East. I expect that it is also the very reason that we have so much road rage on our streets. So much of our manufacturing base has left the country and left many people without decent jobs of which they can be proud and with which they can support their family, decently. So much for the well-being of our masses! And equality? Our national wealth is being more and more concentrated in the hands of fewer and fewer people. How does that lead to equality? And freedom? Well how can a poor person, or even a member of the middle class, feel free when he can't find a job and violence threatens him from every angle, and he is at the mercy of a government which often seems to care more for the people of other countries than for its own citizens.

I, personally, would find it strange if there were no rage on our streets.

55

Sanctions

Let's see. Putin's image at home is soaring, many of his political enemies say, because of the American fixation on Russian meddling in our recent presidential election. Our continuous fixation, as depicted in our media and in congressional sanctions, portray Putin as a wily, strong leader who has the ability to disrupt and completely upset the strongest democratic nation on earth. Our fixation further reinforces the image Putin likes to portray of himself, a strong leader, who has a deep understanding of the technological age and can use it to Russia's continuous benefit, and a "geopolitical genius." Further, many Russian liberals feel that American liberals have become so paranoid about what happened in the election (Mr. Trump became President Trump) that they are desperately trying to pin the cause of their electoral failure on anyone and anything not American, and Russia has become the scapegoat because of meddling that was mainly peripheral and probably did not affect the final vote.

Kim Jung-Un is still leading North Korea in the direction he wants to go. Iran's power in the Middle East is still way up there. So, what does that all say about the US system of sanctions and its fixation on Russian meddling in our last presidential election, the latter of which has of course led to further sanctions against Russia? I think it shows clearly that sanctions don't really work. All they do is penalize the average citizen. But, of course, many disagree, although others do agree.

According to Wikipedia, "A report by the United Nations Panel of Experts stated that North Korea was covertly trading in arms and minerals in defiance of the sanctions.[23]

"The academic John Delury has described the sanctions as futile and counterproductive. He has argued that they are unenforceable and unlikely to stop North Korea's nuclear weapons program.[24]

"On the other hand, <u>Sung-Yoon Lee</u>, Professor in Korean Studies at the <u>Fletcher School</u>, and Joshua Stanton, advocate continued tightening of sanctions, targeting Pyongyang's systemic vulnerabilities, including blocking the regime's 'offshore hard currency reserves and income with financial sanctions, including secondary sanctions against its foreign enablers. This would significantly diminish, if not altogether deny, Kim the means to pay his military, security forces and elites that repress the North Korean public'".[25]

56

School Shootings

Mass shootings, it seems, are becoming more and more synonymous with school shootings. Or maybe it's just that the recent spate of school shootings has biased my memory processes. I don't know. But what I do know is that we aren't any closer to finding solutions to the "mass-shooting" problem than we were years ago. The anti-gun advocates and fanatics come out of the woodwork every time a shooting occurs, no longer simply advocating gun control (or no guns at all) but also advocating laws that would limit, if not completely do away with, gun ownership by the mentally ill, especially if there was any indication that a mentally ill person had a tendency to violence in any way, shape, or form.

I would have no problem with this, with the FBI keeping a list of people who have shown in some way that they might be a danger to society, with other law enforcement agencies (local and state and federal) being required to submit the names of potentially dangerous people to be added to said list, with it being illegal to sell guns to anyone on the list, and with gun dealers being required to consult that list before selling guns to anyone. Of course, this would not keep our children safe from motor vehicles being used as killing machines. Nor would it stop a potential killer from trying to make a bomb, or bombs. Nor would it stop a wannabe mass murderer from stealing a gun or guns to carry out his desire. But so far it has been guns, not bombs or motor vehicles which have committed most of the senseless murders in our schools. So I think such laws just might force a drop in the number of school shootings, which seem to be increasing recently.

I would also accept arming teachers who have the proper training or are willing to undergo such. I don't really like this idea. The thought of our children seeing armed teachers daily makes me shudder. How will that affect their image of the world into which they are growing? How will it affect them personally? Will it make them more comfortable around firearms, much like hunters or soldiers are? Or will it destroy their trust in what is supposed to be a free and open society?

Sex & Human Plumbing

My God! Let me get this straight. Some state governments are starting to legislate how all people have to refer to homosexual and transgender people? That sure sounds like *Brave New World* and *1984* merged into one. In my mind, it is both tyrannical and ridiculous. It is an invasion of religious beliefs. It is tyranny. It is a rewriting of dictionary meanings by government rather than by people who use the language over long periods of time. It is creating speech by governmental dictate rather than linguistic evolution. And, most of all, it is one of the silliest governmental movements that I have witnessed in my lifetime. Going to jail for calling a man him rather than zam or sim or some such nonsense? Frightening.

In the military, if, say, one person in the company does something stupid like disobeying an order or not keeping his "space" as neat as expected or, say, returning late from a weekend pass—in other words, if he's a little lazy or he makes a mistake, the whole company is liable to be penalized. The logic there is that one mistake or one hesitation in battle could mean the death and/or capture of the whole company. It could mean the defeat of the entire regiment. Each soldier is dependent on the soldier next to him for his life and for success in war. The company has to work as a unit, a smooth fighting machine. So I can understand such practices in the military. I too suffered through them, willingly, because they are logical and necessary. But in a country and, more importantly, in one supposedly based constitutionally in free speech? No, I think such dictates are more what one would find in countries like North Korea or the old USSR under Linen and Stalin.

And so, my understanding is that in New York a citizen (or non-citizen?) can be fined up to $250,000 or put in jail for insisting on calling a man "him" if that man prefers to be called "her" or some other pronoun, even a made-up one such as "Ze" or "hir," which, according to *The Washington Post,* "are popular gender-free pronouns preferred by some transgender and/or gender non-conforming individuals." And vice versa for a woman. Of course, they would probably fine me for calling a woman a woman and a man a man, since I tend to go by their plumbing rather than by their wishes. But then, I'm a little old to try on new stripes, especially idiotic ones. So, anyhow, remind me not to go to New York again, especially not soon; the "Thought Police" might just be waiting to nab me, stick their fingers in my billfold, and send me off to the Ministry of Truth, which, of course, would then ship me to the Ministry of Love for a little good, old-fashioned torture until I acquiesced to using whatever language the elite wanted me to. And to hell with someone's sex assigned at birth, or his/her plumbing, or his/her medical history, or the sex typed on his/her driver's license or other identification. After all, if the Ministry of Truth says a "him" is in reality a "ze," who am I to dispute that, especially after a few weeks of torture?

So, I think I'll stay out of New York. I don't much care for a state where 96 to 97 percent of the population accept being ordered to do silly things, and accept being penalized if they don't, for the benefit of three to four percent of that same population, which is the estimated population of the LGBT community in our country, I believe.

Funny. I can spit on the American flag if I so choose. I can even burn it. I can call the President nasty names on public television if I want. I can vote or refuse to vote. I can work or not, draw pay or welfare. Foreigners can come into the country illegally if they want. Football players can kneel during the national anthem. Demonstrators can rob and pillage if they want. People don't have to work if they don't want to; they can draw welfare. But I can't call people by the pronouns (and nouns?) that nature and centuries of linguistic usage by millions of people have assigned them. Maybe I should decide that I want to be a millionaire. Do you think the government of New York would make people treat me as such if I moved there? Or do you think there would have to be a few thousand of us before the New York state legislature would assign us that special status? And what about the money that should go with that status? I demand it! Hmmm, or rather I will when there are enough of us to make the demand stick.

And more, to add the flu to a long-term, debilitating sickness, the California legislature recently passed a law, one similar to the New York law, for people working in long-term care facilities. The staff can be fined $1,000 and/or jailed for up to one year if they fail to use the nouns and pronouns preferred by their LGBT patients. Moreover, the bill requires that LGBT people be allowed to use the bathroom of their choice. Just whip it out there, Mr., uh, Ms, uh, Ze. Don't mind the little girls watching. Or the ones trying to do their business in the open stalls.

Don't say it. I know I'm being facetious. But how else do I describe how ridiculous and perverted I think these laws are, how sick I feel as I read of them, and how fearful I become for the future of my country. Power might lead to a thirst for more power. But corruption leads to destruction, ultimately, simply because it too leads to more and more corruption. I believe that's a lesson we should learn from history, although I realize that many people don't really care for explaining the present by reference to the past. That was brought home to me in a conversation several weeks ago when a person I was talking to said something on the order of, "We're talking about now, not about those old days. They're irrelevant." So, my mouth a little on the slack side, I shut up.

Anyhow, I think I'll create my own sterilized non-gender pronoun forms and see if I can find a legislator in one of the coastal states to turn them into law. We can start with "he" and "she." What we want is to neuterize the forms, which in turn might eventually neuterize all people of both sexes and thus solve two major problems with one swipe—get rid of both sexes so we don't have this continuous increase of the genders and of the sexes chasing each other like animals in heat, and turn those two sexes into one and thus rid the world of the war of the sexes, and rid the good old USA of sexual harassment. Just think how much fun such a world would be. The only sex people would seek would be with themselves. Peace at last!

So, she and he would become "see." His and hers would become "hess." "Her" and "him" would become "hem." We could, of course, change sex nouns also, thus possibly attaining our desired result more quickly, and more smoothly. Woman and man could become "wan." Male and female could become "mamal." Boy and girl could become "goy." Lady and gentleman could become "lentle." Lad and lass could become "ads." Mistress and master could become "mattress." And…oh, well, that song about "what a wonderful world" we live in could also become what a silly nightmare we have created. Correction: are creating.

Sex

Sex? We Americans have long had a dual relationship with sex. On the one hand there is that spiritual belief which has been passed down to us by our Puritan ancestors, along with the totality of our Judeo-Christian heritage—the belief that the physical relationship between the sexes is sacred and, as such, to avoid sinning, we should only consummate the act in marriage, to create children. On the other hand there is the often ungovernable natural urge for a boy and girl, a male and female, to give in to the driving desire of the moment and take their pleasure immediately—not tomorrow, not after a wedding, not a second or two from now, but now, right now and right here at this excruciatingly, painfully pleasurable instant. In the past the majority have fought the urge, putting off until tomorrow what their bodies tell them to do right now. But history (the growth of science in moral and ethical importance and our resultant slow withdrawal from the bonds of our Puritan past) has changed our attitude, slowly but inexorably turning what was once an integral part of our religious creed into a game designed for our pleasure, or as so many of us seem to think anymore, a game in which the natural outcome is not childbirth but rather the orgasm and only the orgasm (or sexual fulfillment, I should say), unless the female of the game accidentally becomes pregnant and then decides to have the child rather than abort it.

This essay is not about abortion, however, nor is it about sex as a religious or moral act. It is about sex as a game of pleasure, pure pleasure, like eating a sweet dessert or taking a dip in cool water on a hot day, or having a beer after a long, hard day at work, or lying quietly in a darkened room on a Friday evening and listening to soft, gentle music. It is about something that has lost its spiritual significance. It is about the loss of part of America's soul, a social and spiritual loss which took many generations to complete itself. It is not just during the past few decades that sex in my country has lost its spiritual meaning. The evolution has developed over many generations.

In some ways this evolution has freed us to enjoy the moment without any sense of guilt whatsoever, moral or religious. Or, maybe I should say, many of us, not all but many, have no sense of guilt about performing the act itself, any time, any place, or getting rid of the possible result. Thus the sex act has become no more nor less than a game like handball or monopoly or chess or basketball although, I must say, considerably more pleasurable. And there are no referees or rules, except those put into play by the participants, put into play as the game proceeds, to enhance the pleasure, not the lost morals.

Loss and gain, I suppose, as in all human development. Our spiritual link with our ancestors and progeny has been weakened considerably. Our physical link to the here and now has been heightened. More and more we are becoming creatures mired in the present, the physical, the here and now, with weaker and weaker links to the past and future, to the creation and to an idealized, ultimate paradise.

Our churches can't seem to control the slide. There are those who might argue that some of our clergy are involved in the slide. There are others who might argue that the church (i. e. our religion) has become too weak. Others might insist that our schools are part of the problem, given their social and cultural and lack of religious bent.

But as with so many of our social problems, it is our culture where the real force for change lies, in a culture driven by science and technology rather than by religion, a science and technology which, I must admit, have brought us to the height of physical comfort and pleasure.

Materially we as a culture are far superior to what we were a century ago. But morally and spiritually? Do we have problems? Of course. Put only a couple of people together in a limited space and you're going to have an occasional problem, a superficial disagreement here, a more profound one there, maybe a spiritual one down the road. Put together over three hundred million people? Add in our rapid transport system of airplanes and cars to make the enclosed space smaller. Put television in the mix. Relax, and keep relaxing, the moral and ethical codes for movies and tv programs. Ignore the exaggerations and biases of the news media, and of the educational system.

Emphasize the physical over the spiritual in terms of repetition and importance, continuously. Make science the shining example of truth and technology the greatest human development. Make....

Oh well. Who is in charge of the morality store anyway? The church? I think I've already excluded it because it has lost its place of dominance in human affairs, to science. Our political leaders? That's a laugh. They don't seem to be interested in much of anything except whatever put them in office and keeps them there, or maybe in some wild political or scientific theory that they don't seem to know how to implement without destroying the economy or our health care system or our educational system or.... Men in general? I don't think men have ever been very good at controlling our moral or ethical values without instituting some form of tyranny, political or spiritual. Women? Well, it seems to me that women have always been the ethical and moral roots of society, of any culture. But, over the past generations, they seem to have been trading that cultural control for material equality with their male counterparts.

So who? The barbarians? Or are we on the verge of a renaissance? I hope.

Sexual Abuse 1

Sexual harassment? I just read an article on the Internet that said Bill O'Reilly of Fox News is being accused of sexual harassment. The Times article was supposedly published in the *NY Times* and written by Emily Steel and Michael S Schmidt.

In the article, I didn't see any listing of the female or females who were accusing O'Reilly, and I didn't see anything about exactly what he had done, but toward the end there was a mention of a specific woman who is supposedly joining others in suing Fox News for sexual harassment and the article did list the companies who are supposedly pulling their ads. So, I would say that here we have another case of good old USA media justice: guilty until proven innocent. But that's neither here nor there, just my show of contempt for our "fake" news media.

The article also referred to NOW (the National Organization for Women), saying "it" had called for O'Reilly to be fired and had asked for an independent investigation to be undertaken. According to the article NOW also complained about so many wealthy and powerful men harassing women in their employ.

And so, the War of the Sexes continues, all the way from Adam and Eve to the present, and in so many different forms. Let me see now. There are all of those cultures, past and present, that arrange(d) marriages between a male and a female who might or might not know each other, maybe even arranging that marriage with the two unwitting participants still in their infancy. Sometimes these marriages are referred to as arranged and sometimes they are referred to as the female being given to the male (like some kind of monetary or titular gift) in order to cement some relationship, tribal, family, between friendly or not so friendly people in order to bring them closer together. The problem is that it usually seems like the female is the chattel here and the male gets a free ride. But you know, that attitude seems to me to be more fictional than real. There are one heck of a lot of females I wouldn't want as my bride (or one of my brides), not for all the tea in China and India combined. And not only because of looks, although in fiction the female is usually a knockout! Shrews and deadbeats and "sell-outs" come in all shapes and sizes, attractive and ugly. So I don't see that it is always the female who gets the raw end of this stick.

What I'm saying is that there is just too much myth and fiction and personal and ideological idiocy attached to the whole idea of male/female relationships. Eve supposedly got Adam to eat the fruit of the forbidden tree. Now, I don't know about all my male colleagues the world over, the Christian world anyhow, but if I had been there in the Garden of Eden with Eve, just the two of us, no other female this side of heaven…well, I just might have done anything she asked, other than commit suicide or self-mutilation, in order to stay on her good side and maybe get a little "loving" now and then. After all, as I see it, Adam was young and testosterone-ridden. So he was probably panting after Eve like a sick dog, with only one thing on his mind and completely immune to the call of anything else. Most of you normal guys know what I'm talking about. We were all young once. The only difference between us and Adam is that we had a lot more females to choose from and, definitely in my time, apples were not forbidden, although the results might be somewhat problematic.

My problem with a lot of this sexual abuse stuff is that I never see any clear-cut definition of precisely what sexual abuse is and is not. It's kind of like alcoholism and rape. What, exactly, makes an alcoholic? I taught English composition to college freshmen for many years. One of my favorite early composition topics was "Discuss your family." And many of you might be surprised to learn how many of my students thought they had alcoholic fathers, or mothers, or parents. Yes, but often that supposed alcoholism amounted to one or two drinks a night, or a father stopping at a bar a couple of times a week and coming home afterwards smelling of booze, or a mother having a couple of glasses of wine as she cooked the evening meal. But of course there were those few who really did have an alcoholic parent, a mother or father who was drunk all the time, maybe a functioning alcoholic, maybe a person who didn't function as anything except a drinker. That's a lot of space to fill, the space between one drink a night and continuous drinking all the time.

And rape? What is rape? Statutory rape is fairly easy to define, although often not very logical given the difference between an arbitrary legal age and our body's sexual growth and desires, and the sometimes strong attraction of the young to older people of the opposite sex And the rape of a female adult by a male adult? That's always been a complicated one, and it gets more complicated all the time, I think, although a lot of people would make it easy to define: If a woman says no, up to and including the very instant before penetration has begun, and the man doesn't stop…that is rape. I actually think many people would consider it rape even after coitus has begun if the woman suddenly decided she didn't want to continue and said stop…and the man didn't stop. What that definition ignores is the male and his inability to stop himself after he has reached a certain pleasure point in the mutual sexual actions leading toward coitus. It gives the female complete control of the sex act and leaves the male completely at her mercy, ignoring the increasing incapability of the male to control himself as his sex drive rises toward climax, especially if there has been some drinking before the petting-gone-crazy.

But enough grousing! I'm no longer a testosterone-driven young man. And I was discussing sexual abuse—rape is but one form of that and <u>I do not believe that men should be allowed to rape women,</u> although I doubt that my definition of rape is close to that given by such organizations as NOW.

So, anyhow, back to sexual abuse. I have a problem here also. So many instances of sexual abuse seem to be related to the work place, as so many public cases of rape anymore seem to be related to party time and/or the close, prolonged proximity of young men and women, like living together in a college dorm, maybe on different floors, maybe not, but close together nevertheless.

So, who is to blame for sexual abuse? The abuser, of course. That's always the answer, isn't it, in fiction and in real-life situations? And that's as it should be, doubtlessly. However, as in the cases of alcoholism and rape, what precisely is a clear and simple definition of sexual abuse? Does it necessarily end in rape or some other sex act? Does it have to do with physical or psychological violence or some other form of harm, like the loss of a job or public shaming? Does it have to do with the groping of a female's private parts—unwanted, of course.

Another question I have, one that will probably irritate some of you, is this: Is it always the abuser who is totally responsible for the abuse, or is it possible that the abused might sometimes carry a little of the guilt?

I don't know. I find it impossible to unequivocally answer that. But let me again point to my personal experiences before continuing: I started teaching in the mid-sixties, in a California community college. That was the time women's skirts and dresses were getting shorter and shorter—miniskirts, tight miniskirts baring the legs up to the upper thighs, and sometimes even a little higher, high enough and tight enough on some women that it was a little difficult for them to sit without showing a little butt and even sometimes a glimpse of panties in the crotch.

I was a teacher, a young man. I stood in front of the classroom. The desks the students sat in were typical, just chairs with a kind of board as a table to put books and notebooks on, no drapes or curtains or wooden fronts to hide the lower body. Soooo, in each class I faced these rows of bare legs, and sometimes more than legs. And to make matters worse, so many of those short-skirted young girls couldn't keep from squirming and pulling at the bottoms of their skirts or dresses to keep them from showing too much a*^. Hmmmm, for a normal male like myself it was a little distracting at times, to say the least. Squirm, squirm, squirm. Legs often showing up to the crotch as the squirming couldn't keep that skirt in place. And the questions were always there in my mind. Do these girls know how squirmy they are? They must be pretty uncomfortable in those skirts. Why do they wear them if they are so uncomfortable? Is it to entice the male of the species? Why else would they wear them? Definitely not for comfort and I hope the girls always in the front row squirming away don't expect to improve their grade by wearing such short things.

Well, my life improved. Or didn't. In any case, the scenery of my classrooms changed. I moved to the Midwest, where girls don't seem to be as modish as the California girls. And then short skirts went out of style.

And where am I going with all this? Fox News has been in the sexual abuse "news" lately, first with Ailes, and then Kelly's accusation and move away from Fox, and now Bill O'Reilly, the man with whom I began this ramble. Me, I'm kind of split here. Fox seems to be an example par excellence of what I see as the manifestation of the sexual abuse problem. Is the cause of the problem the workplace itself, the male, or the female, or is it possible that all three have to share in the blame. Take Kelly, for instance; I can't remember her first name. She wore dresses and skirts that barely covered her buttocks, very tight ones, tight enough that you could pretty well tell the shape of her butt. And she almost invariably showed quite a bit of cleavage and the edges of her breasts. Was that her preferred form of dress? Or was it something that Fox News required of the females it allowed on camera. I can't recall any woman at Fox who didn't/doesn't dress like that, except Greta Van Susteren, and she is long gone. So, who's to blame here? A company that requires its female public figures to show as much of their body's sexual assets as possible without crossing the line into poor taste, or women who use their body to compete in the work world, voluntarily or through coercion, or men in power who require show and tell of their female employees...or, possibly, a public that likes to see women and men being women and men? I don't want to get into that blame game. But I do believe that women will never be accepted equally in the world of work until they dress for work rather than for show and tell. Look at the way successful men dress. No tight pants that show every movement of the leg muscles. No open shirts that show the hair, or lack of such, on their chests. (Of course, who would want to see any part of the body of these men anyway?) However, I truly, truly doubt that women will ever be treated equally until they too dress to hide rather than to show, if there can ever be true equality between men and women… if, that is, the war of the sexes can ever find a way to reach a truce, the possibility of which I doubt, not until the hormonal juices stop flowing anyway, which would be a terribly sad day. Maybe the last day. But maybe we could reach some kind of compromise.

60

Sexual Abuse 2

In my last essay I rambled along about sexual abuse, throwing in along the way a few of my other irritating ideas about rape, the natural tendency of men to be turned on by women, and the tendency of women to dress shamelessly, especially if they are beautiful and have a great body, or are psychologically tied to the latest styles, or find that dressing sensually gets them to positions they might not get otherwise—or at least makes them more competitive. I suspect that many people will disagree with this, and I have to admit that it is no more than my opinion and not necessarily a popular one at that. As for "dressing shamelessly," the adverb is a poor choice of words. What I actually mean is that, relative to the majority of women, some push the fads to a more risqué level, showing a lot more of what is often referred to as feminine charms.

Upon re-reading the above-mentioned essay I found that I didn't give much of a definition of sexual abuse. I did touch on rape, which I think is one of the worst forms of sexual abuse. But I never defined just what I think rape is. What I did suggest is that I don't think a heavy petting party that winds up with the female saying no at the very moment of attempted penetration, and the male not stopping, or being able to stop, but forcing coitus anyway, whether alcohol and/or drugs have been taken or not... I did suggest that I don't really accept such a situation as rape. Unfortunate, yes. Forced sex, yes. An act that should require incarceration, no. A man might force himself upon a woman who has done no more than flirt with him. That would be rape. A man might have consensual sex with a woman and then force her to have sex with a friend of his. That would be rape and incitement to rape. A man might force himself upon a woman who is passed out from drink and/or drugs. That would be rape. Rape, I firmly believe, is a man forcing penetration of a female who has not incited his passion to the boiling point. Prolonged flirtation; a shared evening of dining and dancing; some kissy-face, huggy-bear; even a little petting are not sufficient incitements for a man to force himself upon a woman and then claim that she asked for it. Of course there might be some other extenuating circumstances that I have not covered here. And, when push comes to shove, I do think that women should be more careful about what they do and where they go with men than vice versa, no matter what the call for their equality with men. After all, I've known since I was a young teenager that there are some men I would be better off not getting caught alone with, and that there are some that no woman should be caught alone with. I also learned young that it was best to avoid bullies, and it was in my best interests to avoid certain places—certain areas of cities, certain bars and streets, certain kinds of people. If I wound up in a place I shouldn't have been or with people I shouldn't have been with, I figured that part of the blame was mine. I would be more careful next time. The main question here, however, is whether or not, in certain circumstances, a woman should share some of the blame for being raped. It's a difficult question and I don't think that either an absolute yes or an absolute no is the answer. For a woman to insist that she has the absolute right to go anywhere, any time she wants to and not be molested is a little naïve, to say the least. Of course she has recourse to the law if she is raped, no matter where the act takes place…if she survives.

But enough of this! Rape is more degrading than a black eye and bloody nose or cracked ribs, or even a knife in the ribs or a bullet in the brain.

But what about other, less violent, forms of sexual abuse, like a husband forcing his wife to do humiliating or demeaning things with his or her body, like a father forcing his daughter to have sex with him, like a boss forcing a female employee to have sex with him if she wants to keep her job or get a promotion? Or what about men who invite women to their apartments and use whatever means necessary, short of violence, to get those women into their bed, means like enough booze or drugs to keep the woman from say-ing no, or even being able to say no? And what about companies or bosses who insist that their female employees wear revealing clothing? With re-spect to the actions in the first sentence above, I don't think there's any doubt that they are instances of sexual abuse. With respect to the situation in the second sentence (women going to men's apartments), I think that if the woman took the booze or drugs willingly, knowingly, along with the man, and was ultimately forced into coitus…I'm not certain that I would consider that rape. But if she was given a drug or some form of knockout drop in her booze, without her knowledge, then I would consider that rape (i. e., sexual abuse). The same would be true if she passed out and was then sexually molested.

My feelings about the situation in the third sentence (bosses or com-panies that make their female employees wear revealing clothing) are a little more ambiguous. If there is a clear company purpose for its female employees to wear revealing clothing, then no, I would not consider the insistence as sexual abuse. For instance, if the place of work is a bar, and the primary purpose of the bar having female bartenders and waitresses is to attract men into the bar, believing that men drink more than women and that attracting men will also attract women, then, yes, I think the owners of the bar have the right to insist that their female employees wear reveal-ing clothing. I would say that a clothing store that sold female clothing of a risqué design might want its female employees to show off its wares. I would say that movie companies might, at times, when they are filming certain movies…might want their actresses to wear revealing clothing. On the other hand, I don't think factories or offices or universities should, or would, want the same thing.

But Fox News now? And other television news companies? I see no acceptable reason why they should insist that their female newscasters wear revealing clothing. They must believe that beautiful women wear-ing revealing clothing will attract more viewers, especially men. If such a requirement is or leads to sexual abuse, I'll leave that for the courts to decide. Me, I like to watch sexy women also, like most of my male peers, I expect. But I sure don't tune in to a television news station because of what the women on camera wear. I tune in to listen to intelligent analyses of the latest political and cultural and world problems. Whether I hear those analyses from a male or female is immaterial.

So, if a company like Fox News or any other television news station requires that its women broadcasters wear revealing clothing, well, the question is whether that requirement is actually sexual abuse or just gender bias and a quite unseemly company rule. I personally don't see it as sexual abuse. And it might not be completely immoral. But it definitely is tasteless and verges on being degrading to Fox's female employees.

61

Sexual Abuse 3

Well, now we have Harvey Weinstein. Before Weinstein's peccadilloes came to light, there were Bill O'Reilly and Roger Ailes. And Bill Cosby. And Bill Clinton. And? And then we kind of get back to the Middle Ages of "sexual harassment." Way back there before the news media had its nose in every corner of every famous person's bedroom, bathroom, rumpus room…boat, yacht, car, pockets…whatever. Those were the days when we knew that JFK was a womanizer of the first category and that Ike had a mistress. But, you know, the media stopped there because most people figured that those relationships were simply a male/female thing, that men liked women and women liked men and men seemed attracted to beautiful women and women seemed attracted to men of power and wealth. And what they did together was nobody's business but their own. Oh, we had our hot tamale magazines back then also, but they were pretty tame compared to what so much of our news media is like today. Television and social media and changing moral and ethical values have seen to that.

Those old days of my youth were also the days, it seems to me, when if a woman claimed rape by a certain man or that the baby developing in her womb belonged to a certain man, well, sometimes a number of men would appear to claim that they too had had sexual intercourse, consensual intercourse, with said woman, that she was in actuality a pretty loose woman and so her claims were probably just that, claims. That's kind of like, in reverse, what happens today when a man of wealth and power is accused to taking sexual liberties with women. Out of the woodwork come all these women who claim they suffered the same or a similar fate as that of the accuser. The problem is distinguishing between false and true accusations, just as it was in the past. The problem is determining if some of those accusers acquiesced in order to get something they wanted and only later decided to join the accusatory crowd or if they were physically forced in some way to acquiesce, or if they are simply lying. I'm not very sympathetic toward people, male or female, who use sex today to get something they want and then tomorrow blame the sex partner for abuse.

Another problem I see is that nowadays the media, even *Time Magazine*, often list sexual abuse accusations as if they are absolutely and completely true. So, in public opinion, since so many people seem to form their opinions from what they read in or hear on the news—the accused is judged guilty, without a trial—guilty until proven innocent.

Another problem with all of this is that I no longer have a clear idea of what the law defines as sexual abuse. Or rape even, although from what I read I have no doubts that there is a really wide variance in how people define both the former and the latter. When I was a young man, I thought we were all pretty much in agreement about what rape constituted. If a male and female were playing around and wound up naked without any struggle, any fearful or contentious fight…and after they had stripped, either themselves or each other, they were still playing around, hugging and kissing and touching each other's body—well, the next step was coitus and the female could, or would, in no way claim rape. Nowadays I keep reading and hearing comments like the following: If at the very last moment, when the foreplay has reached the point of no return for the male and he is ready to put it in the female, she still has the right to call the whole thing off. She can say no and, if the male continues anyway, he is committing rape.

Now that I find pretty stupid and naïve, but then maybe it's my age that is speaking, or my prejudice as a male being in the modern ultra-feminist, ultra-sexual world we are talking about. I would think that any male capable of stopping at the last moment would have to have a very weak sex drive. I would also think that any female who would go that far and then say no would have to be what we used to call a tease. Either that or she'd have to be the type of woman who should never have allowed herself to get in such a situation, maybe one with a pretty submissive personality until fear of committing "sin" or of the potential results of breaking certain social values finally seeps into her conscious mind.

My definition of rape is when a male forces himself on a female who has done nothing to egg him on, or who has done no more than flirt with him, or has only done some necking and maybe a little touchy-feely with the clothes on, or maybe rolled around with him on a couch or the floor for awhile, but hasn't done enough rolling or playing to reach what I would consider the point of no return, although that point, I have no doubts, is considerably different for each and every male as well as for each and every female.

Being a male I firmly believe, of course, that it is up to the female to flash the stop and go sign. We males don't have much of a moral panic button when it comes to sex. We don't have to suffer nine months of pregnancy and then the pains of childbirth, and all of the potential social stigma of pregnancy without being married. Nor do we have to suffer the many years of raising a child to adulthood if we don't want to. Most women will not force us to and even if one did try to we could disappear, or marry the woman and get a divorce the next day, or month, or year. In other words I believe a lot of males are not attuned to parenthood as so many women seem to be. Else why so many single mothers as opposed to single fathers in the modern world we have created, when we all know that it takes two to tango.

Another problem with all of these sexual abuse accusations seeping out of the woodwork like the filthy water must have in certain parts of Houston and Florida and, of course, Puerto Rico after their respective hurricanes... another problem with all this is that men and women haven't changed in any essential way since I was a young lad. Oh, I think men liked and respected women more back in those days, since the two sexes were not in direct and contentious competition for the same jobs and the same wages as much as they are today. I think men respected women more back then because women, in the final analysis, were the arbiters, not necessarily of sexual morality in general, but of the implementation of those mores in personal relationships, and they tended to have sex with a male mainly only if they thought of him as a potential mate. Most men were well aware that there were some women who were willing to have sex for the pure pleasure of it, or for some other personal reason, without expecting any commitment in return and without there being any real "love" felt between the two participants. They were also aware that most women expected some kind of long-term commitment before they went too far, a commitment expressed or simply understood. (I realize that there have always been humans of both sexes who have broken the normal social codes and that the above is all pretty much of a generalization, unsubstantiated and bubbling up from my memories of my youth.)

Today though? The ability to control impregnation and the ease of abortion and lax social norms have drastically changed the female role in sex. Sex is definitely not looked upon as something sacred between husband and wife. Men and women live together for short periods, for years, for life without getting married. Boys and girls not long into puberty experiment with sex. Females no longer think a long-term commitment of some type from their male partner is necessary before they, the females, acquiesce to the sex act, or some form of it. Actually, they no longer necessarily leave the aggression to the male of the species, but rather in many cases become the aggressor themselves, thus competing with the male for the role of dominance in the sex chase, or sex war, or whatever you want to call it. For the dominant role in gender relationships.

But back to sexual abuse: I'm not saying that there was no sexual abuse and rape back in those days of my youth, or that men didn't sometimes use their strength in those personal relationships, or that men in power didn't use that power to entice, or even occasionally overpower, female underlings, or that there weren't a sufficient number of women who would do about anything to get a job position they wanted. People haven't really changed over the past 70 years. What has changed are the sexual norms expected by society, by our culture. They have changed drastically, anywhere from how much women are ready and willing to show off their physical endowments to what they are willing to do with those same endowments. That means, of course, that men's expectations of a male/female relationship have changed also. There are always people willing to take advantage of social values, take advantage of those for their own purposes, desires, needs, wants. Some women have always used men's needs and wants for their own purposes. Some men have always used women's needs and wants for their own purposes.

There's nothing new about that. I expect such is older than the oldest profession. If "using" (read sexually abusing) a person or persons of the opposite sex destroys that person's or persons' life or future, then yes, the user needs to face our legal system—if the "using" is illegal. But I do not believe that any person, Harvey Weinstein or anyone else, should be tried in the court of public opinion, where the press assumes the role of both prosecutor and judge.

Sexual Abuse 4

Here we go, again. Or, rather, here we go, still. The "metoo" army is trying its best to keep Roy Moore from winning the Alabama race to become one of the state representatives to the US Senate. But they seem to be having a problem. Their efforts aren't cowing as many Alabama voters as they probably had hoped. The race seems to be close, but the "accused" sexual abuser, Roy Moore, is still very much in the running. It won't be many hours now until we know for sure whether he or the "me tooers" won. (This is the next day: Moore lost, but by 20,000 or so votes—another example of how polarized my country is now; I wonder who actually won and who actually lost; it was definitely not the country.)

Over the past week or so, President Trump had begun a robo call effort to help Moore. Of course (because of that?) women accusing Trump of sexual abuse came out of the woodwork also. Moore's new accusers had tapered off some time back. But maybe there are no more. Or maybe those who haven't come forward don't think that something non-violent, or non-threatening of physical violence, something that happened fifty or so years ago between a male and a female—something of such distance and insignificance should be used to destroy a man's career. I don't know.

What I do know is my own belief system. Excluding rape, I believe that any woman who accepts a man's unwanted physical invasions of her privacy (groping, touching, kissing) without doing something about his invasion, doing something at that precise moment, has to accept some of the blame if he repeats his actions. She can tell him to stop and let him know that a second invasion will result in a complaint, to his boss, to the police, to the public. She can slap him or push him away. If there are people around, she can make his invasion public right then and there. Or, of course, she can walk away and refuse to continue working with him, if that is what their relationship is.

If she doesn't do something to stop him from repeating his invasive action, then she must accept some of the blame if he does it again. If she does nothing because she is afraid of losing her "job," whatever that is… then, as far as I am concerned, she has sold some of her integrity for a price. That, in my belief system, is prostitution. If she does nothing because she is too afraid to, or too meek, or too "childishly innocent" and so incapable of standing up to someone else's overbearing and arrogant persona…, well, I don't know what to say except, again, that she has to shoulder some of the blame that the me tooers are laying completely on the aggressor, sometimes 40, 50 or more years after the incident.

Making an aggression public, a sexual aggression in this case, 50 years after it happened? I wonder if there is a moral or ethical statute of limitations, as there is a legal one. But I expect that I'm being somewhat facetious here, although I can't see myself ruining another person's career, or life, because of something that happened years ago, especially when I did nothing about it those many years in the past, especially since it is one of the experiences of my past that has formed my character, for good or bad. I am what I am because of many experiences and happenings, some of them hurtful, some of them beneficial, although I'm never quite sure which experience was beneficial and which harmful.

Do I have the right, the moral right, to destroy someone's life or career because of something he/she did years and years ago, at which time I did nothing? I did nothing then, maybe because I was alone and did not have the courage to act, or maybe for other reasons. But now, with all the other me tooers, I can pile on this person without suffering any major damage whatsoever, to my personal image of myself or to my public image. What kind of a person does that make me? Does it make me better than the person I have accused, after so many years? Or does it put me down there in his/her category? Does it make me, too, a person who would destroy another in order to satisfy my own cravings—cravings for revenge rather than for sexual favors, but personal cravings nevertheless. After all, most of us, I think, change and grow, even improve, with the experiences that come to us with the passage of time, the bad experiences as well as the good ones.

I suppose my above attitudes are enough to cause some of my readers to want to stomp me into a mud puddle, or maybe just to spit in my face and call me a name or two. But then there are people out there who are ready to destroy anyone who dares disagree, ever so slightly, with a woman's accusations of sexual abuse from a male. Angela Lansbury is a good example. She dared say that women have to share a little of the blame for men sometimes treating them shamelessly, because they have always dressed to attract men. I mean, that's what women do. They dress to show their sexual attributes, often even when those attributes aren't very attractive, let alone very sexy. In office work and positions of authority men wear suits which basically hide whatever sexual attributes they have, or don't have. On television talk shows and newscasts, most men wear suits. Those few who don't, don't wear shorts that show their legs up to their butts and don't wear shirts open wide enough to show plenty of cleavage and some of the man boobs on both sides of that cleavage. I wonder why, if they are sexually abused so much, women don't start dressing like men. You know, wearing trousers that aren't tight on their legs, wearing blouses that cover everything up to the neck, and wearing "unfitted" suit coats that hide rather than show.

Why? Is it because women, as many continuously insist, have the absolute right to do with their own bodies whatever they so desire? Or is it because they are so unsure of themselves that they think they need to use their sexuality as well as their expertise to compete in the business world? Or is it just a natural desire to attract the male of the species, a desire which backfires occasionally because it attracts the wrong man or gives the wrong man the wrong impression of the moral code of the woman in question? Or, and I really think this is the true answer, but one so far removed from potential change, or correction, that it is kind of idiotic to even mention it—is it that men always see women as potential sexual prey (always chase women) and, being the aggressive sex, use whatever weapons they have at hand to catch their prey; while women, being the deciding sex, always see men as potential mates (always dress and act to attract that desired one) and so at times give the wrong impression to the wrong man?

But then, afterwards, to wait 50 years and then say no publicly?

Sexual Accusations

Well, here we are again, or should I say still, ruining lives because of sex, and this time because of something that happened years ago, back when 50-year-olds were hormone-driven teenagers. When I myself was young, it was the males on top. A pregnant, unmarried girl might claim that a specific boy was the father of her baby. Maybe she was being honest. Or maybe she wanted some male of her choosing to take responsibility and help raise the baby. Or maybe she just wanted money from the wealthiest boy she knew. The rumors and suspicions invariably ran rampant. But often, soon after the accusation, out of the woodwork would come all these other boys who would claim that they had had unprotected sex with the girl and so could be the father. Or a girl would claim rape and name a specific boy as the culprit. Again out of the woodwork would come all these boys to claim that the girl was a loose woman who had slept with all of them at one time or another. And so the girl was immediately suspected by many of just trying to get some money out of a wealthy family or of being a promiscuous nut case or some such thing. Even as late as Bill Clinton's political years female accusers could be attacked as liars or the real perpetrators of sexual abuse—as witness what the Clintons did to some of Bill's accusers.

Now with the #Me Too movement, the sexes have completely reversed their roles in the sex-blame game here in the good old "puritanical" USA. A boy (or man, as is often the case) gets a little too aggressive on the petting couch, or gets a little too drunk and gropes a girl (or young woman) who doesn't want to be groped (at all, or maybe no longer, or maybe not quite that much, or maybe not by that specific man) and the next thing you know the girl accuses him of sex abuse. Or maybe it's not the next thing, but rather thirty, forty or fifty years later; you know, after the Statute of Limitations has run out but at the height of cultural rage at male aggression. In other words, when the cultural pendulum has swung from favoring the male in sexual-assault accusation cases to favoring the female. Like with so many things pertaining to sex in my country, we seem to lean to one extreme or the other when it comes to accusations about unwanted sex or its aftermath—mainly its aftermath, I suspect.

I have no doubt that males are generally the aggressor, sometimes the unwanted aggressor since they (I should say we) often misread the sexual signs emitted by the female of the species—for many reasons, including the male ego but also for the simple fact of how women so often dress to show off their sexual attributes (breasts, legs, rear ends, bare skin here and there—does that make them the real aggressor? I wonder what would happen to the future of the human species if males didn't like sex and weren't overly aggressive about getting it and women quit trying to attract males.). Now I'm not saying that I want American women to dress in burkas and cover their heads with shapeless veils or some such thing. Being a normal male, I like to look at the female form, the more of it the merrier—or sexier? As long as there is not so much showing that it's vulgar rather than sexy and as long as what is showing is attractive, which is not always the case by a long shot. But what I am saying is that if girls are going to go to drunken parties with young boys whose hormones are raging (often out of control), alongside the raging female hormones the girls themselves often have, they should expect that they might not come off unscathed. By the time I was a teenager I knew enough not to get caught alone with certain people. I knew enough to avoid bullies and drunks. I knew that there were many places I shouldn't go alone, like certain seedy bars or neighborhoods. I was intelligent enough to know that it was stupid to walk blindly across busy streets just because I had the right-of-way "and it's a free country." Tangling with a 3,000 pound plus vehicle wasn't in my best interests, and getting in its way wasn't either since its stopping power was very limited compared to mine and any kind of clash would leave me the worse for wear, not the vehicle. In other words I was quite aware of many of my weaknesses as a young male of the species, and as a human being. And, if I did say to hell with it and go wandering to places I shouldn't or with people I shouldn't, I accepted my share of the responsibility for anything bad that happened to me; I didn't go crying to police or parents, either then or years later. I accepted the bad experience as part of learning to become a rational, careful, thoughtful adult. After all, I am a Christian and, as such, I completely accept that part of the Christ myth in which Jesus descends into Hell <u>before</u> ascending to Heaven. I don't believe that we can become good human beings, really good citizens and parents and friends, unless we have some idea (practical or vicarious experience?) of the dangers, the evils and the sins and the weaknesses, that exist not only around us but also inside us.

So, you can probably guess at my reaction to a lot of this crap that the #Me Too Movement has brought forth. Not all of it. Rape, either violent or with the use of drugs, is rape and should be punished. But when? That's the question. And who all? And what are the lines between aggression and criminal abuse? These questions cannot be ignored if we really are interested in justice rather than revenge.

And even more importantly, how? Punishment by accusation? No way. But that is what is often happening nowadays. The people who are suffering along with the man accused are the family members, especially the wife and children and parents. Of course, you can argue that the same is true of the family of all accused felons. Maybe so, but I would counter that it's really the convicted felons, not the accused ones, whose spouse and children suffer greatly, unless there is little doubt of the accused person's guilt. Not so, however, in the case of a man accused of sexual abuse. Just think of all the men in the news media and other positions of public or private authority who have recently found themselves without a job after being accused of sexual aggression, <u>without trial</u>. And what about this latest trashing of a man nominated for the Supreme Court? For something done almost forty years ago, back when he was a teenager in high school, a kid moving through the years of raging hormones? For something that was not rape, or even penetration of a female in any way, shape, or form? I mean, forty years ago? And no coitus? Accusing a man who is now in his fifties and has lived an exemplary life, possibly with the exception, or not, of a few wild high-school years? I mean, destroying a man's family and trying to destroy his career over some action so far in the past, over something as trivial as holding a girl down and groping her—supposedly in a drunken stupor? I mean, wow, what do you think the courts would sentence a teenager to for such a hormone-driven simplicity? Even more to the point, what was this girl doing at a drunken orgy in the first place? And don't tell me she didn't know about the potential dangers there. And don't tell me she wasn't there to maybe find a boy she could have a little "sex-time" with. And don't tell me Judge Kavanaugh is guilty just because she says so when she can't remember anything about the party except the faces and laughter of Kavanaugh and his friend, who also denies having done such a thing.

One of the things that irritates me most about the Kavanaugh case (and other such cases) is the timespan between happening and public accusation, not to mention the timing of the accusation, when a man, a conservative, is being considered for one of the highest of judicial positions—and the accuser is a liberal democrat. I'm an independent and have been all my life. I try not to let petty political chicanery and nastiness from either party influence me in any way. But this whole situation really stinks to high heaven. A <u>California</u> liberal democrat accuses a conservative judge of committing sexual abuse way, way, way back when he was seventeen and she was fifteen? Now, tell me. What normal horny young male hasn't pushed the sexual envelope some time in his youth? I personally wouldn't think much of him if he hadn't. But he denies it in this case, and so does his friend who supposedly was involved. And the accuser's friends do not back up her story. And she can give no detail about the incident except that it happened and she is "100% certain" that it was Judge Kavanaugh who was the abuser? Let's see. False memory somehow implanted in her mind? A mistaken identity? A desire to keep the Supreme Court more oriented toward the liberal side of the aisle? A woman driven along by the mob mentality of many in the #Me Too movement and in the far left of our present political reality? And then this Senator Feinstein held off on making the accusation public until there was almost no time left before the vote on Judge Kavanaugh's nomination, knowing full well that the accusation would get a lot more publicity at such a late point in the nomination process and would have a greater chance of destroying Kavanaugh's good name and thus his nomination? I find it next to impossible to think that she didn't also realize that his wife and daughters would be psychologically damaged no matter what the outcome of the nomination.

As far as I'm concerned, the whole process stank of lynch law. In other words the man was deemed guilty by many (mostly democrats, liberal democrats, I assume). The mob rose and demanded "justice," which on their terms meant destroy the man because he is guilty. And, since he is guilty, he should not be allowed time to prove his innocence—which he cannot do anyway since we, the mob, have already decided that he is "100%" guilty. End of story. String him up!

64

Shooting From the Lip

Well, President Trump has been precisely that, President of the USA, for over a month now. His feud with the media continues unabated, nevertheless, and I don't find it difficult to understand why. Obama promised to have the most transparent presidential administration ever. But, of course, his presidency was just as opaque as any before him. I suppose that's what the media means when it keeps citing people who want President Trump to <u>act</u> presidential. Making decisions, discussing matters, disagreement among cabinet members, reacting negatively and off-the-cuff to criticism—as long as all this is done in the back room or some other place out of the public eye, that, I suppose, is being presidential, if I may insert a little sarcasm here, for I personally find it a little refreshing to get a good insight into the real emotions of our President, after six decades of voting for men to fill the slot and later only seeing the public persona of the new president, the public persona as created by his handlers through speeches prepared by professional speech writers and hackneyed comments straight from a teleprompter or memorized beforehand. It's refreshing to see a real human being in the presidency, a man with all the emotions and frustrations and humanity we all have on a daily basis.

But that, I believe, is the problem. Obama promised transparency but gave us the old pap—opacity or, in other words, "presidentialness." President Trump throws every emotion and reaction out there for the public to see. So the media goes into a tizzy fit, a feeding frenzy, and screeches "not presidential." Is it possible that this is because so many of them haven't really liked Trump from the beginning? Well, there have been quite a few presidents in my lifetime that I haven't liked personally, presidents who were really quite good at their job. And there have been some that I kind of liked personally, like Jimmy Carter, but who have in my estimation not been very good presidents.

But Mr. Trump is President, after all, so you would think that the media would slack off a little, would give him a short honeymoon at least. But they haven't. And he's definitely not the type of person who keeps quiet when someone or something attacks him. So the feud goes on, kind of like the movie feud between the Hatfields and McCoys, but with a major difference: no shooting except with words from the lip rather than bullets from the hip. I would like to see it settle down a little, but I don't think the media is about to back off. There are too many money-making stories in attacking a President who attacks back.

Like most successful people, businessmen, politicians, or military men, et al, as far as that goes, President Trump seems to have a pretty hefty ego. Unlike most of our presidents, though, he is not a politician and so has not learned to cope with the media by simply denying everything and then getting some canned words from his handlers to serve up to the public, through the media, of course. How better to pacify them?

But actually, I'm not certain that anything he could do would pacify most of our media. They don't seem to like either him personally or what he stands for.

So they call him non-presidential and he calls them bearers of "fake" news. Fake news. Hmmmm. I think that's an unfortunate choice of words to define our news services. They don't invent news. They just warp it to suit their need to make money while expressing their own personal biases. And that, I think, is really what they are. They, the supposed reporters, are human like the rest of us. They are biased and opinionated, they exaggerate, and they are terribly negative relative to President Trump. Early last December the Harvard Kennedy School's Shorenstein Center on Media, Politics and Public Policy published an article entitled "News Coverage of the 2016 Election: How the Press Failed the Voters." The authors claimed that during the election both Trump and Clinton "received coverage that was overwhelmingly negative in tone and extremely light on policy." They said that during the general election Trump's negative to positive vote was 77% to 23% while Clinton's was 64% to 36%, and that during the entire campaign Trump's were 56% to 44% and Clinton's 62% to 38%. That is upsetting, but not unexpected. Negativity sells more news than positivity does, I expect.

After reading the above, I got to thinking about all the articles and newscasts I read and listened to during the election. I thought the Harvard school was absolutely right, but I decided that they had only dealt with negativity and positivity in a general sense, not taking into consideration all the exaggerated and biased verbiage that the media had used in President Trump's case. And here are some of the "wild" adjectives, adverbs and verbs used to lambaste Trump personally during and after the election process: erratic, chaos, falsely, crush of crises, tumultuous, rowdy rallies, fix is in, unhinged, bluster, bravado, pretentious, obsessed, disturbing, and dubious. Even *Time Magazine*, a magazine I read weekly, one that I have always considered mostly fair, although leaning somewhat to the left of center—even *Time* was not able to keep from bias and exaggeration in reference to Trump, I don't believe. Here are the titles of some of its articles in the March 6, 2017 issue: "Trump's immigration crackdown seems designed to spread fear," "Disruption and dysfunction define the new presidency," "American's experience: fear, loathing, relief and delight."

All of this I find discouraging, although it is to be expected because our reporters are actually "opinionators" rather than reporters, and opinion is invariably laced with bias, in all of us. But maybe that's what the public wants.

Slavery Tax

Just the other day, on the Tucker Carlson talk show on Fox News, a black girl explained a really wild, inconsiderate, and naïve (I almost said racist) proposal that she had made to the college she attends. She attends Western Kentucky University in Bowling Green. She proposed that, in order to compensate Blacks for the slavery that their ancestors had to suffer through, they be given free tuition to the university.

Tucker Carlson appeared somewhat flabbergasted. I guess that those words would also describe my reaction to her proposal. I mean, slavery in the good old USA ended over 150 years ago, with the end of our Civil War. Over 150 years? My God, for my whole life I have thought that debt peonage (I mean the passing of the debts of the father on to the sons; although in this case it would be the offspring)…I always thought that debt peonage had long, long ago been outlawed as terribly unjust. But what she proposed sure sounds like debt peonage to me. It is a debt peonage, though, that jumps many generations to finally start charging present-day taxpayers for the, in this case, "sins' or crimes of the fathers (or distant ancestors) rather than for their "debts." Of course, we have been paying some of that already, with work and education racial quotas.

Her proposal irritated more than flabbergasted me, I have to admit. When people make such outlandish demands they never mention that slavery was pretty much international during much of the time that it was legal in the USA. Moreover, it wasn't only black people who were sold into slavery. The Barbary pirates, who sailed the Mediterranean Sea off the coasts of much of what is today North Africa, captured and sold Europeans into slavery from the 16th to the 19th centuries.

One of the things, or lack of things, I expect, that made me the most irritated was that the girl made no mention, absolutely no mention at all, of the African slave traders who sold their fellow Africans to the white man. She didn't suggest that we slap an annual education tax on any African country that presently exists in an area from which the black slavers came. If we asked her to do so, she would probably sneer and say that we had absolutely no way to sort the innocent ancestors from the guilty ones over there. And I would agree.

But, of course, over here there is a close analogy to "over there." Tucker Carlson asked one of the questions: How do we separate out the white people whose ancestors came to the USA after slavery had been abolished? They shouldn't be made to pay for the enslavement of black people in the USA, should they? I think the girl thought that they should since they are white and therefore part of the racial majority that keeps the Blacks depressed. In other words, I think her proposal came not only because of slavery but because she thinks black people have always been and still are kept downtrodden by white America. I disagree. First, I don't think Blacks are all that racially oppressed any more. The fact that the girl who made the proposal is black and a student suggests this, as does the fact that there are many, many other Blacks who are presently in or have graduated from college. Moreover if there is still any oppression, I believe that white people in general are only a part of it, and a small part at that.

Anyhow, another problem I see in the girl's proposal is that not all Blacks who presently live in the USA had ancestors who were slaves in our country. Many came here during the late 19th century and throughout the 20th, not only from Africa, but also from the Caribbean islands, Mexico, and Central and South America, and maybe some from Europe and Canada. I don't know.

But what I do know is that it would be next to impossible, and wildly costly, to try to separate out those whose ancestors were slaves in our country from those whose ancestors were not. And it would be much more unjust for Whites to pay for the education of all Blacks than only for the many whose <u>distant</u> ancestors had suffered slavery, which would be unjust enough. And the whole proposal is kind of idiotic anyway, about as idiotic as asking Southerners to pay for the education of Northerners because they killed a lot of the Northerners' ancestors during the Civil War. Or vice versa. Or asking Texans to pay Mexico reparations for having taken the state from them through violence rather than through peaceful means, like money. Or asking the USA to pay Mexico for our whole Southwest, which we took from them also by violence (war). Or insisting that we pay reparations to Great Britain, both for the Revolutionary War and for these here United States, the ones we took from them, at least. And where does such idiocy stop?

Then, of course, in reference to the black student's proposal, there's the problem of exactly which Whites actually have an ancestor or two who had slaves. How do you separate those Whites who did from those who did not? In both the North and the South? Ye Gods, what a can of worms! And finally, how do we figure out which black students (US citizens, of course, or should illegals get free tuition also?) had African ancestors who were slavers and make sure these students don't get free tuition?

I have to wonder what the heck kind of an education this girl who proposed such an idiotic thing had, in elementary school, high school, and college. It most definitely failed in teaching her the difference between fiction and reality. And between justice and injustice. And maybe between racism and "reverse" racism.

66

Straight Pride

According to the Washington Post, the vice mayor of Dixon, California "proclaimed July "Straight Pride Month." Hmmm. I'd say that man, Ted Hickman, has a lot of guts. I wish there were more like him, lots more. It sounds like he's already getting guff from everywhere: people wanting him to resign, people wanting the Dixon city fathers to fire him or whatever you do to get rid of a vice mayor, people wanting him to apologize, people wanting him strung up probably…almost anything is acceptable but an expression of pride in straight people. Next thing maybe we'll exile all the straights and thus have a real paradise.

And the really telling thing is that a lot of the people complaining about Hickman's comments, and other similar comments, are straight themselves. But I guess, you know, there are one hell of a lot of people out there who flare up any time someone expresses pride in being normal, or American, or Christian, or…straight.

Yet the irony, as I just mentioned, is that even many straight people don't seem to want any—and I mean any—straight, normal person to express pride in being just that, straight, normal. Is it that they are ashamed of being normal? Or is it that they think any expression of "straightness" makes non-straights upset, or insulted, or sorry for themselves, or feeling less happy, or…what?

I think a lot of people would like to stand up for straight, normal people, maybe brag about them, maybe defend them. Personally I've never seen anything wrong with being straight and expressing pride in being so, in spite of what all the anti-straight people say. But we all know that anyone publicly expressing pride in being straight would bring the wrath of the far left and all its fellow travelers down on him/her. It's simply not acceptable, not to lots of people, not to all the nation's "honkers"—it is simply not acceptable to defend straight people. Some people…many people act like it's a social sin to express pride in being a normal human being, almost like it's a crime, not in being normal, but in expressing pride in that normalcy. For some reason many people seem to think that any expression of pride in one's normalcy is belittling to anyone who is not normal. Yet those very same people smile happily when someone who is not normal expresses pride in what he is. Now you tell me. Why cannot I, an old white Christian heterosexual who has basically lived within the moral codes of his upbringing…why can't I brag about me and my kind? Am I supposed to be ashamed of what I am? Or is it that some touchy/feely people who are something else than what I am will be "hurt" by any public expression of self-pride that I make?

Other kinds of people can march the streets, parading in open support of their homosexuality or bisexuality or transvestitism or atheism or whatever. They can take pride publicly in not being sexually normal and thus not marrying a member of the opposite sex and having babies and living a contented family life.

But then, normalcy is apparently not only passé in our society but kind of like leprosy as well, something to keep hidden and silent even though everyone knows damn well what you have. Maybe people think that just mentioning what you have will be contagious. Meaning the words themselves might just spread the disease. And, oh my God, we wouldn't want to spread that terrible disease of being straight, would we? How destructive for all of us!

But, you know, this indignation at publicly expressing pride in being straight is just one symptom of our society's sickness: Minorities are welcome; let the silent majority remain silent, or else.

67

Teacher Strike & Illegal Immigration

Well, I survived the Arizona teachers' strike, in spite of having to do a lot of babysitting with a kindergartener, although I have to admit that I did enjoy the time I spent with the little guy. I have to wonder how many other grandparents, not to mention aunts and uncles and neighbors and..., and babysitters were saddled with children to care for, and how many older students spent several days staring at the boob tube, alone or with a sibling or friend (plural?), or played internet-type games, or screwed around with the girl, or boy, next door because the parents were all working and they, the students, didn't have to go to school and so were home alone and un-supervised and...how many single mothers had a terrible time balancing child care with their work requirements. Enter The Law of Unintended Consequences.

I would also like to say that I'm glad the teachers got most of the raise and classroom monies they asked for. Being a retired teacher myself, I can sympathize with their frustration at the lack of decent pay and limited funds for giving their students the best learning situation possible.

However, I would also like to say that I'm a little (to say the least) ir-ritated by where a lot of our state's educational budget, as well as the state budget monies in general, goes.

I attend a "talk fest" weekly, a gathering of a group of people to discuss recent events in the news. At the latest "fest" the teachers' strike was one of the major topics, as it had been the week before. Of course, being mostly from the educated classes, the attendees supported the teachers, and the strike. I was the only one who "tried" to bring up Arizona's illegal population and their cost to the taxpayer, not only in the education budget but also in a number of other aspects of our state budget as well. I didn't get far. One other person said, indignantly, that the illegals are humans also. And those words shut off that area of conversation. It seems that for some people in this country, a lot of people I think, certain topics are taboo unless they are approached with a positive or, at the least, acquiescent attitude. Illegal immigration seems to be one of them. Just witness the anger of some people when you use the word "illegal" rather than "undocumented."

Or when you try to point out some of the problems created by illegal immigration. And cost is of course one of those problems, if not the most telling one. In the article "Cost of Illegal Immigration Rising Rapidly in Arizona…" (May 17, 2010, *Fox News*), Ed Barnes says that Arizona's illegal immigrant population cost the state "a whopping $2.7 billion in 2009." He further cites the Federation for American Immigration Reform (FAIR) as saying that, annually, "illegal immigrants take $1.6 billion from Arizona's education system, $694.8 million from health care services, $339.7 million in law enforcement and court costs, $85.5 million in welfare costs and $155.4 million in other general costs." FAIR, in an article entitled "Immigration in Arizona" (published in April of 2012), says that nearly half of Arizona's foreign-born population is made up of illegal aliens, that 6% of the state's total population is illegal, and that between 1996 and 2010 the illegal population of the state rose by 213%. FAIR further points out in the same article that 10% of children enrolled in public schools K-12 "have parents who are in the U.S. illegally." That is one in ten school children. Now I think that is a little problematic given that we are in 2018 and some of that rising trend has likely continued to the present.

To add a little scary note to those numbers, in the same article FAIR cites the Arizona Department of Corrections as estimating that "17% of its prison population" and "22% of felony defendants in Maricopa County are illegal aliens." That's right at one in five. The CPRC (Crime Prevention Research Center) insists that illegal immigrants "are at least 142% more likely to be convicted of a crime than other Arizonans." "They also tend to commit more serious crimes and serve 10.5% longer sentences," are "more likely to be classified as dangerous" and are "45% more likely to be gang members than U.S. citizens." According to *Breitbart Connect* (Report: 'Dreamer'-Age Illegals Have Crime Rate Double Young Americans) our DACA "dreamers" population, as well, doesn't seem to be as replete with innocence and righteous social ambition as we, the general public, have been led to believe. According to *Breitbart Connect*, "DACA age eligible immigrants are 250% more likely to be convicted of crimes than their share of the population" in general.

In spite of all this, of course, there are many who insist that illegal aliens are needed to fill jobs that native citizens will not, especially jobs in the farming and fruit-growing industries. We are all aware, I expect, that illegal immigrants fill many of the jobs having to do with housekeeping, public and private, and general property care. What would many of our wealthy homeowners, and even middle class, do without "cheap" labor to be their maids and gardeners and general "lawn cleaners"?

Doubtlessly the wealthy would suffer price increases for their personal labor needs around home and property if we could somehow get rid of most if not all of our illegal immigrants, but the American blue collar workers might actually benefit from such. According to the same article by *Breitbart Connect* cited above, when Arizona began labor immigration reforms in 2004 "and the state's population of roughly 450,000 illegals gradually dropped by roughly 180,000 people from 2007 to 2012...," wages for the average citizen "rose significantly," as per *Moody's Analytics* and the *Wall Street Journal*. Income for "low-skilled whites" rose about 6%, for Arizona farmworkers about 15%, and for construction workers about 10%, all between 2010 and 2014. As well, during the same period, annual Arizona government costs dropped significantly: welfare by roughly $430 million, education by $350 million, emergency room costs by $60 million, and prison costs by $202 million.

The problem here, as I see it, is the word "illegal" relative to immigration. It is not immigration in general. From the references to "legal immigration" that I have come across in my limited research, it seems that those immigrants who are in our country, and state, legally are a boon to rather than a drain on our budgetary and other resources. So, there is no doubt in my mind that we as a state and country must (and I emphasize must) come to terms with our immigration system, somehow halt, completely halt, illegal immigration and increase <u>as needed</u> legal immigration. But with so many people throughout the nation for "open borders," and with so many sanctuary cities and even states, how can we possibly do so?

68

The President & The Media

Can you believe it? This press corps character Acosta tries to take over a press corps assembly led by the president of the USA. He refuses the president's order to give the microphone to another reporter. He keeps asking questions when the president has told him to be quiet. He refuses to give the microphone to a presidential intern, a female, keeping the microphone from her by pulling it away and putting his arm up to keep her hand from taking it. Such rudeness! And now his "news" company, CNN, is planning on suing the president because he had the reporter's White House pass revoked? They also seem to be claiming that the tape of what happened is doctored. As far as I am concerned, this shows the sorry state of some of our news media. Little respect for the truth when it criticizes them. No respect for the president of the United States of America. What next? Does the press corps begin to disrespect the American flag? And then any member of government who disagrees with them?

And now, just today, I read that a judge has ruled that the president must allow Acosta back in. What? Wow! Talk about disrespect? I can't believe that this judge is politically unbiased, any more than a lot of the press corps is. And I can't believe that the president will have even the slightest control over his press conferences in the future, although he says that he will set up specific rules for the reporters to follow and, if they don't follow them, he will evict them or halt the press conference (walk out himself). If I were him I know what I would do. I would cancel all future press conferences until CNN promised that Acosta would not be reassigned to the White House press corps.

And just what is the problem with people like Acosta? Fanatic hatred of the president, I would say—what has been called the Trump Derangement Syndrome in the past. I find it difficult to believe how much hatred for President Trump there is in our culture, personal hatred, not necessarily hatred for some of the things he believes in or does, although there is plenty of hatred for that also. And disrespect. And belief that he is not capable of being president of the nation. Yet he is a man who increased a family fortune into a mega-fortune? A man who helped raise a couple of really capable children? A man who became the president of the USA in spite of all the odds against him—women who wanted a female president, Blacks and liberals who claimed that he is racist, Democrats who hated and still hate his guts, women who consider him a sexist, and even many members of his own political party who figured that he didn't have a snowballs chance in hell of making it in the 2016 election and didn't like him either. And the Washington DC swamp was against him. And the news media (and the "clowns" from Hollywood), the majority of whom hate his guts and show it continuously in the nasty and negative press he gets and the ways they talk about him? Just look at all the insulting adverbs and adjectives and nouns and verbs (and supposed funny jokes and skits by supposed comedians)… the verbal trash the media uses when writing or talking about him. He must have a great deal on the ball to have completed that obstacle course I mentioned above and come out the winner, and still to this day continue with his head up. Yet so many people ignore that, ignore his many accomplishments as president, both political and personal.

I know, many people say that he's not <u>presidential</u>, which, it seems to me, means that he isn't a robotic extension of a teleprompter, as his more recent predecessors were. And this brings up another irony. Obama promised that his presidency would be completely transparent, the most transparent in history. Yet he did almost everything behind closed doors and seldom said anything controversial in public. And, like most if not all politicians, he told lots of lies and made not a few exaggerations while in office. Now President Trump hangs a lot if not all of his reactions and feelings out there on Twitter (extremely transparent) and all his detractors complain about it. Yet many of them are the same ones who complained about President Obama not being transparent like he said he would be. What hypocrisy!

Me, I wish that President Trump would be more careful about what he says in all his tweets. But I also wish the news media would be less fanatic in their hatred of him. And I also wish that they would exaggerate less and be less biased. When he makes a comment about our trade imbalance with our friends in Europe, or mentions that he disagrees with some specific leader (of England or France or Germany), about what they did or said, I wish that the press would be honest and say he made a comment or point out that he disagreed, rather than rant that he "bashed or trashed" a specific leader, or cry that he's leading us to doom and damnation. I really dislike personal attacks on anyone, and especially on the president of the USA.

But, many people will say, a democracy needs a free press in order to function "freely," even if that means a specific news media is excessively liberal or conservative politically. I disagree. A democracy does not need a free press which is also dishonest. It does not need a press corps which is biased toward one political party or another. It does not need a press which continuously exaggerates in order to sell more news and thus make more money. Rather it needs a free and honest press, one that keeps bias and exaggeration to a minimum. Otherwise, yes, like the president says, the press does become an enemy of the people, and thus the nation. It helps lead the people in one specific political direction. And, sorry to say, that is the state of much of our press corps today.

The Whining Goes On

Well, I thought maybe the political childishness was winding down. I thought the anarchic destruction by the inauguration demonstrators in Washington, D. C. just might be the end of it. But no, now we have the women's march and what did I hear some famous female singer say? She said (she really, truly did) that she had thought seriously of blowing up the White House. All I can say is, the spoiled brats just aren't going to give up.

Just what is going on in my beloved country, I ask myself, what terrible disease has overtaken us? Why can't the people of the political left accept the fact that President Trump is precisely that, the duly elected president of our country? Why do they want to subvert our democratic system simply because they don't like the man who was elected? Why do they keep expressing, in public no less, their oh so petty anger and frustration? Why do they keep pouting and whining and stomping their feet and throwing tantrums? The game is over. Donald Trump won. The game was not rigged. The refs were not paid off. Both teams played their best and the nation's Electoral College made its choice according to voter instructions from the people. So I wish they would just quit bellyaching and go home. If they don't like what is going on politically, they can join the political system, support those who feel as they do and try to legally bring about the changes that they want. If they don't like the Electoral College, they can use the system to try to change it. But let them please quit their noisy whining. It only incites others who are braver than they are and less inclined to use the cover of the law for their purposes…it only incites them to further rioting and destroying the property of honest citizens, some of whom just might be on their side of the political spectrum. And, most importantly, it threatens the very fiber of our nation, of our democracy, which is the peaceful transition of power from one elected official to another, which has been going on for well over 200 years.

I for one feel that the Electoral College worked just fine this time. It, I believe, actually worked as it was meant to. It gave the smaller states and the voters outside the major cities a winning voice. Why should the most populous states and our major cities rule over our nation, which actually does stretch from shining sea to shining sea, which has fifty states, not just a half dozen or so, and which has a huge, huge population living in towns and small cities and in the countryside, although I sometimes wonder if our politicians from a few coastal states and a few of our largest cities consciously accept that? Why shouldn't the less populous states, the smaller cities and the towns, as well as the country folk, have a shot at electing someone who will look out for their image of where the country should go, no matter how myopic or mistaken or dangerous some might think that image is?

I realize that people will be hurt. You can't make laws or do much of anything without the law of unintended consequences raising its ugly horns. I would suspect that some if not all of our most basic laws have that consequence. Just take our driving laws. Say the speed limit is 75 and three men are caught doing 85. They are all fined $200. One man earns $300 a week. Another earns $1,000. And the third earns $10,000. Just ask yourself, are these men being penalized equally? I don't think so. The first man must pay two thirds of a week's salary, the second only one fifth, and the third only one fiftieth. The fine for the first man is maybe his family's food for the month, or a big percentage of his rent money. But for the third man, the fine is pocket change.

What about Civil Rights and the quota system that tried to equalize the number of African Americans in college? Some white kid gets hurt if a specific university has only a certain number of openings in its freshman class and has to meet a quota of minority students. And that hurt just might be compounded if a certain amount of the federal aid a college has must go to minority students, might it not?

And then there's the draft during our past wars. It's a lottery system and so is based on the luck of the draw. One kid's bad luck is that his number is drawn. He goes off to Germany or Korea or Vietnam and is killed in action. Another is lucky and his number is not drawn. He lives.

Now, I'm not necessarily advocating a change in our laws or the way we do things. What I am trying to point out is that we too often ignore the fact that many people are hurt or upset no matter what we do. You can't promote one person without passing over at least one other. You can't elect one candidate for the presidency without rejecting at least one other candidate. You can't allow illegal immigrants to flood into the country without hurting the legal citizens, from taking their jobs and forcing wages down to increasing criminal activity and violence in our cities and towns. You surely can't allow American manufacturing companies to continuously flee the country without hurting the entire population. Yes, foreign-made goods will be cheaper when they are sold in the USA, cheaper than goods manufactured in the USA, but many of the workers who had those jobs when the companies were in the USA now have no jobs or jobs which pay much cheaper wages. So, for them, buying the cheaper products might actually be buying more expensive products.

I could go on rambling like this, I suppose. But the point I'm trying to make is that no matter what we do somebody is going to suffer while others benefit. The President's latest edict, the ban on Muslims from certain countries is a case in point. The people who want to come to the US from those countries will, naturally, be adversely affected. The countries on the ban list will be angry. But people from other Muslim countries will possibly benefit by being more readily accepted as immigrants. And American workers will benefit because the influx of foreign workers will be slowed, an influx that would have brought in many workers who would have competed for jobs and probably helped lower wages in general. And then, of course, there was the potential for future terrorists coming with the influx. Some of that just might be avoided by the edict.

So, what does all this have to do with the whiners? A lot! President Obama brought in many refugees from the very countries that President Trump has put on his banned list. President Obama made his decision supposedly based on humanitarian principles, while President Trump based his decision on nationalistic principles. But in the final analysis, as I see it, President Obama's decision potentially harmed his country and its workers, while President Trump possibly saved his people, the workers of his country, from lost jobs and lower wages and, possibly, terrorist attacks. Is that not humane, a humaneness oriented toward the citizens of our country, not toward the citizens of other countries, which often seems the case anymore.

I do not dispute that President Obama's heart was in the right place. But what I do dispute is whether his decision was in the best interests of his country and its citizens, now and in the future. So, what do people really have to complain about? That one president should put the welfare of his country before the welfare of a few immigrants? Isn't that what a president is elected to do, defend his country against all dangers? Or are people crying because they don't like President Trump's personality? Or are they crying because they don't like some of President Trump's ideas? I personally didn't like some of Mr. Obama's ideas and actions. But I didn't march on Washington. I didn't try to sue him and the federal government he represented. I, like many who must have agreed with me, waited and used the legal political process to make a change. I just wish that all these present "nay-sayers" would do the same.

70

Trump Jr. Meets With Russians

Some of the Trump campaign, his son specifically, met with Russians during the past presidential election campaign, hoping to get some dirt on Hillary and therefore improve the Trump chances of winning the election. So what?

Well, it seems like there are two main arguments against the legality of such a meeting, or is that morality or ethicality or some other such nonsense rather than legality? I'm not at all certain what such a meeting has to do with the law, unless some secret American documents or information were traded to the Russians for the information President Trump's son wanted, or rather hoped to get.

Anyhow, one argument against Trump Jr. attending such a meeting goes something like this: It is illegal for any of our government officials to accept anything of value from a foreign government, or a representative of a foreign government. Jeez, receiving helpful information from a foreign entity is of such "value" that it is illegal? And in a country that prides itself on its freedoms? And how was Trump Jr. a government official during the election?

A second argument goes something like this: It would have been acceptable for Mr. Trump or one of his representatives to meet with representatives of a friendly nation, like Great Britain or Australia or Sweden or Canada, but it was not acceptable for any of them to meet with an enemy nation like Russia. It's okay if my friends pass me helpful information but not if my enemies do? What balderdash! I'll take helpful information anywhere I can get it. Besides, I doubt very much that any government official would reject helpful information from <u>any</u> source. If they would, then I don't think they should hold their jobs after being found out. There is no doubt in my mind that we humans learn much more from those with whom we disagree than from those we agree with 100%. Just close your eyes and imagine a round table at which eight people sit. They are talking about one subject, Russian interference in the recent American election. Each one explains why President Trump colluded in the interference. No one denies it. They all say the same thing: Russia tried to get Trump elected, not Hillary. They all use the same exact argument. They all use the same words. Then each one repeats exactly what he said the first time. And so on. What does it sound like? To me it sounds like television news about President Trump and Russian interference in the 2016 election.

But let's get back to the real essence of the self-righteous indignation (or should I say "political indignation"?) that led to first the Trump and then the Trump family investigation in the first place. It was the supposed interference of the Russians in our election process. It was the belief that the Russians had interfered in order to help Trump and hinder Hillary. At least it was framed that way by many Democrats, and not a few Republicans were indignant that Russia would have the "evil" nerve to interfere in such an inherent and important American process. Of course nobody, that I can recall offhand, offered any solid proof that the Russians did actually interfere, and on Hillary's side. There was lots of innuendo and finger-pointing, but any substantiating facts were conspicuously absent, although the scramble still goes on today to find President Trump and family guilty. However, I recently read a more substantive article that points the finger in another direction: that Russia really did try to interfere in our presidential election, but not necessarily to get Trump elected. Rather its purpose was to instill in us, the American people, doubt about the inviolability and integrity of our election process, although even in the article there are a couple references to the "possibility" that Putin did want to help Trump—or is that possibility actually no more than hope. And there is a kind of sloughing over of one of President Obama's red lines.

The above article was published in the July 20, 2017 issue of *Time* and is entitled "Inside the Secret Plan to Stop Vladimir Putin's U. S Election Plot." It can also be found on the internet. I found it an interesting and somewhat refreshing article as articles on Russian interference in our 2016 presidential election go, interesting because it contains both factual data and logical insights into both Russian hacking and our governmental and political reaction to the same and to the election process itself. However, it does not offer incontrovertible proof that is was the Russians doing the hacking.

Lacking in the article is the self-righteous indignation so inherent in many of the articles and television panel discussions I've come across over the past months. I found that quite refreshing. Why? Because we Americans have no moral right to get indignant about another country interfering with our elections. I'm not saying that we have no right to fight back, only that our indignation is hypocritical.

According to *The American Spectator*, June 14, 2017, while a US Senator Obama "illegally used a taxpayer-financed trip to campaign for far-left presidential candidate Raila Odinga in Kenya's 2006 elections." Odinga was a distant relative of Obama.

Later, as President, Obama transferred millions to Odinga's government and ultimately caused hundreds of millions to go to the same place. In the 2015 Israeli elections, the Obama administration "funneled State Department grants "to opposition groups in an attempt to defeat Netanyahu. Other countries in whose elections Obama intervened are Macedonia, Libya, Honduras, and Egypt.

Moreover, according to an article by Nina Agrawal in the *Los Angeles Times* of December 21, 2016, the "U.S. has a long history of attempting to influence presidential elections in other countries—it's done so as many as 81 times between 1946 and 2010, according to database amassed by political scientist Dov Levin of Carnegie Mellon University." I might add that we also have a long history of simply interfering with other countries' inner workings. We separated Panama from Colombia in order to more easily build the Panama Canal. We took most of our Southwest from Mexico. We took Cuba, Puerto Rico, and the Philippines from Spain in our war with Spain. We have sent armies to a number of Spanish American and Caribbean countries, like Grenada. We have been responsible for regime change in countries like Chile and Nicaragua. And of course we tried and failed in Cuba, at the Bay of Pigs. It seems to me kind of naïve for us to ignore that our CIA is often involved in trying to bring about regime change in other countries or that some, if not a lot, of our foreign aid goes to opposition groups in countries whose ruling regimes we wish to depose.

In this context, as far as I am concerned, to persecute the Trump family for talking to Russians is simply political chicanery and part of the political and ideological "Resistance" to the American President. After all, he is President. His success or failure is America's success or failure. So, I say to the Democrats and others, please stop the obstructionism and the concentration on something so irrelevant. Let's get to the things that are important to the country: the economy, jobs, illegal immigration, our infrastructure, and the problem of polarization in our politics (and among the people).

71

Trump

In some ways many Democrats are right. Donald Trump has startled a lot of people in a negative way. But he has turned on just as many, according to the vote, especially blue collar workers and people who don't live in the "wealthy" coastal states, and people who want us to return to the economically sound country we were before all the "outsourcing" to foreign countries and all the lousy trade deals (like NAFTA) destroyed our manufacturing base. I've just finished reading a book entitled American Hunger. I'd like to quote a sentence from it: "The government food stamp program has tripled in size during the last decade, growing to serve 47 million Americans at a cost of nearly $80 billion each year." I don't know the detailed history of the food stamp program before the last decade, but its growth during Obama's reign is pretty startling, to say the least. 47 million? That's about one sixth of our population. If you add in us old codgers who aren't working? And all the children? And the women (and some men nowadays) who are stay-at-home moms (or dads)? That doesn't leave much of a work force, in percentages. It's the kind of situation that leads to economic disaster like Greece's. It's the kind of situation that leads to deep anger and frustration among the poor and lower middle classes, even a lot of those who are on the dole—those forced onto the dole anyway. All I hope is that Trump changes the trajectory, as he has promised to. If he doesn't...I shudder at the thought of what kind of life my grandchildren will have.

Obama, like Trump, turned off a lot of people during his two runs for the presidency. The Republicans shouted and moaned about his terrible lack of any experience in managing anything larger than a family budget, let alone a government the size of the USA (Trump, after all, has built and managed a multi-billion dollar, international company). They growled about the tax dodgers he appointed to important government positions. They loudly doubted his citizenship and his academic credentials. That's par for the course, I believe, the finger pointing from the Dems and Reps at a new president, although it seems to have gotten a lot worse since the press joined the "biased" fray on one side or the other, and since they started delving deep into the personal lives of presidential candidates. What is happening, it seems to me, is that our country is polarizing. Obama promised to bring us together. But he actually separated us even more than we were. Now Trump is promising the same thing, but from the sounds of all the people still trying to keep him from assuming office in January, we are just as divided as we were, if not considerably more so. What really bothers me about all this is that most people want to lay the blame (for everything bad?) on the other side. Nobody wants to accept any of the blame. Yet, as far as I am concerned, Bill Clinton, the Bushes, and Obama, and other previous presidents are all to blame for our economic plight, as are both the Democratic and Republican parties, and as is Congress. Clinton was the first president to take the Democratic Party away from its blue collar base and over to Wall Street. Of course he, and Hillary as well, still pretend that they are one hundred percent for the worker, which more and more workers don't believe any more.

I believe Obama also promised that his administration would be one of the most transparent ever. Well...no need to delve deeper into that. I think he made most of his deals on the golf course (just kidding, somewhat). I think Trump has been criticized even more by the Democrats than Obama was by the Republicans, and considerably more nastily. As for his cheating on taxes, he can't help it if the government has opened so many tax loopholes for the wealthy; he wouldn't be much of a wheeler/dealer, a doer, if he didn't take advantage of them. I know I don't pay any more taxes than the law requires, and I don't really consider myself a tax cheat. I don't know about his deferments for the Vietnam War, as has been alleged, but there hasn't been a war since WWII that I would have gone willingly to. Who wants to go fight a war in which we don't have the will to win? Korea is still divided. Vietnam is ruled by the North (Hanoi). For how many years have we been fighting in the Middle East, without resolving anything? I mean, in Korea we let the North and China bluff us out. In Vietnam we were afraid to blockade Hanoi's harbor, and to destroy Hanoi if necessary. And in the Middle East we are doing the same thing—fighting with fear of world opinion riding on our shoulder. Oh where is another Harry Truman, who knew, like FDR before him, that you don't defeat a nation by defeating its army or killing its leaders? The nation can simply raise another army. Other leaders can replace those lost. You defeat a nation by destroying the will of the people to support the army any more. FDR and Churchill must have known that, as suggested by their bombing of German cities. I suspect that that was one of the reasons for the destruction of Hiroshima and Nagasaki. And, I might add, Bashar Assad and the Russians fighting at his side definitely know that. If America and its allies would get out of the way, that civil war would be over quickly, which would save a lot of lives and bring peace to the region—a dictatorial peace, but peace nevertheless.

As for Trump cheating on his wives, as I maintained with Bill Clinton's sexual escapades, that is a matter between The Donald and those very wives. I don't think Clinton was any more or less of a president because he cheated on Hillary; the Starr Commission was a terrible and vindictive waste of taxpayer money and government time. I would say the same thing about FDR, Ike, Jefferson, and any other president who couldn't keep his do-floppy in his pants. I've never been wealthy or powerful, but I suspect that there are a lot of women strongly attracted to men of power or wealth, and men, sexually normal men, are like Adam, more susceptible to the wiles of women than not. If that's not a main characteristic of human nature, I don't know what is.

As for Trump's intelligence and knowledge, no man who has done what he has can be stupid, like some people insist. Moreover I doubt that he has developed his multi-billion dollar business without being an excellent listener and without knowing how to attract capable people to his side. Witness the people he is selecting for his cabinet. I don't agree with all his choices (I think here should be more manufacturers) but I have to admit that, if the press is right, they are all pretty capable people, people who express many of the general attitudes that Trump himself has expressed in his run for the presidency, which is the kind of people presidents usually gather around them. And I really doubt that he cares what others expect of him over the next four years. He has said what he is going to do. The people elected him supposedly to do what he said he was going to do. So he knows what he is expected to do—what he wants to do, if he has been truthful (which most politicians are not, including Obama). Me, I don't expect him to be some kind of self-effacing diplomat like his predecessor. I want another Harry Truman. You know, a man who says what he thinks and does what he says. The problem I have with Trump is that he is already starting to make compromises. But, then, that is what democracy is all about. That is one of the main characteristics I have been looking for in a president for decades—pragmatism. I say out with ideologues, in with pragmatists; up with good old American pragmatism. It has been a long time. It has been a long time since compromise has been one of the key ingredients of our government. About time it returned from the dark, I say, even if I don't think I could be a friend of the man bringing it back. Our personalities would clash. But then, nobody asked me to run for the presidency. It would really be a laugh if they had.

72

UCLA Ballplayers in China

What the heck is going on here? A person holding one of the most powerful positions in the world, President of the United States, is in a spitting contest with someone as insignificant as this Ball fellow. I find the whole thing very childish and idiotic. President Trump should know better. He should be above such childishness. After all, he has had the ability to turn a few million dollars into a few billion. He has raised some really capable children. He has a very attractive and apparently capable wife. And he has become the president of the United States and begun to make some inroads into resolving some of our country's major problems in spite of not only the "resistance" of the Democratic Party but also that of many in his own party, the Republican Party. I cannot understand why he would let himself become embroiled in such a petty faceoff with such a petty person as Ball—I can't recall Ball's first name and am not interested in checking it out.

Part of the problem is, of course, the President's. It was noble and bighearted of him to speak to the president of China about the three members of the UCLA basketball team who committed an act of shoplifting while in China. Without that short discussion on his part, the three ball players might well have wound up in a Chinese jail. After all, the sentence for the crime they committed was three to ten years, I believe. It was also decent of the president of China to look into the situation. I have little doubt that he was the reason that the three shoplifters were set free to return to the United States.

Of course, I don't know for certain that a Chinese judge would have sent the three shoplifters to jail. The three were foreigners, after all, and

271

they were guests of China; they were basketball players and China enjoys its basketball just as does the United States. And they are still teenagers. All of this might have led to some kind of clemency for the three. But it might not have, also. No one probably knows for certain, least of all the self-centered father of the Ball kid, a father who didn't even have the grace to thank our president for his attempt to help the man's child. That I find verging on the nasty. But then, the Ball father showed very little grace during the year his oldest son played at UCLA, last academic year. And from what I read, he, the father, is about as self-centered as they come, self-centered and nasty to anyone who doesn't cater to him and his three boys. I wonder what it must have been like for his sons to be raised by such a father. They are definitely good ballplayers, although the oldest is not yet doing so well in the pros—because he turned pro after only one year of college, too young and unseasoned? But how is the three sons' self-esteem off the court, I wonder. Or did their father develop in them the same egotism he himself has?

Be that as it may, I still find it unsettling that the president of the United States would stoop to exchange insults with such as insignificant person as what's-his-name Ball. But then, President Trump seems to have a very thin skin, and maybe a fairly large ego inflated by his great successes in life. He involves himself in such silly controversies sometimes, with his continuous tweets, and often causes gossip, rumors, and problems where none really existed previous to one of his tweets.

I'm not saying that President Trump should be "presidential," whatever that means, but only that he shouldn't instigate controversy where, without one of his tweets, none would exist except in the imagination of the Trump haters and bashers. He should try not to give them any fodder for their "basher mills" except what they can invent on their own. Lord knows, fanatics can usually come up with enough trash on their own.

Wall

A wall between the good old USA and Mexico, all the way from the Pacific Ocean to the Gulf of Mexico—what do I think of that?

In some ways I think it is a necessity. In other ways I think it is simply a waste of money. Where there are border cities, especially where the border cities overlap both sides of the border, like Mexicali and Calexico, Tijuana and San Diego, or Nogales (Mexico and USA), of course there should be a fence to separate the two parts of "the city," as there already is, separating the part on the USA side and the part on the Mexican side. Without a fence, trying to enforce national laws would be ludicrous, either in the courts or on the streets, and, as far as I am concerned, enforcing the laws of each country would include not only the laws of tourism and visitation for other reasons (like work, business and study) but also the laws of immigration. No fence, no barrier except like the mental barrier (and signs) one encounters when traveling, say, from Arizona into Utah, or Indiana into Illinois, would result in pure anarchy. One of the two governments involved would have to cede control to the other. The only other alternative would be war, or the two governments simply allowing the area under consideration to form whatever it might out of the political and legal and social chaos, no matter what the consequences (the outcome).

I would also advocate non-scalable fences in all areas of heavy population "near" the border and in areas where highways and other easily used US roadways come within a few miles of the border, as well as in areas where the terrain lends itself to the easy movement of drugs and illegal immigrants. As for other areas, where roads are not easily available and the terrain makes covert passage difficult and dangerous, I would beef up the border patrol and technological devices in these areas, devices designed to pinpoint human or mechanical movement.

All in all, though, I doubt very much that we can stop all illegal immigration into our country by these methods, and I don't know but what much if not all of the above is already in force, but I think to expand a fence and any other border protection methods beyond what I have mentioned would be a waste of money.

Illegal immigrants will continue to enter our country…nay, pour into our country…as long as they live in dire poverty and danger south of our borders and elsewhere, and as long as there are jobs and/or government help available here—as long as hope for a much better life and sanctuary await them here in the USA, for as long as they believe that our arms are open to them. Why would they not?

The problem is that you can't cure a cancer by only treating the symptoms. You can't mend a broken bone by only using pain medicine. You must attack the cancer at its source. You must set the broken bone and keep it stable until it mends.

In the case of illegal immigration, we cannot always attack the problem at the source of its beginning. We cannot go down to Mexico and root out all the drug cartel problems. We cannot go down to El Salvador and destroy all the gangs that make life so terribly dangerous for the law-abiding citizens. We cannot go down to those countries and turn them into such peaceful and thriving economic countries that their citizens can and will remain there and prosper. We have a tough enough time doing such in our own country.

So, we can't do that and, as far as I am concerned, an inclusive border fence, an expanded border patrol, and technological devises will not solve our problem. So what should we do? We should attack the problem at its American source, at its destination—jobs and government aid in the USA.

But first let's talk about all the illegal immigrants already in our country. How many are there, really? Of course there were all those who were occasionally granted asylum during the last half of the 20th century. Then, from what I read, there was a huge surge in our illegal population during the decade of the 1990s, from over three million to over twelve million. Then a slight decline set in, supposedly. Julia Preston, in an article in the *New York Times*, September 23, 2013, said that about "11.7 million immigrants are living in the United States illegally…" but that the number might be on the rise again, according to the Pew Research Center, although that is not actually conclusive.

However, the Research Director at the Center for Immigration Studies, Steven A. Camarota, in June 2016, wrote that an "analysis of new government data…shows more than three million new legal and illegal immigrants settled in the United States in 2014 and 2015, a 39 percent increase over the prior two years." He further said that about 1.1 million of those were illegals, which was an increase from 700,000 in the preceding two years.

So, you can blame the rise and fall of illegal immigration on the government or specific politicians, or on the economy and the general social attitude, or on the lack of an inclusive fence, but I think the only logical solution is as follows: 1) Reinstitute something like the Bracero Program with work visas for those who join the program; 2) Make it illegal, with stiff and enforced penalties, even with respect to those illegals already here, to hire illegal immigrants unless the immigrants have proof that they belong to the program (i.e., have work visas); 3) Determine with the appropriate government departments just which labor areas in the country cannot staff their labor force with legal residents; 4) Make all people in this country illegally sign on to the program or face deportation; 5) Make sure that those here on work visas do not begin taking jobs from our actual citizens; 6) Deport any illegal immigrant who commits a felony; 7) Enforce all the above; otherwise, this would simply be another program of futility.

74

War

So, we bombed a Syrian airfield, destroying a lot of the machines and buildings but leaving the runways intact. I understand why we sent the missiles—to let Assad know that we wouldn't put up with him using chemical weapons on his own people. I'm not sure I agree with what we did and the reason for it, and I'm not sure that the bombing will be all that effective. But it was the President's decision and I for one am glad we have a person in the White House who is willing to make tough decisions, whether I agree with them or not.

I do think, however, that it was a more rational decision than the one President Bush made to invade Iraq. It was more on the order of President Reagan's decision to bomb Gaddafi's palace. Gaddafi became considerably less antagonistic after that bombing. So Reagan silenced a belligerent and potential antagonist before that man got out of control, silenced him by showing him that he, personally, <u>was</u> vulnerable. The message President Trump sent was not quite as personal and direct, and will not silence Assad's weapons of war, I don't think. But they might keep the dictator from continuing his use of chemical weapons. We'll see.

My problem here is not so much with the potential outcome or the method. It is with the reason for the bombing and desired outcome. And even more so, it is with our national attitude toward war in general, if the attitude I see in many of our leaders, in Washington and in state capitals, really does reflect the general public attitude.

We have not had a war within our national borders since the mid nineteenth century, since our Civil War. We have not had a major war to fight since WWII. I think that we as a people have forgotten what war is all about, so much so that we sometimes seem to treat it like a game, a game with "humane" rules, and "moral" referees, and kudos for the waging of "civilized" warfare (i.e., sportsmanship). Of course there are the Geneva Convention and the United Nations. And there is world opinion.

And then there is war. We didn't win World War II by following "humanitarian" rules of conduct. If we had, we would now be speaking German or Japanese, at least in our schools, if not in our homes. We won WWII by our armies defeating the armies of the Axis Powers. Yes. But even more importantly, we won by bombing German factories, by destroying their war effort, even when they were placed in civilian neighborhoods, no matter the cost in lives of women, children, and older people. We also won WWII by firebombing German cities, killing multitudes of "innocent" civilians and destroying their will to continue supporting the war.

I wonder if our present military and civilian leaders would have the guts to do the same, if we somehow got involved in WWIII. I kind of doubt it. But who really knows.

We also blasted Japanese cities from the air, as we had done in Germany, but the Japanese did not surrender. So, knowing that multitudes of people (American military and both Japanese military and civilian) would die if we invaded Japan, we dropped two atomic bombs on two Japanese cities. The decision to do so came from no other than President Harry Truman. Some people nowadays call him a war criminal. I call him a true American hero. Why? Well, as far as I'm concerned there is only one purpose, one aim, in a war and that is to win, unconditionally and at all costs. And that is done by winning as many battles as possible, killing as many enemy soldiers as possible, and, most importantly, destroying the will of the enemy, military and civilian leaders and the general population, to continue to wage war. And that means that many civilians will have to die. Furthermore, there is always one major question that is very difficult to answer: How many more people might have died if we had not bombed German and Japanese cities and had allowed the war to go on and on for another five, ten, or more years? How many more Jews and people from other European countries?

How many non-Japanese Asians and peoples of the Pacific islands? How many more Germans and Japanese and Americans?

Since that time we seem to have lost our appetite for waging all-out war. We allowed the Korean peninsula to be split between north and south, and look at the cost in military aid and antagonism with the North. We fled Vietnam with our tail between our legs, and after a few years of purging the north and south have become united. We invaded Iraq and deposed a tyrant, which led to a prolonged struggle with Al Qaeda, and probably to our present war with ISIS, and maybe to the Arab Spring and the rise of all these Muslim extremist groups in the Mideast and elsewhere. Would we be better off to leave and let them solve their own problems?

One of the worst things about the Atomic Age is that we have the ability to destroy cities and kill thousands of people with just a bomb or two. A major outcome of the above is that, even though many countries have weapons of mass destruction, no one is willing to use them except as deterrents. This, I believe, has resulted in the world having many regional wars, wars in which the super powers (the US and Russia) may or may not become involved. Other questions I often ask myself are the following: Would the occasional use of nuclear weapons reduce the death, starvation and general suffering that so many local wars have produced? Or would it simply increase such many times over?

I haven't the slightest idea how to answer such questions. But I can't believe that allowing a war to go on and on does not add greatly to the death, starvation and suffering in the war zone. I cannot believe that we have not helped cause a lot of unnecessary death and suffering in Syria because of our insistence that Assad use only conventional weapons and not destroy civilian neighborhoods. Just think of all the Syrians that have fled Syria, some dying in the flight, many others suffering from lack of food and amenities in camps. And the innocents left behind in Syria to suffer through year after year of war? I sometimes ask myself if it wouldn't be more humane to let Assad do what he needs to do to win the civil war and return his country to peace once again. We might have another South Korea. Or we might have another North Korea or Cambodia or East Germany. But would fewer people suffer and die over the long haul?

75

War 2

A couple of blogs ago I talked about war, using our attack on the Syrian airfield as a starting point. I also said that I am glad that we have a decisive president in Trump, even though I don't always agree with his agenda. The attack on the Syrian airfield didn't lead to any further hostilities on our part, but it has led to Russia flexing its muscles by sending its bombers into our Alaskan coastal waters. I don't know whether the bombers are a face-saving gesture by Putin, whether he is actually trying to provoke us into some kind of hostile act, or whether he is trying to find out what kind of a leader Trump actually is? I do know that sending the planes so close to our shores is kind of scary, and stupid, unless Putin really does want to start a war.

Of course, Syria doesn't present any kind of a threat to us or our allies. Nor do I think Russia does, although there could be a bumble by one of the Russian pilots, or by one of the American pilots sent up to intercept the bombers, that leads our two nations into a physical confrontation. Or, more likely, a war between us and Russia might start in Syria.

We want to get rid of Assad as Syria's leader. I understand why. He's a nasty kind of person. But he seems to understand more about war than we do. It isn't a game with rules derived from sportsmanship and humaneness. You either win or you lose. If you win, you not only get to decide the future of the conquered, but you get to decide the history of the war and how, in the future, it will be remembered. If you lose…well, to the victor belong the spoils. The other guy gets to decide your future. Besides, I really think it's silly of us to insist so strongly that Assad has to go. We are partially to blame for the problems in Syria, Libya, Egypt, Iraq and other Mid-eastern countries. By our meddling (and our ouster of Saddam Hussein)…our <u>inconsistent</u> meddling, I might add, we are to a great extent responsible for the Arab Spring and the many rebel groups like ISIS that it has brought to the fore. Our meddling has also got us embedded in a war that seems to have no end, unless, of course, we decide to use all we have to destroy the enemy, which might just bring us into more confrontation with Russia.

I don't really think we will do that, though. We haven't used all our might to destroy an enemy since World War II. We gave up in Vietnam, saying we just couldn't win the war, when we all know that we had the bombs and ships to destroy Hanoi and all its military bases, and to blockade the city's harbor. What we didn't have was the will. We had the might. We did not have the political will.

And then there's North Korea. We allowed the Koreas to be split by giving up on the Korean War, backing off of a full-out commitment to destroying the North and uniting the country. Now look what we have. We have a North Korean government that is not only developing nuclear bombs but also trying to develop long-range missiles that can reach the USA. We have a North Korean government that is threatening South Korea and Japan. We have a North Korean government that is antagonistic to the USA and could care less about the sanctions imposed upon it by us or the United Nations. And, I might add, we have a North Korean government that is led by a man who acts like a spoiled brat who doesn't have much sense and whose ego has elephantiasis.

Me, I'm not an isolationist, I don't believe, but what I do believe is that we need to quit meddling in the interior affairs of other governments. We need to quit playing world policeman. And we need to use our military might only when our interests or our closest allies are threatened. And last, we need to let our allies develop whatever weapons they think are necessary to protect themselves, nuclear weapons included. After all, in the case of nuclear weapons, there is no way we can keep countries who truly want such weapons from developing them.

76

War or Peace

War or peace? That is the problem (or question?), the either/or problem that has probably haunted us humans forever and will doubtlessly continue to haunt us until we sprout wings and halos and the civilizations we create become settlements in heaven.

The rise and fall of civilizations—another problem we humans seem not to be able to solve. We have no problem building civilizations. Lord knows, we've built enough of them. But we sure can't seem to keep any specific one around forever, or even for a millennium or two. Not thus far in human history anyway.

Why? I ask myself, why? The historians, of course, have given us any number of answers to the question, from the rise of a new barbarian horde just waiting for the right leader to lead their invasion; to the slow corruption and decay of both the civilized governments themselves and the will of the people to remain loyal to those very governments and nations over the centuries; and on to the immigration of "foreigners" into those civilizations in search of a better, safer life, "foreigners" whose "basic, unconscious" loyalty is to the culture, nation, and/or religion they left behind (or rather, actually, took with them consciously or unconsciously) in their quest for a better life for their children and themselves, not to the nation, the culture, and often the religion to which they have immigrated.

There are lots of reasons, I suppose, why all our civilizations have declined or have been destroyed. I could talk about the reasons why the Spanish empire declined, or the Roman, or why Texas ultimately fought for freedom from Mexico, or why the USA now has in its essence a lot of land that was once Spanish territory and then Mexican territory before becoming part of the USA, and, of course, before becoming Spanish territory it was "Indian" territory, different "Indians" at various times, I expect.

I could, but there are a number of reasons why civilizations fall and nations change, sometimes drastically, and I expect that the reasons for the demise of each and every past civilization has some characteristics in common. I expect that one of the primary common reasons lies in human nature itself, in our inability to live at peace with each other for any extended period of time. Our civilizations are built by war and sacrifice, and then periods of relative peace because we are unable, as nations as well as individuals, to sustain wars for extensive periods of time, not only because of the high cost in lives and money, but even more importantly because of the emotional costs. So we move from peace to war to peace in a never-ending cycle.

Can we live at peace with each other for extensive periods of time? I don't think so, relatively speaking. Ever since the end of WWII there have been regional battles around the globe, some which we have been involved in, like the Korean War, the Vietnam War, Desert Storm, Operation Iraqi Freedom (still going on against other foes?), some of which we have not, at least overtly, like the Russian War in Afghanistan, the Chinese Civil War which ended with a communist takeover in 1949, La Violencia in Colombia, The Dirty War (1976-1983) in Argentina, the present Paraguayan People's Insurgency (2005-ongoing), the conflicts in Central America and the Caribbean and Africa, and so on, and on, and on.

Then, of course, we could take this all down to a personal level, from nations at war to individual violence, and consider what happens to personal relationships when there is or has recently been no war to cleanse the anger and frustrations from our souls. We could point to road rage, violent demonstrations in our streets, fathers and mothers killing their babies, interracial violence, dismissed employees returning to the workplace and going on a shooting spree, and, by all means, terrorism from the likes of Timothy McVeigh and Terry Nichols in Oklahoma City to our present-day terrorists, often Muslims, locally bred or not. The essence of the human soul has something violent buried deep down inside it, some hatred or anger or yearning for violence that erupts like a volcano after a long period of dormancy, after a period when no war has fed and pacified its explosive needs.

What do we do with individuals who commit acts of violence? In a democracy like ours we lock them up in prison, expecting that to be a deterrent for others who might opt for violence, either consciously or unconsciously. Does it (locking them up) work? I don't know. It definitely doesn't stop all the violence. How many people the legal threat of prison actually keeps on the straight and narrow, I doubt if there is any way of knowing.

Would an eye for an eye…would an instant and unchangeable death penalty for all murderers work? I doubt it, but I don't really <u>know</u>. I do really suspect, though, that the death penalty, if carried out at once, might just slow the carnage a little. As for nations, I believe the same.

I truly believe that wars are won, not by defeating armies, but by defeating peoples, by destroying the will, the emotional capability of one of the belligerents to carry on with the fight, to continue to suffer the financial sacrifice, the privation, the death and crippling of their young soldiers, and the destructive fear of those who have not yet lost a son or daughter to the war, but have one or two or more in the military or at an age when they will soon have to join up or be drafted. To win wars, I strongly believe, you have to go after the civilian population that supports the enemy war effort, whether that support is active or passive, like we did in WWII. But, many people will say, the fighting we are presently involved in in the Mideast is not like normal wars. Many of the people caught up in the area of battle are innocent. They are just as much victims of Muslim Extremism as we here in the USA are.

Many of our leaders insist that the fighting in the Middle East is not like the fighting of old, not like WWI or II, not even like the Korean or the Vietnamese Wars. I agree that it's definitely not like WWI and II. In those wars we clearly knew who our enemies were and went after them. We didn't avoid killing civilians who were in the way, especially in WWII—firebombing German cities and dropping atomic bombs on two Japanese cities. There are those today who might consider such acts as war crimes, especially the dropping of the two atomic bombs. I disagree. The above acts probably helped hasten the end of the fighting and so, in the long run, possibly saved lives and more suffering, even among the enemy.

But then after WWII we seemed to lose <u>our will</u> to win at any cost. We backed off and let Korea be divided between North and South, and look at the problem we have today. And in the Vietnamese War? Instead of waging all-out war to win, instead of bombing Hanoi and destroying its harbor, or even blockading the latter, or using the weapons of mass destruction at our disposal (which I am not here advocating), we put our tail between our legs and ran for home, leaving thousands of civilians in the region to either flee or be imprisoned or slaughtered. We did not have the stomach for a real war. It was really silly of us to get involved in the war in the first place, and then, worse, we let it become more of a political war than a real one, which was, in my view, the major reason that so many American military lives, and the lives of many South Vietnamese, were frittered away for little or nothing, in a war that meant so little to us as a nation.

And, I fear, the political inconsistency that defined our war with North Vietnam defines our war, our lingering, drawn-out war, in the Mideast. Of course it's a different type of war. The enemy is not so easy to ferret out or come to grips with as in normal warfare. However, it stands to reason that somebody is helping finance the ongoing war. We need to find out who these people, or companies, or nations are and go after them, not just financially, but with killing weapons, like President Reagan went after Gadaffi. We need to go after them and the leaders of ISIS not only as President Obama did, with drones, but also with everything else at our disposal, financial, cultural, or military, excluding at this point in time weapons of mass destruction. And we need to put an overwhelming army of troops on the battleground, enough to destroy the enemy no matter where they are and no matter how many civilians get hurt in the process. Otherwise we need to pack our bags, put our tails between our legs, and run for home. We cannot keep up the war we are engaged in, not for many more years. We do not have the will for such. So? We have to destroy the will of the enemy, soldiers and civilians alike (enemy sympathizers and neutrals), or we will eventually <u>lose our will</u> to continue the fight. The loss of will in Vietnam didn't cost us much as a nation, except in national prestige. But the North Vietnamese were not and are not a people who want to dominate the globe. ISIS and their forebears are. Can the free world, the Christian world, lose this war and still remain free for many, many years, and Christian?

77

What is Happening in Our Country

What is happening in our nation? Just the other day I saw a video on the internet in which two neighbors got into an argument (about what I don't know). One pulled a gun and started firing at the other one. The neighbor who was being fired at then pulled a gun and started firing back at the first one. What? Pulling a pistol and trying to kill a neighbor, or anyone, over an argument? It sounds a lot like the Wild West of fiction, like someone saying something that Billy the Kid doesn't like. So Billy says, "Draw!" And the fight is on whether the other man wants it or not. Personally I have a problem with all of this "hidden carry" thing. What with all the anger out there, all the road rage and family rage and gangs and drugs and terrorism—so many people are simply too ready to draw and shoot at the least little "imagined" insult or danger. Yet would the killings be worse if guns were illegal? Would that mean that only the "bad guys" would have guns and nobody else would be able to protect himself? Over the weekend of July 4th more than 100 people were shot in Chicago, and that city is supposedly a gun-free zone.

The sad thing, and yet the lucky thing, I guess, is that in the above "gunfight" between neighbors, only one was wounded. Sadly I don't even know which one—the one who fired first or the one who fired in self-defense. Is that a weakness in me? Do I care so little about people who get into gun fights that I easily forget who won and who lost, who got wounded and who didn't? Or do I even care at all unless they are family or among my friends and acquaintances. Am I becoming so immunized to the senseless killings taking place in my country that my moral or humane or whatever trigger that makes me a caring human being no longer functions very well.

Then (was it just yesterday?) I read where some woman, some illegal immigrant mom, stabbed to death her husband and four of their children, only a nine-year-old daughter surviving. And today there is a picture of this murder-mom in court smiling for the cameras and giving them a thumbs-up. The article with the picture says that she refused a lawyer, saying that the people were her lawyer. A person who destroys children, her own, thinks that "the people" will exonerate her? Is there something in our legal or cultural system that motivates such a belief?

That's a hell of a lot of confidence in the people, and the court system. But maybe she's right. Our court system, as well as our culture, has become somewhat more permissive in some ways and yet more hard line and arrogant in others, and not always in the way it should be in a world ruled by common sense and compassion, I think.

And then there's the young man who shot and killed a college girl because she wouldn't give way as they both exited a freeway. And the man who shot and killed the female cop just the other day, with no apparent reason except that he dislikes police officers. Well, there are lots of people in this world that I dislike, but if I attempted to destroy them all, I would have a few years of labor ahead of me and, moreover, doing such would make me either a nut case or a pretty nasty and arrogant individual, and definitely a lot worse human being than anyone I wanted to destroy. To destroy one person because that person belongs to a large group of people I dislike would make me some kind of evil, warped product of what our culture, and the world, has been spewing out over the past few decades?

And there's the G20 Summit. Let's see: protestors burning cars and trucks and buildings, protestors attacking police lines, protestors injuring 200 or more police officers while the latter are simply trying to keep the peace and keep people as safe as they can, some protestors advocating concerns over such as the environment and globalization but others seeming to be there for the sole purpose of disruption (attacking the police lines, trying to storm the building where the Summit is being held, robbing and burning stores). And, of course, we would be very upset if the police attacked these "demonstrators" with anything that might do them real damage, although we don't seem to get very upset at how many police officers get hurt.

We human creatures are, primarily, a selfish bunch. Our first instinct is for self-preservation. When threatened we protect ourselves, through flight or fight or whatever other means we find necessary at the time. But we are not just instinctual creatures, nor are we completely selfish. We are loyal to family, friends, community, nation, and our God. We can remember the past, in one form or another. We think about the future. We assess the present in terms of both past and future. We care for family and friends. We protect and nourish our children as they grow into adulthood. We protect our spouses. We have ambitions and desires and plans for the future.

And, of utmost importance for our civilization, in the present and the future, we are mostly loyal to our nation and are often willing to give our lives so that it may continue to exist and thrive.

And no nation, that I recall, survived and thrived without a military, to protect it from outside dangers, and a police force, to protect it from inside dangers. We ask a lot of both. And to both we owe a lot. Yet we do a lot of quibbling before paying our debt to either or before strengthening laws that will better protect either or both groups.

From what I read, as of July 5 of this year 68 police officers died from duty-related problems ranging all the way from sicknesses they contacted on the job to vehicular assault. Of those 68, 25 died from being shot. Last year (2016) 145 police officers died from duty-related problems, 63 of those by gunfire.

According to the National Law Enforcement Officers Memorial Fund, "gun-related deaths have risen by 9 percent" over this time last year. They further say that "50,000 law enforcement officers were assaulted" in 2016, assaults which ran "the gamut from pushing officers to shooting them and causing disabling injuries."

I know that there are probably rotten police officers. I expect that such is true of all professions, from politicians and lawyer and teachers to plumbers and electricians. In all working groups there is probably a small percentage that are outstanding in their job and another small percentage that are lousy. And the majority? Average to decent, I expect. That is true of judges as well as legislators. If a judge makes a mistake and sentences an innocent person to jail or, worse, death, and we find out about it weeks or months or years later, we don't try the judge in court and sentence him to prison or worse. If one of our elected legislators proposes and gets passed a bill that destroys lots of people, financially or socially, or maybe even takes some lives, we don't demand that the legislator be tried and thrown in jail. I could say the same thing about businessmen, firemen, anybody who works in a job that can cause destruction of any type. Yet we do so for our police officers. They have to make split-second decisions. In today's violent social climate, they must be on edge, nervous, a lot of the time, even when they do something supposedly as non-dangerous as stopping a car for speeding. And, in many cases, because of the anger and even rage of the people they (the police) confront, the anger and nastiness that most police officers face weekly if not daily, their emotions, and fear, must be riding on their sleeves. And then one does something he/she shouldn't have.

And many segments of the public demand that this officer be thrown in jail or condemned to death.

My feeling: The only difference between the police officer and all the rest of us who make mistakes, simply because we are human, is that his/hers is much more apt to cause physical harm or death, oftentimes his/her own. That's the essence of the job. However, I do not believe that accidents, even emotional failures, should be punished by imprisonment or worse. People who spend their daily work time protecting the rest of us should be allowed a lot of leeway. Otherwise they (the police) might begin to lose that drive, that emotional drive which makes them want to serve and protect the rest of us. Moreover, honestly, we cannot expect other human beings like ourselves (the police) to put themselves in harm's way day after day while <u>living with the fear that any mistake will be punished in the courts</u>. To do so is asking way too much of a human being. It is also endangering, maybe even slowly destroying, one of the groups of people most essential for the survival of our nation, the police. Without them, without their service and loyalty and continued effort to serve and protect, we live in anarchy.

78

White Privelege

White privilege? How many times have I heard those exact words, or something similar, over the years? The most recent group to spout them is Black Lives Matter? The insistence on those very words, and the anger when some person has the nerve to say that all lives matter, suggests that many blacks believe that for whites in general, not just those whites in blue, black lives are not as important as white lives and, thus, even in life and death matters, white privilege holds supreme.

Me, I have to agree, at least to a general extent, with the idea that many whites would consider white lives more important than black lives. I believe that most blacks would feel that black lives are more important than white lives. I have no doubts that most people of any race, way down deep, would be more moved by the loss of an unknown person of their own race than that of an unknown person of another race. That seems to me to be logical. We tend, I believe, to be more emotionally connected to the familiar than to the less familiar. Most of us would be more upset by the loss of a family member or a close friend than by the loss of a neighbor with whom we had only an occasional interplay, maybe an occasional brief talk while we were both working out in the yard, or maybe a more extended conversation when we happened to run into each other at a local park or movie theater or restaurant. Most of us would be more upset at the loss of our own child than at the loss of a neighbor's child, or of a sibling's child, or of a cousin's child. I would consider that human nature.

So, white privilege? I don't doubt there's some of that out there. What can one expect in a country in which whites outnumber minority groups? However, I don't think white privilege holds true in all cases. I recall teaching in the Imperial Valley of California back in the 60s. One ability was in high demand in the valley, in many jobs that required dealing with the public. That was the ability to speak both English and Spanish. In other words, being bilingual was an advantage when applying for many positions. And, of course, the vast majority of bilinguals were of Hispanic descent. Being Hispanic certainly did not mean that one was not "white" in the actual sense of how we tend to use the word but it usually did, I expect, in the cultural sense and, I further expect, in the majority of cases of bilingualism, again because of cultural norms rather than reality, and because of the Moorish occupation of Spain for a number of centuries and because of the mingling of Spaniards with the natives of the New World.

Later, after I returned to the university to complete my PhD studies, I again ran into a situation in which hiring preference was not given to white males, but rather to minorities and women. This was back in the very early 70s. I finished my PhD studies and set out to find a college teaching position. At that time I had a wife and two little children to support. I sent out over 700 letters of inquiry around the continental USA. I did not keep track of how many, but I received many rejections simply, as stated in the rejection letters, because the college I had applied to was looking for a minority member or a female. They were pleasant letters, but they sure didn't assuage my worry about finding a job, which I might not have found if not for a lot of luck and some help from one of my ex-professors.

So, what does this all have to do with what many people of all ethnic groups consider a pervasive cultural tendency toward white privilege? Well, I attended school in the forties and graduated high school in 1952. I lived in a small town. There was only one black person I ever saw in that town and he lived a couple of miles out of town on a small farm. I played on the school basketball team. I only remember competing against one black kid in my four years playing. I passed newspapers and so had free passes to the four movie theaters in the small city twelve miles away. Needless to say, I went to lots of movies. I recall the black spectators all sitting in the balcony.

Nowadays, when I go to a movie, I see lots of black people, and other minorities, sitting anywhere in the theater, and using the same restrooms as the white people. When I watch a high school or college ball game, basketball, football, baseball, male or female, I usually see more black players than white players, or Hispanic players, or Asian-American players. Many of our highest paid professional athletes are black. When I turn on the television, I find programs with people of all races on them, on news programs as well as fiction programs. I see channels in Spanish and channels with all black casts in some of the fiction programs. I go onto university and college campuses and I see students, professors and administrative workers of all races, including the black race. And of course there is the ethnic quota system that many of our public higher education institutions have. Moreover, I recently had eye surgery to remove cataracts. My doctor and some of the nurses were black. My heart doctor is of Asian descent. I live in a neighborhood of mixed ethnic groups. The couple across the street (east) is of Hawaiian descent. The couple across the street (south) of them is from India. Just north of them is a Hispanic family, with an Anglo family north of them. To the north of us live three young people, a white woman, a white man, and a black man. Just north of them lives a Hispanic family and north of them another Anglo family. To our south live five young people, two of whom are black. And south of them is a family which, I believe, is Muslim. The whole neighborhood is mixed. When I go to the grocery (no matter which one of the three within two miles of us), I run into black customers and, in two of them, black employees. And then there are our educational system, our government, and our military, from the highest to the lowest levels. All you have to do is watch television awhile to see that there are quite a few blacks at all levels of those systems.

What I'm getting at here, I guess, is that for me, with my past, I find it a little irritating for blacks to complain a lot about White Privilege. In my mind, the relationship of the races has changed drastically in my lifetime. Are there still problems? Of course! Are some minorities hurt by racial problems? Of course! Are some whites also hurt by racial problems (like educational or job quota systems)? Of course! Are there still things that should be improved? Of course! But violent demonstrations and surly complaints tend to bring about negative reactions rather than positive ones. Our citizens of all races need to work within the system to bring about true equality. I believe that a lifetime of work and decency bring about more positive change than do sporadic, violent demonstrations or public complaints.

79

White Privelege 1

White Privilege? I read an article on the internet yesterday in which some white model was admitting (confessing? whining?) that she was only where she was, as a paid model, because she was white. My first reaction? Why doesn't she quit the job and get a less high paying one, a really menial one in fact, if she doesn't think she should be there simply because she's white? Or is it that she's only being a hypocrite? I believe it was Don Quixote who said that the Biblical Good Samaritan might have given his whole coat to the beggar if the season had been summer. I suspect that this model is something like the Good Samaritan, except she is just talking, just offering words, not actually giving or giving <u>up</u> anything. If she really wanted to do something rather than do nothing but pay lip service to a problem of inequality, she might spend her days at work carrying a sign that reads: "Fire me and hire a black model!" But I doubt if action rather than words ever entered her pretty head. Of course it's possible that she just wants to be liked and thought of as a very nice person, without any racism even in her sweat.

As far as this white privilege matter goes, it doesn't stand alone in the privilege category, not by a long shot. I'm not saying that there's no such thing as white privilege. Of course there is. There are many jobs for which Whites are much preferred over Blacks, most for business reasons, I suspect, some for racial reason doubtlessly, just as Blacks are probably preferred in all-black neighborhoods for jobs which require dealing with the public.

But let's go back to this privilege matter. It seems to me that I've run into this problem since I was a young tad growing up in a small town. I still recall my first day in the first grade; we didn't have kindergarten back then. I was ready, and really, really willing. I had learned my ABCs. I could count to 100. I was ready. And what happened. I was put in the back of the room and the teacher explained that the front rows were for the better students and, as the semester progressed, those who proved themselves would move up. Well, the thing is, I did not move up, the whole year, in spite of my being ready, able, and willing, with raised hand, to answer the questions she posed to the class, about homework or any other matter.

I never moved up. And it was only years later that I learned who those up in the front of the class really were. They were the privileged. They were children of the town's rich and powerful.

But learn I did, in various ways, that there is such a thing as wealth privilege. The wealthy can buy their way into the best schools, the best universities, and, of course, through that method and the good old boy system, which is as you know an integral part of that system, they can pave the way for their offspring to get a lot of privilege here and there, along their path into adulthood. And those of us who are born into poor families, we can only complain and hope that someday someone like the model above mentioned will come along and throw a sop our way. We can dream, of course, that the thrown object will be much more than a sop. <u>Or we can ourselves struggle our best to rise as far as we can and so, possibly, overcome some of that privilege.</u>

There's also the privilege of power. President Obama's daughters went to a private school during the eight years of his presidency, I believe, while President Trump's children have had the benefit of his wealth and now have the privilege of his power, which has helped them become power brokers also. Just think what all that power and wealth will do for President Trump's youngest son and his grandchildren. My question here, Should those grandchildren maybe throw over the privilege they have, admit that it is a "sin" to be so blessed, so lucky, and take up the medieval sackcloth instead? I doubt if they do and just hope that at least one of them transcends the upper limits that his/her grandfather has reached.

Privilege? Let's see. There is the privilege of race, of wealth, of power and, by all means, the privilege of birth, not only relative to race, wealth and power, but of nationality. I was born here in the good old USA, a democracy with lots of freedoms and relatively high economic levels. Should I apologize to all those people who weren't so lucky, poor people born in Venezuela or Bolivia, North Korea or Laos, Kenya or Chad, Iraq or Afghanistan? Should I maybe ask them if they want to trade places? I don't think so. I don't mind being lucky, or in having at least some privileges which help me get a step on the guy next to me.

I always thought that being competitive in life was taking advantage of what "privilege" you do have, whether that privilege is of place, race, social status, physical ability, laws, or whatever. I mean, we are not all born equal no matter what the Constitution says. Nor are we born with equal rights. The wealthy and powerful have more rights than do those in the middle class, and the latter have more rights than do those in the poorest class. It's pretty naïve to think otherwise. That downward progression also pertains to birth. Those born at the top of the social heap have more privileges than those below, and this pertains in descending order.

Of course there are exceptions. These are just generalizations. Some people are born much more intelligent than others, of whatever social class. Some people seem to be born with the knack of making money, others with an affinity for science at its most profound, others for politics at the highest levels. Their genetic "endowment" gives them a special "privilege" which many of us do not have, which is not to say that they don't have to work hard also. Should they apologize to us for this mental superiority which was none of their making? I doubt that they would think so, no more than I think the model I began this essay about should apologize for being white and beautiful. And she must be beautiful, which is a privilege not all women get to share. Does she think she should apologize for that? Or is she only worried about beautiful women and all the people of other races

I would like to end this "irritating" essay on the note of black privilege. We, meaning my country, are now and have been for some time in a phase of social engineering. One of the catch phrases of this is "diversity." Colleges and universities, businesses, government, and the media have been working on this for some time, to a greater or lesser degree, I must admit. And, of course, affirmative action is still in effect in many of our colleges and universities. I have to admit that I don't know a lot about affirmative action, but there seems little doubt that in many cases minorities with lesser academic standards are accepted as students ahead of better prepared Whites. That seems to me to be a privilege. And I have to ask myself if that privilege (preference) also holds true for federal and state monies which go to students, as grants or loans. If so, Blacks share in that privilege. And then there are the black athletes who are accepted to colleges and universities on the basis of their athletic prowess alone, to play football, baseball, basketball, or track, as of course are good white athletes. Their numbers compared to the number of white athletes in those sports, when the relative number of Whites and Blacks living in the country are taken into consideration, suggest that Blacks have some kind of genetic privilege here. One has to wonder, if Blacks began playing other college sports, like soccer and volleyball, would their superiority show there also? Or am I just imagining that it takes both genetic superiority and environmental determination to excel at most things. Oh well, God, government and society all grant privileges to some of us and not others. But I don't think I'd have the world any other way. It would be terribly boring if we all had the same physical and psychological "privileges." Just the idea of such reminds me of some kind of zombie movie.

World Policeman

I am sick and tired and sick and tired and sick and tired of people around the world depending on us to police their problems. I am sick and tired of our own people who insist that we need to police the world's problems, and what they really mean is that we want to superimpose our style of democracy on the world. I am sick and tired of us getting involved in wars around the world and then getting out of those wars before they are resolved, and so leaving our local allies to fend for themselves with the enemy. I am sick and tired of us thinking of ourselves as the world's policeman. policeman.

Police. That's the key word. Not soldier, but police. And what's our American image of a policeman? Definitely not that of a man or woman who goes out to fight the bad guys with all he's got, no matter how dirty, underhanded, rule-less he/she may be. Definitely not that of a man or woman who does anything, <u>anything</u>, to win—<u>anything</u>, no matter how destructive, unethical or immoral. Definitely not that of a man or woman who would use any weapon to win—hydrogen, atomic, poisonous: no matter the consequences in human destruction and cruelty as long as the only object is to win. Just think for a moment about what happens to many of our own policemen who will go to any lengths to stay alive in what they consider (at the moment, the dicey, scary moment) a life or death situation. Woe to those who judge incorrectly and shoot someone who just acted like he had a gun. Second-guessing by the news media and self-appointed social judges seems to be the final arbiter for many in such situations. You know, Saturday quarterbacking,

No, our idea of policing the world is definitely not soldierly or warlike. Even in war we insist that both sides follow all the Geneva and Hague and chemical and atomic Convention-like rules. We insist that our soldiers treat the enemy humanely, even when the enemy itself acts inhumanely. In other words, we tie our soldiers' hands much as we do those of the policemen inside our borders. Add to that the political bickering and back and forth that accompanies any war that lasts over a few months…and what do you have?

Let's see. We didn't have so many rules tying our hands during WWI and WWII, in spite of their length. And we won. Then came the Korean War. Our first political war, as I see it—meaning our first war fought not only on the front lines in Korea, but also in the political halls of Washington, D.C. When China entered the war, we stopped in our tracks, let North Korea go communist, and started pushing the South toward our brand of democracy. Korea is still divided. Then came the Vietnam War. Eventually our politicians decided that we could not win the war, so we tucked our tail between our legs and ran for home, leaving our allies in South Vietnam to their fate at the hands of the not-so-humane North, which still runs all of Vietnam. Our reasoning? We couldn't win the war, not in such unfriendly terrain. Of course, the apologists ignored our ability to blockade Hanoi harbor, or even completely destroy it if we so wished. After all, we did have plenty of bombers and bombs, and could have destroyed the harbor, or much of it, if we had had the desire, the will power, even without weapons of mass destruction. We also had plenty of atomic and hydrogen weapons to destroy the harbor, or Hanoi itself, if we had so wished. But we preferred to be humane and turn tail, I guess, leaving our allies in the area to their fate. That's being humane? Maybe to the enemy. But what about to our friends? And what about to all of our soldiers who spent time on the front lines? What did we do to their sense of self, of self-worth and psychological stability? And was Vietnam, and Korea before it, just one more bit of erosion of our national self-worth? Not to mention the same for our allies, nations who trust us to stand up for them, through thick and thin. Or is that trust eroding also?

And what about all the tens of thousands of American soldiers who died in the above two wars? And their families? Do they have the same sense of worth and national pride as did their predecessors in WWI and WWII, in spite of their loss? I doubt it. And what about all the Vietnamese and Korean soldiers and their families, and all the devastation of business and land in those two nations, and the displaced families and...?

I hate to say this, but I don't think we understand as a nation how the "humane" prolongation of war year after year leads to much more death and devastation than does a quick, vicious, even inhumane war. I think that our politicians and citizenry are too removed, geographically, from the real effects of war. I think they need to study the Syrian civil war, without pre-conceived attitudes. Every year, it seems, tens of thousands more Syrians die in that war.

Anyhow, some estimates put our financial cost for the Korean War at $15 billion and for the Vietnamese War at $584 billion. That, of course, probably doesn't take into account how much it has cost us to maintain a military presence in South Korea since the end of the fighting in, what, 1952 or 3.

Continuing this line of thinking about our world policeman role, *The Balance* estimates that the Iraq War (2003-2011) cost us $1.06 trillion. Reuters (March 14, 2013) raises that cost a little: "The U. S. war in Iraq has cost $1.7 trillion with an additional $490 billion in benefits owed to war veterans, expenses that could grow to more than $6 trillion over the next four decades counting interest...." On January 1, 2015, *Time* said about our wars in Iraq and Afghanistan that "A truer measure of the wars' total costs pegs them at between $4 trillion and $6 trillion. This fuller accounting includes 'long-term medical care and disability compensation for service members, veterans and families, military replenishment and economic costs" as pointed out in 2013 by the Harvard economist Linda Bilmes.

And then there's the following from the Mint Press News Desk: The US spends "over $150 billion annually on overseas military bases."

And yet, when most of the news media and our national politicians talk about foreign aid, they only talk about the $50 or $60 billion we spend annually on aid for health and economic reasons. They ignore the costs of our wars "of support" for our allies. They ignore the costs of our economic trade deals with such as China. Me, I agree with President Trump in his criticism of our deals with China and of such hopefully gone trade deals as NAFTA. And I wholeheartedly agree with what he supposedly said to Kevin Lemarque of *Reuters* (May 1, 2018): that we as a people are losing our interest in being the world's policeman because we are spending excessive amounts of money doing so. And, I might add, getting nowhere. The president supposedly further said that, instead of policing the world, "We want to police ourselves. We want to rebuild our country."

I say, we want to fix our deteriorating infrastructure. We want to help our own poor: our homeless, the hungry children of our slums and impoverished rural areas, our students burdened with debt, our economy's manufacturing base and our citizens who would love to service that base, our ecology and water systems, and the pollution of our land, lakes, streams, and oceans. Let others solve their own problems. We have enough of our own. We can't keep kicking those problems down the road for the next generation, and the next, and the next. We need to stand up and quit the continual bickering that goes on in Congress when someone tries to get something done.

YMCA

Somebody told me the other day at the Tempe Y that a Pennsylvania YMCA had dropped Fox News, CNN, and MSNBC from the television stations on its exercise machines. Startled, I asked him why. He said that too many people were arguing and even coming to blows because of disagreements about the news. That, it seemed to me, was just too childish to be true. So I checked. And sure enough, I found an article about that specific Pennsylvania Y, the Greater Scranton YMCA. They had dropped those three stations because of too many arguments almost turning into fights. Not only that, but I also learned that some YMCAs have not allowed those stations for a long time, for the same reason as above.

I thought oh well, if people of certain views can't speak at our universities without others shouting them down, and even worse, what should I expect in a gym? Then I thought about conversations I have overheard at the Y, in the fitness room while exercising or in the locker room while dressing. Most of the extended conversations that I recall have been about sports and sport figures, or have been a discussion by two colleagues about a work situation. Conversations about politics are usually brief with a comment, another comment, and then another comment or nothing. People who disagree with what has been said must hold their tongue. Even during the recent election process I can't recall any extended political discussions. If a comment was made about Trump or Hillary, any answering comment was usually in agreement. Any disagreement was usually abrupt, followed by silence or a change of subjects. There are exceptions, of course. There are several guys at the Y who belong to a discussion group led by one of the Y members. They meet one evening a week at a Starbucks, to discuss recent news items. (I also hear them at the Y occasionally discussing politics or some other news item.) I've attended their weekly meetings several times although the hour at which they meet is difficult for me. It's an interesting group and one in which all get to express their views about the subjects under discussion, often controversial and even volatile subjects. They express a wide range of views, mostly toward the left of center, yet they are always polite and listen to what others who disagree have to say.

All of these thoughts got me to thinking about my own past experiences. I come from a blue collar household. Nobody but me read anything except *True Romance* magazine and the Union news sheet, the latter my father's bible, the former read by one of my sisters. Any type of intellectual discussion simply did not exist in our family. As far as I was aware, the same was true of my friends and their families. My friends didn't talk about much of anything except ballgames, sports figures, movies, and movie stars, and, of course, girls and who was doing what to whom in our little town. I really doubt if they were much different from other kids, then and today. Every school probably has a few kids who like to discuss all kinds of subjects, but they are in a small minority, I expect.

In high school we didn't talk much about current events either. The subject matter of our history classes never reached into contemporary times. Even government class didn't often apply current events to analyses of government and the Constitution. That would have to wait for college classes, which, my being a "late bloomer," were quite some time in coming, and not really much different from the high school classes except in depth and amount of work required, and the more controversial figures and subjects we were faced with.

Then there were the Army years. No real difference. My fellow soldiers were only interested in drinking and chasing the female of the species. When they weren't talking about the latter, or our duties (work), the topics of conversation were ballgames and sports figures or movies and movies stars. Of course, once I wound up in Germany, travel, skiing jaunts, and, occasionally, Germany and the German people and where to go on our next weekend pass, or what a great time we had the previous weekend or night, were often added to the conversational mix. If some political or philosophical or artistic or literary topic did come up, it was there for a few moments and gone the next, a comment or two, agreement or disagreement, and the subject was complete.

On the other hand the Germans in the neighborhood bars or on the trains or on the ski slopes, during a moment of mutual rest, were always interested in talking about the United States, its daily life, its politics, the life of its famous people. The same was true of the people I met in other European countries that I visited on leave. And it was true in Mexico City, where I spent some time a few years after being discharged from the Army. People of other countries seem to be fascinated by the USA. I always wondered why we didn't have a similar interest in other countries, until I became a full-time student at university and later a professor of English and Spanish. Over those years I learned that there are Americans curious about the daily life and customs of other countries. But they are in the minority, even on college campuses. It slowly dawned on me over the years, dense as I am, that the same is probably true of the people of other countries. Those I met showed an interest in us. But that's probably why I met them. They were interested in me because I was American. Those who weren't interested in the USA doubtlessly avoided me and other Americans, or at least didn't try to make personal contact.

So, where am I going with all this rambling? The thing is that people avoid talking about controversial subjects. Politics, religion, sexuality, and other topics like abortion are not only controversial because of the emotional interest people invest in them, but they are volatile for the same reason, simply because what people believe in these subject areas defines the very essence of their life—their soul as they see it. To deny their beliefs is to negate what they have become over the years and what they have learned about life and the human experience. And that, of course, makes them more worthless in their own eyes. The only logical reaction to such negation is anger, the anger of self-defense or, maybe, self-preservation now and forever, as they see it.

You Know

You know, I get awfully tired of all the hype against the police, especially the hype that comes roaring out of the woodwork every time an officer kills someone he/she shouldn't have, a volatile roar that is easily combustible around the nation if the victim happens to be a black person, not so easily if the victim happens to be Native American, Asian American, or European American. It doesn't seem to matter to some people that it is the police officer who is putting his/her life on the line to keep the rest of us safe. We aren't out there putting our lives on the line to protect the police, or our neighbors, or other citizens. And I don't see any of us out there helping protect the police, nor do I see many of us out demonstrating to keep the police safe, nor even marching in their favor. They, the police, are the men and women out on the streets patrolling to keep us safe…us, the average citizens They protect us from the criminals of our society, those who would steal from us, molest our children, rape our daughters, murder us, our friends, our neighbors, or those other people who are related to us only as fellow citizens—the criminals put us all in danger, and they put the police in danger. Many of those police officers are our neighbors, neighbors trying to do their jobs as well as they can. Moreover those who would continuously denigrate the police, rightly or wrongly, put us all in danger. For they turn many of us who think with our emotions into police haters.

Even without a lot of police haters scattered around the nation (or any nation), it doesn't take much for a peaceful demonstration to turn into a violent, destructive mob, which is not the only way demonstrations cost us.

During any demonstration the police must take time from their normal jobs (protecting us) to protect the demonstrators, as well as to protect innocent citizens from those demonstrators who could turn unruly for one reason or another, which we all know happens often enough in demonstrations, spontaneous or not; we know this not only because we have seen it happen over and over throughout the years, but because emotion is the driving force which puts demonstrators on the streets in the first place, and it doesn't take much to turn an already emotional bunch of people into an unruly bunch of people, and then into a completely out-of-control mob.

So, who pays for the police to protect and try to control a pack of demonstrators filling our city streets? We the citizens of the city, the state, the nation do. Who else? We pay in two ways: financially through our taxes and through sacrificing our safety by means of a reduction in the number of police officers in our neighborhoods and through the exponential increase in the danger in the area of the demonstrations. And those of us who have a business in the area, where demonstrators turned uncontrollable, might just pay with our livelihood as well, might just lose everything, everything, because our business was not just robbed and vandalized, but vandalized and then set on fire. And our mortgage payment on our house, and our monthly payment on our car, depended on that business. Without it, overnight we have become paupers. But who pays the most? Well, of course, the police officers. Often they have to protect demonstrators who call them names, insult them, throw things at them—demonstrators who try to hurt them in any way possible, psychologically and physically. My question is, how do they live through it and still keep that short fuse from disappearing altogether. How do they keep from wading into that mass of demonstrators who spit and throw bottles and rocks at them—how do they keep from wading into that mob with truncheons and chains? How? All I can say is that I will never make a police officer. My fuse is way too short. I have a lot of admiration for those women and men in blue. It must take the temperament of a social worker as well as the valor of a soldier to be a perfect police officer, if there is such a being this side of heaven. But then how many of you people out there in my country are perfect, no matter what your job? Or lack of a job? Are there any Mother Theresas out there reading this? I doubt it. When most of us make a mistake, or blow up, it's no big deal. Mostly nobody gets killed or maimed or put in jail. Maybe we overcharge somebody. Maybe we send a shipment to the wrong address, possibly on the far side of the country. Maybe we make a defective product (which might kill or maim people). Of course we could make a mistake and fire the wrong person, a person who ultimately winds up homeless and dies on the streets, penniless and lonely. Or maybe we make a major mistake, one that destroys our business and puts a lot of people out of work and some of them on the street. Does anyone demonstrate against us? More than likely not. Even if a friend of ours, an airplane pilot, miscalculates a takeoff and winds up killing everybody on board except himself and two passengers, the most he will probably get is an investigation, definitely not an angry mob chanting, "Kill the pig! Kill the pig!" No, the rabid anger of mob abuse is mostly reserved for the men and women in blue, those people whose job it is to keep us and the mob safe, no matter what the cost to themselves, psychologically and/or physically. Yet, they are human, like you and me. They like some people and dislike others. They make mistakes. Some are good at their jobs. Some aren't. We forgive those weaknesses in most people, unless we already dislike them. But not in police officers. Am I exaggerating or are there lots more people who dislike police officers than like them, people who dislike them not as individuals but as sub-humans who wear blue uniforms, people who refuse to forgive them their humanness?

Me, I sure as ever wouldn't want angels using halos to fight our criminals. I have no doubts that the criminals would win hands down, and this country would swiftly become like the Mideast, maybe Iran or Syria, or the land of the IS.